Herman Haeberlin Regained

Anthropology and Artifacts of Puget Sound 1916-17

Jay Miller, PhD

CULTURE

KING COUNTY LODGING TAX

2020

Lushootseed
Press

@ 2005

Thankful Acknowledgments

Haeberlin has been regained through the kind and generous help of translator Ulrich Fritzsche MD; archivist extraordinaire Gary Lundell, SAM curator Dr Barbara Brotherton, Dr Astrida Blukis Onat, facilitator (Dr) Holly Taylor, ethnobotanist Dr Brian Compton, folklorist Dr William Seaburg, ethnomusicologist Dr Laurel Sercombe, and Vi Hilbert, elder extraordinaire. Dr Zeke Zalmai Zahir provided meals, vast knowledge, tech support, and boundless friendship.

Herman's Ohio roots and gravesite were located by the awesome help of Patricia O'Flaherty, Kurt Reidinger, Jay Willenberg, Linda Ward Willenberg, and Stanley Ward. An eighty-year-old living in Akron, Stanley Ward took the photographs of the tombstone that proved the paper trail correcting Herman's birthdate, before my own personal pilgrimage to his grave in 2005. Ira Jacknis miraculously saved his photo (see title page).

Contents

contents

MYTHOLOGY 150 – 206

DR HERMAN HAEBERLIN REGAINED

PREFACE

Herman Karl Haeberlin's name appears as the first author of *The Indians of Puget Sound* (1930). The second is Erna Gunther, who inherited his fieldnotes and translated this work from German. They were born sixteen years apart. Both were students of Franz Boas at Columbia University in New York. They may have met because she entered Barnard about the time he was finishing his graduate degree, which was based on library research. But actual fieldwork with living people was a must for any serious career, and it was such research among Salish natives around Seattle that brought their efforts together, even after Herman (HKH) had died.

Thus, Haeberlin came to coastal Washington in 1916 to establish his reputation as a consummate anthropologist. Driven to add to scholarship, his health failed as diabetes killed him.[1] He intended to cap his training and experience as an anthropologist by fieldwork among the Snohomish, Snoqualmi, and members of other tribes settled on the Tulalip Reservation near Marysville, learning from native speakers of what was then called Puget Salish and is now known as Lushootseed (from its own native name).[2] He had already done international-scale scholarly research in German and US museums and as an archaeologist trying to keep up with Boas in Puerto Rico, as well as comparative work about interrelations among the Salishan language family.

---

[1] His death is particularly ironic because of the high incidences of diabetes among modern Lushootsed elders, who undergo dialysis weekly. Appendix H on insulin and the bizarre quirks of medical discovery is intended for them.

[2] The native language of Puget Sound has northern and southern dialect chains, called dəxʷləšutsid and txʷəlšutsid. In the north were Skagit (including the Sauk-Suiattle), Swinomish, and the Snohomish (including the Skykomish); while, south of Whidbey Island, dialects were Snoqualmi, Duwamish (including Muckleshoot), Puyallup, Nisqually, and Sahewamish, together with Suquamish on the west shore.

Important dialect distinctions are separate names for salmon species, respective accents on the first or second vowel of the basic root of a word, and the use of 4 as the pattern number (done four times) in the north and of 5 (five times) in the south (matching tribes along the Columbia River into the Plateau).

Over a century ago, Lushootseed and nearby languages (Twana, Chimakum, and southern Nootkans (Makah and Ditidat, called Nitinat in English)) shifted away from nasal sounds so that M became B (m > b) and former N became D (n > d). Thus, any snowcapped mountain is now called taqʷʷoba, though settlers heard it as *takoma* (Tacoma) and applied it to Mt. Rainier and a nearby city.

Decades before there had been fierce competition for artifacts from the Northwest Coast to fill world-class museums (Cole 1985, Jonaitis 1988). Most of these objects came from the Pacific's Far North, but Haeberlin was to fill out the Coast Salish collection at the American Museum of Natural History (AMNH) in New York City. This collecting helped to pay for his research project. Further, these artifacts provided important and very tangible evidence of how natives used "what nature provided" at a time when machines, metal, and soon plastic were beginning to alienate all people from their local environments.

Indeed, this was not an easy time for Germans in the US, since these nations were on the brink of World War I. Fluently bilingual, Herman was an American by birth (though later scholars did not know this). His mother's German family had settled in Akron, Ohio, and worked as roofers. His father was a German engineer who came there to work. The Haeberlin family soon returned to Germany for the education of their son and daughter in the rigors of science and music.

In college, young Herman became attracted to anthropology and pursued this interest in German classrooms and museums. He did well, and made the acquaintance of the leading anthropologist of that day, Franz Boas (Pierpont 2004), a naturalized German who had a special affinity for the Pacific Northwest. Papa Franz, as he was affectionately known, was spearheading the premier (and for a time only) department of Anthropology at Columbia University in New York City. Barnard, where Erna Gunther was an undergraduate, was once its sister institution for women. For his PhD, Herman became a Boas student, and quickly acquired the mantle of an heir. After a variety of training experiences (explained in his biography below), he was sent for the decisive test of fieldwork with wise native elders, concentrating on defining distinctive features of Puget Sound's native cultures, and collecting language materials for comparative Salish studies.

Everything that is presently known about Herman and his Puget research is presented within this booklet. It was occasioned by a recent discovery that finally fills out his consummate research. Though he died of diabetes on return from his second field season, his notebooks have remained a goldmine of information. But one number (#13) was always missing. Only 41 of the 42 notebooks, in Washington DC since 1936, have been known and used. Having identified the missing #13 in New York City, it here provides the core of this booklet. Combined together with notebook #32, this work is intended to be a self-contained source for the artifacts he collected. While the notes are vital to understanding native Puget Sound, basic background has also been provided as a context for these notebooks. Appendices provide thumbnail sketches of persons and contexts, and footnotes amplify the text. Where necessary, brief comments by Miller are inserted within the flow of the text; these are set off by curved brackets { }. Uncertain words are marked by double {??} question marks.

England and Germany, given their intertwined royal houses, have been major forces in American History. Germans, however, have taken the secondary role as settlers and shopkeepers rather than as pioneers. In the two decades before and after 1900, Germans were well placed in the US. During World War I, famous German-Americans took leading roles, such as John (Blackjack) Pershing (born Pfoerschein) and the Ace Eddy Rickenbacker. Both Boas and Haeberlin worked during trying times when Germany had imperial ambitions that they did not share. Boas was a pacifist, but many of his students enlisted in the war, to his ire. Many had ancestry in Germany, such as Alfred Kroeber, Esther Schriff, and Robert Lowie.

In Washington State, Germans were long stalwart citizens. They played leading roles in all of the key regional industries and institutions. Principally, they were John Jacob Astor in the fur trade, Henry Villard (Heinrich Hilgard) in the railroads, Frederick Weyerhaeuser in lumber, Gustave (Gustavus) Sohon and Lt Augustus Valentine Kautz in the US Army, Carl A Sander in ranching, Schwabacher brothers in Seattle sales, and a host of brewers.[3] Some of these men made their own contributions to native research. Sohon left a series of native portraits and treaty scenes, Villard provided funds to Boas for local fieldwork, and Kautz's Nisqually children became tribal leaders.

In south Puget Sound, prosperous Germans included Willibald Alphonse Kunigk, Tacoma waterworks engineer, Arthur Jacob Weisbach, Tacoma mayor during the 1885 anti-Chinese riots, Gustave Rosenthal, Olympia oyster developer, William Bremer, who sold land to the Navy for a shipyard in 1891, and Louis Gonter, a hop king of Pierce County. Fertile Eastern Washington wheatlands were resettled by Volga Deutsch. These were German farmers, often pacifists such as Mennonites, who had relocated to Russia. They came to the Northwest fleeing Russian Army conscription despite an official exemption granted when they were invited to farm along the Volga River by Czarina Catherine the Great, herself a German noble married to the Czar.

Above all, Germany prided itself on scientific rigor, which was instilled in HKH and reinforced under Boas. Haeberlin had already earned his PhD based on library research about the Puebloan Southwest. As fulfillment, HKH undertook to confirm his professional reputation by fieldwork with the native Lushootseeds of the Sound, during a proverbial "calm before the gathering storm".

The world has changed since the death of HKH. In his trilogy of novels set just after World War I, John Dos Passos (*1919* 1930: 246, 248) listed its after effects:

> "War brought the eight hour day, women's votes, prohibition, compulsory arbitration, high wages, high rates of interest, cost plus contracts and the luxury of being a Gold Star Mother. If you objected to making the world safe for cost plus democracy you went to jail with {Eugene} Debs." {Above all}, "oil was trump."

Grasping for oil reserves continues today, having dominated world conditions for over a century. Among modern Lushootseeds, this same modern world intrudes into their own traditions, estranging some people from their deeply rooted past. Haeberlin and his legacy helps us all to recall and reaffirm the richness of these cultures in detail.

As tribute to his work, this booklet is arranged into four sections. The first tells the life and work of HKH. The second presents both his notebooks (#13, #32) documenting his entire artifact collection, through gift and purchase, from locals. The third presents his letters, sometimes with responses, in English. Many were translated from the original German by Ulrich Fritzsche, MD, a native speaker and medical doctor. Since German has both technical and folk names for the same disease, he has critical insight necessary for such translations. To amplify information beyond that in brief

---

[3] Dale R Wirsing, Builders, Brewers, and Burghers, Germans of Washington State 1977.

footnotes, as well as to present relevant extracts contained in the other 42 notebooks, appendices have been provided at the end of each section. The fourth section, bringing together an overview of Lushoosteed research, lists Lushootseed researchers, begins to locate their papers, and ends with background references and bibliography.

Analysis, either academic or otherwise, will have to come later, building upon this straight-forward compendium of materials about HKH and his collection of artifacts. Many details remain vague, and other comparative data have not been assembled, but the outlines and gaps for them are provided herein.

Dr Herman Karl Haeberlin
(11 September 1890 - 12 February 1918)

American born but German educated, Herman Karl Haeberlin (HKH) was once the hope of US Anthropology. His tragic death robbed the Northwest of a bright beginning and contributed to difficulties that still plague regional research. His Puget Sound fieldwork was to be the confirmation and consummation of his career. He intended it to bring together all of his prior efforts in museums, archaeology, and comparative linguistics. After arriving in the 1916 summer at Tulalip, however, increasing illness resulted in a diagnosis of diabetes in Seattle (see Letters). Various strict remedies were tried, and he improved. Able to continue fieldwork in 1917, he died shortly after returning East.

HKH was born, started school, and is buried in Akron (Ohio) while his namesake father, an engineer, was working there. By the time he entered university, however, his family had returned to Germany. He began his college studies in Leipsig and then Berlin. His father explained family background to Boas, in a letter of 2 November 1919, while he was trying to reenter the US to mourn his son.

In the spring of 1883, I emigrated to the United States, after finishing an academic - technical education. I received my US citizenship in 1888. My papers were issued February 6, 1888 by probate Judge CR Grant, Akron, Ohio. I married my wife, born Alma Fedderson, in 1885. My two children, Elsa and Herman, were born 1886 and 1890 in Akron. In December of 1906, I left Akron for Duesseldorf, where I entered into the service of a large machine producing factory. My return to Germany was mainly guided by my desire to give my children a superb scientific education. My daughter studied music. You know about my son.

Boas met Herman in 1913 in Berlin, where his fellow students included a Pole, a Russian, and other Germans. Karl Lamprecht and Wilhelm Wundt were their teachers, inspired by the work of Adolf Bastian and the Ethnological Museum. HKH transferred to Columbia University in New York to work with Boas in 1914, completing his PhD with a study, based on published sources, of what would today be call "gender symbolism" on a cosmic scale (Father Sky, Mother Earth) among the Pueblos of the Southwest.

At that time, Boas's premier student, Alfred Louis Kroeber (1915: 283-288) published his "18 professions". These axioms addressed what he regarded as the irreconcilable differences between the two branches of research which were both important to anthropology. One was biological and psychological, and the other was social and historical. To bridge this chasm, he instead looked to a third branch that was uniquely anthropological. This was the no-man's-land between the two which he said was capriciously used as a "picnic ground by whosoever prefers pleasure excursions to the work of cultivating a patch of understanding". It attracted those without rigor, and this could not go on.

Kroeber's basic aim was to delimit the scope of history from that of science. In this regard, he said, the aim of history is to know the relations of social facts to the whole of civilization, not its varied impulses. It is the entire work of humans, rather than "man as individual", except as someone serves as a specific illustration. The organic whole is greater than its parts. Humans have species characteristics. True instincts and heredity lie at the bottom of social phenomena, but they cannot be considered by history because it is only concerned with the particular. Biology is not destiny. Environment is subject to civilization, not its shaper. All human cultures are absolutely equal (by the doctrine of cultural relativity). "All men are totally civilized," the savage does not exist.

All of this was before genes, DNA, and genomes took center place. All social types, stages, and pseudo-species were "arbitrarily selected facts". Cultures react by sequencing among themselves, not according to universal laws nor causes. Science does not exist for history, and each field should follow its own complementary methods.

It is significant for his growing place in anthropology, that, later in the same volume, HKH (1915: 756-759) responded with "Anti-Professions". That he could do so in print, albeit with a certain puppy-dog naïveté, indicates his standing in the profession. He was probably encouraged by Boas to react to his most illustrious protégé. HKH correctly calls this Kroeberian enterprise dogmatic, particularly his lumping of psychology with biology within science. HKH countered that, neither a picnic ground nor a no-man's-land, science is open minded.

All humans are inherently part of their works, they can not be arbitrarily separated off from the culture-whole. While there may not be laws like those of science, parts of anthropology, such as linguistics, discover regular correspondences that are very similar to these laws. Similarly, sequence is itself a kind of causality, rather than its antithesis. Once set in motion, outcomes become limited by statistical possibilities. "Dr Kroeber's psychological bugaboo is a gnome of subjective making ... All scientific work ... is only specialization," within the totality.

The exchange solved nothing, but it did call attention to Herman and added to the stature of Kroeber. As the letters reveal, Kroeber was impressed enough to offer Haeberlin a job at Berkeley, but he turned it down in favor of returning to the East.

Increasingly, HKH's own interests became "manifestations of the aesthetic life," beginning with Pueblo art in published illustrations and held in Berlin collections. He next turned to Northwest Coast art, James Teit's data on Salishan basketry, and pottery from Culhuacan near Mexico City. He also developed an interest in Nahuatl, the spoken language of the Aztecs.

"The character of his work was determined by a keen psychological interest founded on a broad philosophical and historical training. He was never a mere collector of facts, but the material of anthropology served him to understand the relations between the individual and society. Anthropological observations were interesting to him because they throw light upon the relations between individual thought, feeling, and action and social environment. In this sense he was interested in the application of the results of anthropological study to the social problems of our day, because the attainment of true freedom of thought and action presupposes a clear understanding of the social determination of our own activities" (Boas 1919: 72).[4]

Like others of his time, HKH deduced that culture was all-embracing, a mental outlook that served to filter and organize everything. As such, he joined with Boas in opposing the enthusiasm for diffusion and transcultural borrowing then in vogue in anthropology. At the same time his strength was sapped by the onset of diabetes.

Finally, having built upon the work of others, Herman was ready to undertake his own research. He first went to Puerto Rico, where he excavated two sites. But this did not provide the acid test of actual fieldwork with living peoples. For that milestone, he was sent to Puget Sound. Boas had already provided the background for understanding the region, and he had become keenly interested in the Salishan languages because they provided a discrete grouping that occurred in both the Coast and the Plateau culture areas. Other language stocks, such as Algic, were too far-flung and complex for such analysis.

Based at the Tulalip Reservation, he began his studies of Puget Salish (now called Lushootseed) in 1916. From these notes, he was able to publish an article on the major ritual of the region (formerly known as the Spirit Canoe but better titled Shamanic Odyssey ~ Redeeming Rite, Miller 1988a, 1999a). He also produced bulky comparative studies of features of Salishan linguistics. Only his work on reduplication (doubling up of syllables to shift meanings) appeared quickly.

In his letters, HKH seems determined to stay on the East Coast, near the intellectual centers of the US and Europe. I feel certain, however, that Boas wanted to place HKH at the University of Washington (UW) to pursue local fieldwork and look for interested natives and students to take up such research, as he did elsewhere with key native scribes such as George Hunt, William Beynon, and Ella Deloria. The death of HKH was a serious setback for all Americanists, and especially to the Seattle region.

At HKH's death, Boas had something to do with the funeral arrangements and became literary executor. He gave all 41 notebooks − except # 13 which he poignantly kept − to Erna Gunther. She brought them to Seattle when Leslie Spier (her husband via a legal contract not a marriage license) took a job at the University of Washington in 1920. Later, he moved on to the University of Oklahoma, and was rehired by UW in 1929. Leslie went off to the Pacific for fieldwork and Erna filled in as his substitute and stayed on. Herself Alsatian, from families fluent in both French and German because of the political shifts in this mining region, Erna published an ethnographic summary of these materials in German in 1924, at the same time as she published HKH's collection of native stories in English. In 1930, after her own fieldwork in the Sound and her "divorce" from Spier, Erna published an English version of the ethnography, which

---

[4] This official obituary by heavy-hearted Boas (1919) has HKH's birth date off by a year in 1891. Both his father and the tombstone report 1890.

remains in print. The oldest people who had worked with HKH a decade before were dead, so she worked with their children and grandchildren. As Erna once explained, HKH's original overview summary was in English, which she translated into German for the 1924 edition. When she got ready to publish it in English in 1930, however, she could not find the original and so had to back translate from the German.[5]

For unknown reasons, in 1936, though the 41 notebooks had been in Erna's keeping for almost two decades, Leslie sent them to the Bureau of American Ethnology in DC. Presumably he knew that Puget Salish materials from TT Waterman were already there. HKH's song materials went to Helen Roberts, who published them in 1918. Some remaining pages may be in her collection at Yale University.

Many of the "good ole boys" at local historical societies, especially in Tacoma, were deeply suspicious of Spier and Gunther, viewing them as Eastern academics invading their turf. Yet the couple got on well with several self-trained researchers who grew up among local natives. Among these so-called "sentinels" were Nels Bruseth of Darrington, and, especially, Arthur Ballard of Auburn.

Boas was not one to let research materials languish. He gave Herman's material to people who could use it, often without any explanation. The massive compendium on Salishan lexical suffixes is now in the papers of Gladys Reichard at Indiana University. Long on the faculty at Barnard, Reichard received it from Boas because of her work with Coeur d'Alene, an Interior Salish language of Idaho. A dividend of her work there was the college degree earned by Lawrence Nicodemus, a native speaker who continued analysis of his language for decades. In a real sense, Reichard took the place of HKH as the Boas heir.

Stanley Newman, long at the University of New Mexico, received a copy of Thompson (Nlaka'pamux) suffixes when he began work on Nuxalk, the northernmost Salishan language famous for its many vowel-less words. "Boas sent me the ms. In the early 30's (when I started working on Bella Coola) {now Nuxalk} with no explanation or comment – he wasn't a man to waste words" (Newman in Thompson 1974: 220). Other materials are scattered throughout the collections of Erna Gunther and Melville Jacobs at UW Special Collections (until 2004 UW-MSCUA, Appendix A), usually identifiable by the handwriting, topic, or subject rather than any attached HKH name.

His grave is with the Feddersens {headstones are written as ending in both -sEn and -sOn}, Section G, Plot 63, in Glendale Cemetery, 150 Glendale Avenue, in the old and Germanic section of Akron, Ohio. The slanted grey granite stone reads

H.K. HAEBERLIN
SEPT. 11, 1890
FEB. 12, 1918

---

[5] Wayne Suttles identified one German paragraph and a diagram on the trawl net (šabəd) that did not get translated back into the 1930 English edition.

The records from this plot tell of both longevity and sadness. His grandmother Anna died in 1925 at age 92 of senility, his uncle Kuno Feddersen died at 85 in 1952 of pneumonia, as did two others buried in the 1960s. His youngest uncle died at age 76 of infected gangrene, and his grandfather John/Jonathan died at 60 of poison.

Census records indicate that in 1880 the Feddersen males were roofers. They emigrated from Prussia. Their oldest child, daughter Alma who became mother of HKH, was a milliner. Elsa was a female name continued in each generation, as with HKH's own sister. Herman (Sr) and Alma married in Summit, Ohio, on 19 March 1885. His profession is indeed listed as engineer.

There are no obvious indications of religion. St Bernard's Cemetery adjoins Glendale on the southwest, so Catholic can be ruled out, as can Jewish. At this point, non-sectarian or Lutheran remain possibilities. The fellowship set up in his honor was specifically non-denominational, and funded by American assets of the father. Erich Schmidt used his award for Arizona archaeology, though others have yet to be identified.

Boas himself was from a liberal Jewish family. His students included Blacks, Jews, women (sometimes both), and others at a time when colleges were a bastion of Anglo males. His supervision of the son of roofers and engineers speaks to the tolerance of both Boas and anthropology from its very academic founding.

Appendix A: Known Writings

List of known publications, recordings, and manuscripts

of Dr Herman Karl Haeberlin

Franz Boas and Herman Haeberlin

> 1924   Ten Folktales in Modern Nahuatl. *Journal of American Folklore* 37: 345-370.

> 1927   Sound Shifts in the Salishan Dialects. *International Journal of American Linguistics* 4: 117-36.

Haeberlin, Herman K

> 1916-17   Puget Salish, 41 of 42 Notebooks. DC: National Anthropological Archives # 2965.

> 1916-17   Puget Salish, Notebook 13. NY: American Museum of National History, Anthropological Archives.

> 1918   "SbEtEtda'q, A Shamanic Performance of the Coast Salish." *American Anthropologist* 20 (3): 249-257.

> 1918   Principles of Esthetic Form in the Art of the North Pacific Coast: A Preliminary Sketch. *American Anthropologist* 20 (3): 258-264.

> 1924   "Mythology of Puget Sound." Prepared by Erna Gunther. *Journal of American Folklore* 37 (143-144): 371-438.

> 1974   Distribution of the Salish Substantive (Lexical) Suffixes. Edited by M Terry Thompson. *Anthropological Linguistics* 16 (6): 219-350.

Haeberlin, Herman, and Erna Gunther

> 1924   Ethnographische Notizen über de Indianerstämme des Puget-Sundes. *Zeitschrift für Ethnologie* 56 (1-4): 1-74.

> 1930   The Indians Of Puget Sound. University of Washington Publications in Anthropology 4 (1): 1-84.

Herman Haeberlin K, James A Teit, and Helen Roberts

> 1928   Coiled Basketry in British Columbia and Surrounding Region. *Bureau of American Ethnology - Annual Report* 41: 119-484. For the years 1919-25.

Roberts, Helen, and Herman Haeberlin

> 1918   Songs of the Puget Sound Salish." *Journal of American Folklore* 31 (122): 496-520.

> HKH MSS at American Philosophical Society, Philadephia (Freeman Guide 1966)

450. Franz Boas and HK Haeberlin. Bella Bella suffix list [n.d.]. D. 322L. 5 slips.

Preliminary organization of morphological treatment; heavily exemplified suffix list. On reverse side are ethnological materials: Land of the Dead (the sbetedda's {sic} ceremony and the conception of the Land of the Dead); the ideal of fertilization in the culture of the Pueblo Indians; Hopi Sky-Father and Sky-Mother. In notebooks; notes added after 1925. Some offset printed sheets, pp. 1-171 of Boas (1928a).   [30(W1b.4)]

1538. Haeberlin, Herman K. Notes on the composition of the verbal complex in Haida [n.d; 1915?]. D. 17L. A critical reworking of a portion of Swanton (1911a).

[30(N1b.3)]

2341. Franz Boas and Herman Haeberlin. Nahuatl texts. [1912-1924]. Typed D. and A.D. 1 notebook. 314L. In Nahuatl with English, Spanish, and German translations. Texts collected by Boas in 1912 from Milpa Alta natives; verified by Haeberlin. Includes type copy of Simeon (1889): 25-26.   [30(U7b.4)]

Printed, Boas and Arreola (1920) and Boas and Haeberlin (1924).

3211. Franz Boas and Herman Haeberlin, and James A Teit. Salishan dialects [1920]. Typed D. 12L. Data relating to the Salish languages, their distribution, and the distributions of neighboring languages.   [30(S.10)]

3212. Haeberlin, Herman K. Correspondence with Franz Boas [1913-1918]. L. 24 items. Relating to Haeberlin's graduate studies at Columbia, and his field work at Tulalip, Everet[t], and Mayville {Marysville}, Washington.   [31]

Haeberlin MSS at UW Special Collections

MSCUA until 2004

in Erna Gunther Collection, in English, Box 6-4, in German Box 6-5.

in Melville Jacobs Collection, Box 107-7 top & carbon Peter Sam, kinds of mats, Skookum George, Star Husband, Little Sam

Songs

Six Wax Cylinder, Ten Strips

Archives of Traditional Music, Indiana University

Kookum George, Snoqualmie > Love Song

James Percival, Snohomish > Snohomish Song, Warrior Song, Lummi Warrior, Woman's sqaip, Man's sqaip, Snohomish Love Song, Woman's Love Song, Doctoring Song

Peter Sam, Snohomish > Gambling Song, Echo Song

SUMMARIES of all 42 Notebooks

* The name before the > is the source ~~informant~~, capitalized letters indicate titles of epic or mythic texts, (to, from #__) indicate continuations to or from other notebooks. Though annoying, this jumping between notebooks saved paper and time. Dates are included because HKH so rarely noted them.

1 William Shelton > Snohomish features

2 William Shelton > Deer and Loon, burials, constellations, sweatlodge

3 William Shelton > animal people, Lifting the Sky, Fox and Mink (on to #11, #12)

4 Snoqualmie Jim > genealogy, traps for bear & salmon, Star Husband, Wolf & Bear

   Frank Le Clair > genealogy, baby teeth

   Alphonso Bob, son of George Bob, son of Old Bob > tool diagrams

5 Charlie Jules > women's gambling game, Snohomish villages, remedies, money, clothing

6 Charlie Jules > Lushootseed terms for anatomy, landscape, reduplications

7 Charlie Jules > Odyssey / smetnaq, tools, clothing

8 William Shelton > genealogy

   Snoqualmie Jim > flounder.

   Little Sam > worths (values), pheasant, powers, clams

9 Charlie Jules > immortals

   Little & Annie Sam > 3, 4 Nov 1916, oven, fern root, (forced reply)

10 powers, immortals (to #19, #36)

11 William Shelton > Fox and Mink (from #3)

12 William Shelton > Fox and Mink, Black Bear and Grizzly (to #22)

13 missing ?!?, in NYC {see full text, published after a century}

14 Josephine LeClair > Grandfather Carrot, 4 Dec 1916

15 Snoqualmie Jim > Star Husbands, Wolf Brothers, Winds, Basket Ogress

16 George Bob > reduplications {9 Oct 1916 decision to write N as D, M as B to end confusion} {Of note, these intermediate sounds also plagued Boas}

   Snoqualmie Jim > terms for anatomy, weather, terrain, housing, animals

17 Josephine LeClair > Wolf, Raven, Skunk, Frog, Leprous Boy (to #14, #36)

18 Josephine LeClair > Leprous Boy with Sores (to #17, #36)

19 William Shelton > terms, baskets, foods, games, spinning, Odyssey 7 Nov 1916 (to #10)

20 Skookum George > Star Husbands, Wolf Brothers, Mink and Frog, mats, shredding bark

21 Skookum George > canoes, games, herbs, birth

22 William Shelton > Black Bear and Grizzly (#12, #36)

    Charlie Jules > housing, tools, time, verbs

    Skookum George > verbs, pronouns

23 Skookum George > songs

24 Skookum George > Star Husbands

    Snoqualmie Jim >

    Little Sam > Wolf

    Peter Sam > war

25 Peter Sam > Rabbit and Deer, mats, canoes (to #24)

    Snoqualmie Jim > Lion and Rabbit

26 conjugations, tools, paints (to #25)

27 reduplications, Thompson Beaver and Coyote

28 Henry Sicade (Nisqually) > birth, names, potlatch, tamanous + immortals, medicine house (to #30, #36)

29 Henry Sicade > newspaper clippings, wapato, Star Husband, baskets on 21 April 1916

30 Squalli villages, Leschi, traps, kin terms, canoes, teas (from # 28)

31 Joe Swayle > powers, immortals, doctors, baskets

32 Puyallup specimens, shipment tallies {see full text}

33 Henry Martin > First Salmon, Odyssey

    Sally Martin Jackson > Sister of Henry, a doctor

    Henry Sicade > kin terms

34 Cashmere Sam > trade, clothing, Odyssey, immortals, the dead

35 ghosts, Winds, Skagit Mink and Raven, feather blankets

36 tides, Changer = dukʷibəł, Skykomish Mink and Grandmother, burial, souls, summer (from #17, #18, #22, #28}

37 cunning stitał = Fraser River Thompsons, tools, wool dogs, Snoqualmie from Wolf, Snohomish from Tyee {King} Salmon, Skykomish from mountain goat; constellations, immortal doctors

38 Snohomish from blackfish, herbs, Little Sam genealogy, wergild, games

39 Holmes Harbor, games, Skagit chiefs, woodwork, slaves

40 Little Sam? > Grizzly, loon,

      Henry Sicade > marmot blanket,

      Kate Mount (Nisqually) > kin terms, pregnancy, foods, names

41 Kate Mount (Nisqually) > utensils, mourning, class, rank, acorns, slaves, potlatch

42 Pheasant

Native People in Notebooks #13, #32
Mentioned by Name or Kinship

Old Anne (ts!ait), Muckleshoot reservation

Old Bob

wife of Charlie Boston

wife of Celestine

Edward Percifal

son of Georgie Bob

Henry Martin

Jack Wheeler

Joe Swayle

Mrs Johnson

Mrs Josephine LeClair

mother-in-law of Charlie Jules

Mrs Jules

Morris Lobehan

Pete Kalama

Little Sam & wife Annie Sam

Peter Sam

Sokum George & wife

Snuqualmi Jim

Swinomish woman, brown goat wool blanket

Herman K Haeberlin # 13 1916-82

FROM THE BOAS COLLECTION 43

{Stamped on outside Cover}

Martha Washington
Composition Book
No. 154

Page 1

Specimens marked √ were sent to New York Oct. 27, 1916

Information concerning broughten specimens[6]

50.2/

√ 1-   435 $5.00

basket (spɛtcu')[7] Snohomish make, brought from wife of "old Bob." Grass for white imbrication and sample of stick used for black imbrication[8] added gratis

√ 2 -   436   .30

round greenish stone, found on Camano Island by little grandson of Old Bob.

√ 3   437   spoon of horn $1.00

---

[6] Each page has many numbers. In the upper right is the number HKH put on the notebook page itself, numbers added within [ ] correct for the proper sequence, along the right side are the prices he paid in dollars $ and ¢ cents .00; along the left side are number from 1 > for each artifact as he collected it, then numbers in the 400s which were tentatively assigned to him from the potential AMNH inventory until a final cataloging provided a fixed number as well as these field-assigned numbers.

[7] In the modern spelling of Lushoosheed, this is spəču? "watertight cedar root basket" in NL, syalt in SL (Bates, Hess, and Hilbert 1994: 160). Though the dialect names look different (northern NL dxʷləšutsid and southern SL (t)xʷəlšutsid, Whulshootseed), it is a matter of the accent on the schwa. Along the Skagit River, NL speakers used this word only upstream from Bacon Creek, below there they used yiq̓ʷus (Collins 1974: 68). The dialects of NL and SL differ in accent on the first or second vowel of the basic root of a word, basic terms like salmon and basket names, and a preference for 4 or 5 as the pattern number.

[8] Dr Brian Compton (BC), 17 December 2003, suggests the grass is *Xerophyllum tenax*, bear grass, and the stick is *Equisetum*, horsetails.

This spoon was brought from Mrs Jules. She got it from her old mother or some other relative. It was used to eat soup. The whole family would sit around a "Klickitat" basket with soup in it and would dish the soup out with such spoons. Shelton says

6.30 [$ sum]

2

this spoon must be very old. ƛamqɛs = spoon of this type.[9]

√ 4   438   hunter's basket $1.50   made by Mrs Jules. Shelton says that this is the old time hunter's basket. The twilled work on the bottom is also old. When the hunter went out to hunt he would put meat or fish into just such a basket. He would close the top by lacing a tump-line through the loops. The woven band of the tump-line he would put over his forehead and let the basket hang on his back. Such packing baskets were often much larger.

3

√ 5   439   mat of twilled work $1.50

made by Mrs. Jules. It served as "tablecloth." It was laid on the floor with the light-colored side up. Fish or meat would be laid on it, ready to be eaten. The people would sit around the mat and eat directly from the mat. These mats were often much larger than this one.

X 6 -   440   paddle $1.50

This is not a racing paddle.

They have broader blades

For men only. Very old paddle. Brought from Old Bob.

√ 7 -   441   sleeping mat $1.00

4

√ 8 -   442a-b spindle $1.00

brought from Old Bob

√ 9 -   443   needle $ .50

for making mats like No. 7 bought from Old Bob

√ 10 -   444   adze $1.50

This was used for making canoes. The blade used to be of stone. Brought from Old Bob.

---

[9] Zeke Zalmai Zahir (ZZ), SL expert, gives spoon as łabqs 'swish + nose, point'.

√ 11 -   445   points $1.50

of a salmon spear

These two points were put on the two prongs of a spear. The points were originally of stone. Those for sturgeon & seal had a "Widerhaken," those for salmon did not. Brought from Old Bob.

5

√ 12   446   old imbricated basket $8.00

brought from Old Bob's wife

√ 13   447   wicker basket $1.50

brought from Old Bob

√ 14   448   blanket $6.00

(Snohomish work) Made of mountain goat wool. Jules says that the blankets of dog-wool were made just like this one.

√ 15   449   ear-pendant $ .75 See Book 5, p. 27[10]

xᵘtci'łqs.[11] Made of shell which is highly prized by the Snohomish. Three or four whole shells of this kind were worth a slave. It was

6

traded down from the North as these shells were not found in the Snohomish country. Pieces like this specimen were worn as ear-pendants. Sometimes they were also attached to necklaces. Brought from Mrs. Jules.

√ 16   450   clam shell   gratis

Shell of which shell money tc!au'wai was made.[12] See Book 5, p. 23[13]

√ 17   451   fern with roots   gratis

Indian medical herb. Mixed with cherry bark it was good for colds. Good for stomach and moves bowels. See Book 5, p. 11.[14]

---

[10] Book 5, p. 27 xᵘtci'łqs this is the shell of a very large clam found in north and traded down to Snohomish from the northern Indians. It was not found in Snohomish country. The Snohomish prized it very highly. Two or four large shells were worth a slave. These shells were also cut up and used as ear ornaments (See No. 15 of this collection). Jules said that a big chief would have to have one [p28] of these on each ear. Sometimes such pieces would also be worn at the end of a necklace.

[11] Abalone is xʷčiłqs ZZ, Bates, Hess, and Hilbert 1994: 73.

[12] Any shell is čəway? NL, čuwəy? SL, ła?x is plate, platter ZZ, Bates, Hess, and Hilbert 1994: 69, 141.

[13] Book 5, p. 23 "Jules tells me that two kind of shell money was used: tc!auwai and s'o'lax." See Appendix B for full extract. See note 7.

√ 18   452   a large basket $5.00

Mrs Celestine showed me a basket with apparently the same design as the one on this basket. She said the pattern represented "boxes".

Used for berry picking. Brought from Mrs Josephine LeClair. It was made by a "grandmother" of Mrs LeClair. This "grandmother" was partly Skagit and partly Snohomish, she was cousin of the grandmother who had the Wolf sla'letut[15] and who told Mrs LeClair the story taken down in Book 17, pp. 13 et seq.[16]

Mrs LeClair says that the name of the design is xatske'los[17] which means "step-wise."

√ 19 -   453   small square basket $2.00

brought from daughter of Mrs LeClair. The design is sL!iɬtc [18]

which means a tattoo-mark. The design is in imitation of the tattoo-designs that the women used to have on their arms.

√ 20   454   fish basket $6.00

Used by fisherman to put their fish in. brought from Mrs LeClair. The design is uyomatc which means "butter-fly wings."[19]

---

[14] Book 5, p. 11 <u>For Colds</u> Crush the little nodules (look like fish eggs {bacteria}) on the roots of the alder tree. Something* else is mixed with this, but Jules forgot the English name for it. He promised to get some for me. From his descriptions it seems to grow as a parasite {licorice fern} on the maple tree. These two ingredients are mixed with cold water and drunk. It is good for colds, also good for the stomach and moves the bowels.

    * See in Coll[ection] No. 17 Root of a fern.

{BC suggests licorice fern, *Polypodium glycyrrhiza*, while the nodules are "formed by filamentous bacteria (Actinomycetes), i.e., *Frankia*, that are symbiotic with" alders, here probably red alders (*Alnus rubra*) "involved in nitrogen fixation". Cherry is *Prunus emarginata*.}

[15] Immortals are sqəlalitut < from = 'dream, vision' Bates, Hess, and Hilbert 1994: 175, 357.

[16] Book 17, pp. 13 et seq [p13-16] true story, retold after false start, See Appendix C.

[17] Unknown term, though ZZ suggests xack=il=us for ? + 'become' + 'face'.

[18] Tattoo is sƛ̓iƛ̓č ZZ.

[19] yubəč provides the name for both a butterfly (yuyubəč) and king salmon (in NL, SL is saċəb) which appear at the same time of year, in the Spring (Bates, Hess, and Hilbert 1994: 278).

√ 21   455   salmon club $ .25

Such a club was used in fishing to kill salmon by striking them over head. Bought from Snuqualmi Jim.

9

√ 22   456   model $5.00

of racing canoe

brought from son of Georgie Bob

√ 23   457a-k slaha'lb {slahaləb} $5.00

Game with shredded cedar bark used in game. The game consists of 10 discs one of which has no black on the rim at all. Brought from Edward Percifal. Wrapped up in a white bag.

√ 24   458   Instrument $1.00

used in making mats {creaser}

The groove was rubbed over the mat as the needle (No 9) was passed through the mat. This grooved instrument was rubbed over the

10

needle. This gives the mat the longitudinal "ribs."

√ 25   459   spoon $1.50

brought from wife of Charlie Boston

√ 26   460   basket $1.50

brought from wife of Sokum George.[20] Kokum George and his wife are both Snoqualmi. This basket, they assured me, was made by a Snoqualmi. The large designs

thus: one are sxalo'ltc which means "ferns." I could not find out what the black design near the rim (thus) means.

11 [10 written]

The other designs, namely the vertical lines and the dots scattered here and there, are xai'o'xua[21] = "flies." This information was given by the wife of Kokum George.

√ 27   461   twined basket $1.50

brought from wife of Celestine. She said that this basket was made by the Skykomish. It is a xᴇlai'otsid,[22] not a spᴇtcu'. A spᴇtcu' is a hard coiled basket. The dark brown cedar bark used for ornamentation on this basket is called ts!ayu. Mrs Celestine said that these twined baskets were not used for berry-picking, but

12 [11]

for storing goods in house.

√ 28	462	basket	$2.50
√ 29	463	spoon	25.
√ 30	464	basket	.50
√ 31	465	red ochre	.25
√ 32	466	wooden spoon ˇgot last!ˇ	.25
√ 33	467	spoon	.25
√ 34	468	spoon	.25
√ 35	469	basket	1.00
√ 36	479	basket	1.00
√ 37	471	basket	1.50
√ 38	472	basket	1.00
√ 38	473	basket	1.00
√ 40	474	basket	3.00
√ 41	475	basket	3.00
√ 42	476	basket	2.00

13 [12]

√ 43	477	basket		1.00
√ 44	478	mat maker	{creaser}	.50
√ 45	479	basket		2.50

---

[21] Sword fern is sx̣ax̣əlc but HKH wrote sx̣aləlc; Fly is x̣ayux̌ʷaʔ ZZ, Bates, Hess, and Hilbert 1994, 313. Gunther (1973: 13) has sx̣ax̣lc.

[22] Marked rim, mouth is x̣alayucid; while bark is łuway; ts!ayu is unknown.

46	480	basket	7.00
√ 47	481	shell money	.75
X 48	482	paddle (men's)	.50
X 49	483	paddle (men's)	.50
X 50	484	women's paddle	1.00
		brought from Little Sam	
51	485	frame for drying ground hog skins	.50

The skin is that of cau'ł = groundhog.[23] Blankets were made of these skins. 20 or 25 skins of cau'ł to each blanket. The inside of these skins were cleaned with a rough stone. Name of this trap is Leq!tid.[24]

14 [13]

52	486	spoon	.25
		brought from Little Sam	
√ 53	487a-e	model of hoop for	gratis
		catching pheasants	

for description Book 8 p. 22 et. seq.[25] The real hoop is larger and stronger than this model.

15 [14]

cau'ł is mountain beaver according to Peter Sam. According to another man it is a groundhog. A cau'ł skin is on the drying frame #51.

cau'ł comes in from side as shown by arrow. He nibbles at bait "a." See herb in envelope. This causes the "b" to snap out and this again makes the poles

---

[23] Mountain Beaver {šaẇk^{w}ł, šaẇł} though it is usually misidentified in publications as hedgehog, beaver, badger, etc. See appendix G on this fascinating species.

[24] Leq!tid suggests 'side lure' from łəq̇=təd side + tool, implement, though łaq 'lay down' might also apply. The prey approaches the trap from the side ZZ, Bates, Hess, and Hilbert 1994: 145.

[25] Book 8 p. 22 et. Seq [p22-30] diagram and description of a pheasant trap from Mr Little & Mrs Annie Sam. See specimen # 53, pheasant story. See Appendix D.

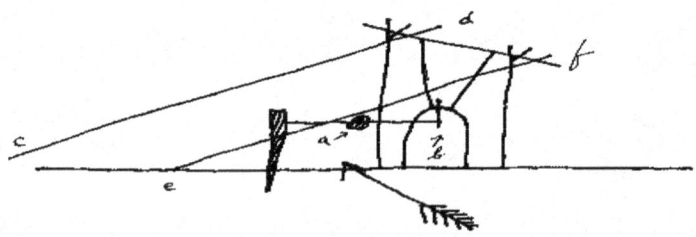

| #54 | 488a-1 | model of cau'ł trap | gratis |

16 [15]

c-d and e-f fall down. Over these poles lie strips of cedar bark and on top of these are heavy stones (not shown in diagram). The weight kills cau'ł. On the ground under the trap lie a number of sticks in the same direction as c-d and e-f. This prevents cau'ł from digging his way from under the weight.

Little Sam made this trap for me. It is the actual size.

#55	489	twined basket	$1.50
#56	490	handle of chisel	$ .25
#57	491	wicker basket	$ .50 {clam basket}

17 [16]

| #58 | 492 | Instrument | $ .25 |
| | | for making mats {creaser} | |

| #59 | 493 | model of bailer | gratis |

made by Little Sam & his wife. This is just a small model of a bailer. The actual bailers were about 1 ft long, Annie Sam says.

| #60 | 494 | wedge | $ .25 |

= gwādāk^u from Little Sam's description it also seems to have been used as a chisel. It was struck with a stone hammer (= skātcīd)[26]

| #61 | 495 | roll of cherry bark | $ .25 |

Annie Sam said that this was the usual way to keep strips of bark {wound diagonally on crossed sticks}

---

[26] ZZ, from the oldest dictionaries, provides gʷadaʔkʷ = 'antler, wedge'; š(ə)qačid = literally 'lift hand'.

#62	496	spoon	$ .25
#63	497	spoon	$ .25

The two examples #62 and #63 are Klickitat spoons. Little Sam's mother brought them from the Klickitat when Little Sam was a little boy. Little Sam appears to be at least 70 years old.

#64	498	dish	$1.50

= kᵘlayōltc.[27] This dish was brought by the Sam family from Canadian Indians for 5 modern blankets 16 years ago. The Sams stated expressly that the Snohomish and Snuqualmi do not make dishes of this make.

#65	499	model	$ .75

of a Snohomish lᵘłyōltc wooden dish

made by Little Sam. The real dishes were larger. This is a typical Snohomish dish. The Snohomish made these kind of dishes out of alder wood, sometimes also of cedar wood. The Snoqualmi made them of maple wood. (Annie Sam)

#66	500	tumpline	$ .25

of dried rushes[28]

made for me by Annie Sam. Annie Sam said that this was the old kind of tumpline. The woven tumpline commonly used now is of late origin. The woven tump-line is not

woven on a loom, it is made by hand. Annie showed me how these woven tumplines are made.

#67	501a-e	model of loom	$1.00

used to make blankets

---

[27] Log, stick, wood + container is qʷəłayʔulč NL, sɨək̓ʷabulč SL ZZ.

[28] BC suggests common rush ~ *Juncus effuses*.

The actual loom is much larger, about 4 ft high and the width corresponds to the width of the blanket. Annie Sam although very old did not know how to weave. Neither did another old woman who was around. The only one who had an idea of it was Little Sam himself. From him I got a general idea of

21 [20]

the mode of weaving, but not all details. The warp is wound around the loom in the following way:

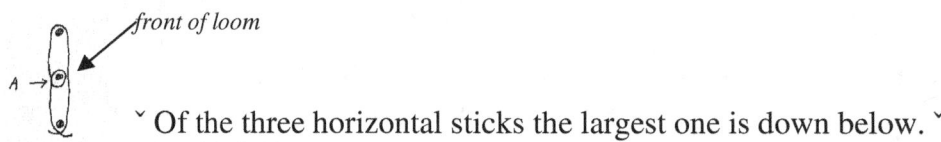

˘ Of the three horizontal sticks the largest one is down below. ˘

The horizontal weft is woven through the warp in a twined weave. When the blanket is finished the warp strands are cut at the point A. The loom was always made by a man.

22 [21]

#68   502   stick   gratis

on which clams are stuck for roasting. See p 35 book 8.[29]

#69   503   birch bark fire brand   gratis

  see book 9 p 30[30]

#70   504a-c model of firedrill $ .50   made by Little Sam, for descriptions see book 9, p 28 et seq.[31]

---

[29] Book 8, p 35 Diagram of fire in front of a log deflector, with clams impaled on sticks leaning against a crossbrace. "The two forked sticks would be about 6 ft apart, sometimes less. If the clams were larger, then would be about 7 on each slanting stick. When the clams on the [p36] lower end of the stick were well roasted, these sticks would be turned around quickly so that the clams at the other end would now get the greatest heat.

[30] Book 9 p 30 Annie's grandfather timed each of Little Sam's quests by the number of days (10, 14, 15) that each firebrand (~punk) was set to burn. See Appendix E.

[31] Book 9, p 28 et seq firedrill, See Appendix E.

#71   505   fernroot   gratis   preparation of
which see book 9, p 35.[32]

#72   506   fernroot

preparation of which see book 9, p 36.[33]

23 [22]

#73 – 507, #74 – 508, #75- 509 different kinds of bulbs, for the preparation
of which see book 9 pp 32-35.[34]

#76   510   Cowlitz basket $4.00

brought by Tulalip woman from a Cowlitz woman.

#77   511a-d model $1.50

        of bows and arrows

The bow is made of tsxbēdats. The shaft of the arrows was made of cedar
(= xpai' {x̣pay}). The Snohomish made the point of the arrows either of
bone or of qatsāqwats.[35] Qatsāqwats is the same kind of wood used to make
needles for mats. One man called it "arrow wood" in English. Little Sam

24 [23]

said that the Snoqualmi ordinarily made the point out of stone. He said that
the Snohomish never used stone for the point. The point is lashed to the shaft
with wild cherry bark. The feathers on the shaft are duck feathers. The
arrow of this model is of the actual size. However for war the arrows were
somewhat longer. The actual bow was about 7 inches longer than the one of
the model. The same kind of bow was used for war and for the hunt. The
string of the bow was made of twisted nettle. See next number.

25 [24]

---

[32] Book 9, p 35 cooking fernroot, See Appendix E.

[33] Book 9, p 36 cooking fernroot, See Appendix E.

[34] Book 9 pp 32-35 cooking bulbs Annie Sam (Nov 4, 1916), See Appendix E.

[35] BC suggests the wood for a bow is western yew, *Taxus brevifolia*, and for an arrow is
oceanspray, ironwood, *Holodiscus discolor*. ZZ gives q(a)cagʷac for ironwood, also
Bates, Hess, and Hilbert 1994: 172.

#78   512   twisted nettle string   gratis

    for bow (= stsa'dzax)[36]

   Nettles are split open with a sharp piece of qatsāqwats. It is then dried and twisted in double strands like this specimen.[37]

X #79   513   paddle $.75

   brought from Annie Sam. She said it was a woman's paddle but Peter Sam, 36 years old, said it was a man's paddle. Oakwood.

#80   514   root-digger

    made by Little Sam (called sqā'lax, the handle is called saxwā'qed)[38]

X #81   515   model of war spear $.50

   made by Little Sam. It is

26 [25]

called sqwē'L!es.[39] This was never used for the hunt, only for war. The actual spear was twice the length from hand to hand. That is to say about 10 f{ee}t long.

#82   516   cradle $.75

#83   517   stick for holding cradle

   cradle = skākē'ił.[40] The baby was laid between cedar bark as shown by the model. Cedar bark was also laid into the armpits, otherwise the baby would become rotten there. Some cedar bark was laid under the neck and head. As shown by the model, some cedar bark lay over the head and some was strapped over the

27 [26]

---

[36] Bow is ċaʔsuč NL ċaʔċus SL, ZZ, Bates, Hess, and Hilbert 1994: 293.

[37] BC suggests nettle is stinging nettle, *Urtica dioica*; sċədʼx ZZ.

[38] Dibble or digging stick is sqaləx; səxʷukʷəd is holder, to hold with ZZ.

[39] This is a long spear, also used for bottom fish, sqʷiƛəb ZZ, Bates, Hess, and Hilbert 1994: 192.

[40] Cradleboard is NL skəkiʔiʔł from skəki 'any unnamed child' + iʔł 'infant' while SL is sxal=təd 'mark' + 'tool' presumable because it flattened the baby's forehead ZZ, Bates, Hess, and Hilbert 1994: 302.

forehead. This caused the deformation of the cranium. The projection at the lower end of the cedar bark is meant for the wrapping for the feet. All the thongs in the cradle are of deer skin. Before the baby is tied into the cradle, it is washed in cold water.

The cradle is hung inside of the house on a pliable pole called dzākidiɫ, see #83.[41] All the thongs on this are likewise of deer-skins. Beside the two loops for the cradle, there was one long strap which was tied to the foot of the mother. By means of this strap she could rock the baby. The dzākidiɫ was

28 [27]

stuck into the ground.

The baby was also covered with some hide (represented by the little cloth blanket of the model). This was laid over the cedar-bark covering. This hide blanket was raised up over the head of the child by mean of a hoop represented by the wire in the model. This was done to let the baby get some air.

X #84　518　house mat　　　　　　　$3.50

from Annie Sam. She says it took her a whole month to make this mat and three days to make the border. This is the kind of mat used to hang

29 [28]

on the walls of the winter-house and to make the summer house.

X #85　519　boy's paddle　　　　　　　$.75

　　　of yew wood brought from Little Sam

#86　520A,B S,T deer trap (model)　　　　　$1.00 made by Little Sam

The tiōɫbaxᵘ sklālētut {Wealth} showed this trap to labxqēdE≡. It is a trap for deer and elk. All the strings were made of nettle rope. The trap was called χuōtEd[42] and was used by the Snohomish, not by the Snuqualmi. The animals were chased into this net by people (Sam said 20 boys, with clappers like that of #87). The deer would

---

[41] Baby rocker stick is dᶻakʷitədiʔɫ ZZ.

[42] ZZ suggests x̌ʷutəd without ready translation except for -təd = 'implement, tool'.

become entangled in the meshes of the net.

Men would lie in the bushes at the poles A and B. As soon as the animals

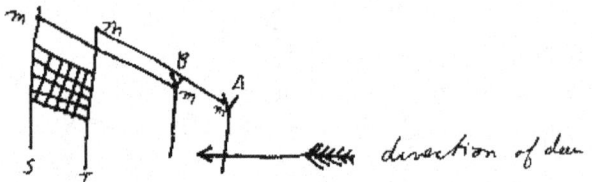

became entangled in the net, these men would pull at the strings m-n so that the poles S and T would fall down and the net would cover the animals. Then the men would run up to the deer or elk and cut the sinews of both hind legs of the animals.

#87   521   clapper $.25

Made by Little Sam

   Struck with a stick to scare up the deer and make them run into the trap #86. This clapper was called tc!ā'xwādid.[43]   The string on the clapper takes the place of wild cherry bark.   The men who followed the deer with these clappers shouted hē, hē, hē.

#88   522   imitation of the stick $.25

   which stiqāyu sklālētut gave to s-dē'u≡ (see Book 10 pp 3 & 4).[44] The end represents a deer foot {hoof}.[45] This stick is called sq! ōsid which is also the general name for "cane." It is painted red. Little Sam

said (Nov 8??) that he did not have such a stick. I believe however he only said this so that he would not have to explain the details of the stiqāyu sklālētut {Wolf}.

#89   plant   gratis

   the root of which is used for black imbrication (see book 10 p 7).[46] The root was split open and the inside of the bark cleaned by scraping.

---

[43] Meaning 'side strike, to hit on the side of something' čaxʷadiʔd ZZ.

[44] Book 10 pp 3 & 4 Wealth Power = tiōɫbaxᵘ, see Appendix F.

[45] Wolf is stiqayuʔ < from 'bushy' ZZ, Bates, Hess, and Hilbert 1994: 226.

#90   grass   gratis

used for white imbrication, see book 10 p 7.[47] The ridge on the convex side of this grass was cut off with a knife. The woman began cutting this ridge off at the

33 [32]

narrow (top) end of the grass-blade.   The opposite side of the grass, dimmest?? the concave side, was on the outside of the basket when the grass was used for imbrication. There are two blades in this specimen, on one the ridge is still present, on the other the ridge has already been cut off.

#91   525   coiled basket $1.00

brought from Johnny Skwāx[u]

#92   526   coiled basket $1.00

made by the <u>aunt of the aunt</u> of Little Sam according to Annie. The maker of this basket was a dukwē'L!babc[48]

34 [33]

(= Pilchuck tribe). It was patched by the aunt of Little Sam, the woman from whom I brought this basket. The tump-line was made by a Snuqualmi woman.

#93   527   basket $.75

This kind of basket is called lɛkwā't.[49] Annie said it was a very old type of basket and was used exclusively for keeping dried salmon. It was used by the Snohomish as well as by the Snuqualmi.

#94   528   basket $4.00

---

[46] Book 10 p 7 Coiled Basketry (Sam & Annie) Nov 19, 1916, See Appendix F.

[47] Book 10 p 7 Coiled Basketry (Sam & Annie) Nov 19, 1916, See Appendix F.

[48] Pilchuck is Chinuk Wawa for 'red water', as is the term dxʷkʷiƛ̓əbabš 'reddish people' ZZ.

[49] A soft basket of cedar bark is ləqʷa ZZ.

made by a Snohomish woman 5 years ago. The woman from whom I bought the basket (not the maker) thought that

35 [34]

the design was that of a snake.

#95   529   rope   gratis

(= stēdgwad) of cedar twigs.[50] This was used to make traps for the deer (Jack Wheeler). If a canoe was to be patched, the pieces would be bound together with this rope, holes having been bored for the rope to pass through.

#96   530   basket $7.00

with Snuqualmi sgᵘdēlētc sklālētut[51]

#97   531a-b Klickitat moccasins $.50

#98   532   model $.50

       533   of moccasins

made by Snuqualmi, Skykomish, Sdōdōhomc. Not made by Snohomish but sold to them by other tribes for shell money.

36 [35]

#99   534   comb (model)

Third box sent to Museum Nov 14, 1916 Charges for this box

Making of box $1.75

Transfer to station   .55 > .75

In this box all specimen were sent which are <u>not</u> marked √ or + . Complete cost of 3ʳᵈ box $34.25 > $34.50

37 [36]

The price of the specimens sent to Museum in box on Oct 27, 1916 was

        $87.05

Specimens marked X were sent to Museum on Nov, 8 1916 (second box)

---

[50] A cedar limb is stidgʷəd, on old growth they were very long and supple ZZ.

[51] These powerful objects are sgʷədilič Bates, Hess, and Hilbert 1994: 100.

The following is a copy of the charges of this second box:

#6	paddle	$1.50
#48	"	.50
#49	"	.50
#50	"	.50
#79	"	.50
#81	model of spear	.50
#84	house-mat	.50
#85	paddle	.50
boxing of specimens		.75
total		$9.75

total charges

1st box	$ 87.05
2nd box	9.75
3rd box	34.50
	$131.30

{The following appendices (B > M) repeat the footnotes added to Notebook 13 itself, then provide HKH's full commentary for each extracted from other notebooks.}

Appendix B: Note 10 Shells

#10.   Book 5, p. 23 Jules tells me that two kind of shell money was used: tc!auwai and s'o'lax.

1 − tc!auwai was made of clam shells found in Snohomish country.   See shell of collection No 16. Of this shell round disks were cut about 1 cm in diameter. A hole was made in each bead so that it could be strung up. These beads must be white and quite round. They were carefully smoothed and rounded on a rough stone on the beach.

2 − s'o'lax this was made of little tubular shells shaped thus XX {dentalia}. This is about the natural size. They were strung {double} as shown above, always [p24] two side by side on two strings with a round bead between the pairs. The two ends of the string of beads were always joined so that the string was in form of a loop.   The measurements are taken for the <u>double</u> line of beads. Thus a fathom of so'lax means the length of a string from one hand to the other and then back to the first constituting the loop. The shells of so'lax were not found in Snohomish country but were traded from northern Indians. For this reason so'lax was considerably more expensive than tc!auwai the shells of which were found at home. Jules said that so'lax was always valued just twice as much as tc!auwai.* see opposite page [p24b]

* Jules said that while so'lax was always measured in a loop that is to say double, tc!auwai was always strung on a thread with two ends and was measured "single." Now if so'lax (measured double) is worth twice as much as tc!auwai (measured single), then the two are really of equal value as far as the actual length of the string strung with shell is concerned. Jules could not comprehend this & persisted in saying that so'lax is just twice as valuable as tc!auwai.

tc!auwai is always strung on one string, not on two like so'lax. [p25] Thus Jules said that a good canoe would be worth about 4 fathoms of so'lax, but 8 fathoms of tc!auwai. A very large canoe would cost more than this.

An ordinary basket was worth about 1 fathom of so'lax. A very good one about 2 fathoms of so'lax. Jules never heard of teeth of animals (= dentalia) being used as money among the Snohomish.

20 fathoms of so'lax might buy a slave. A very good slave would cost 30 or 40 fathoms. The price varied with the size and strength of the slave.

A very important feature about so'lax was to see whether there were [p26] any shells broken on the string. If any shells were at all broken, they would be discounted from the total value of the string. A person who was getting so'lax was very careful to ascertain how many shells were defective. {lists measures of money by span (chest to thumb) and fathom (outstretched hand tip to hand tip). Printed in Haeberlin and Gunther 1930: 29}

Cf also Book 9, page 28 Annie same Nov 5, 1916

The old people used to use shells (tc!auwai') as spoons. With these they would dip the food out of the basket. The shells were used just as they are without handles.

When soup was boiled in basket with hot stones, the stones would be left in the basket when the people started to eat. Then when the basket got empty, they would take the stones out. Finally the people would lick out the basket with their fingers.

Appendix C: Note 16 Wolf

#16   Book 17, pp. 13 et seq [13-16] true story, retold after false start, See Appendix C.

      Grandfather & grandmother went out to travel.   One fall the grandfather, grandmother, and uncle went up river in canoe. They came to a portage. They came up to a place where they heard a wolf howling. Grandma went up to wolf & found that wolf was in misery. Wolf had a big bone in mouth & could not close mouth. Grandmother took a digging stick, shoved it between teeth & pulled out bone. She patted wolf & said, You need not pay me now, but you think of me & give me something later. Next year when they came back there was a fine buck dead lying at the [p14] same place. This happened for 5 years, after that the Wolf must have died. This woman had a Wolf as her skālitut which she got as young girl when she bathed & fasted.

      {retold pp 14 et seq}   {Retold from pp 13 and 14}

                        Told by Mrs. Josephine Leclair

This is a "true" story according to Mrs. Leclair.

      One fall the grandparents and uncle of Mrs. Leclair traveled up the river in a canoe. They came to a portage. One day the grandmother came to a place where she heard a wolf howling. The grandmother [p15] went up to the wolf and found that he was in misery. The Wolf had a big bone which was sticking in his mouth in such a way that he could not close his jaws. The woman took her digging-stick, shoved it between the wolf's teeth, and in this way pulled out the bone. Then she patted the wolf and said: "You need not pay me now, but remember me and give me something later." When they got back to the same place next year, they found a fine dead buck lying there. They found a buck of this kind at this place for five years. After that the Wolf must have died. The ska'letut of this woman was the wolf. She got [p16] it as a young girl when she was fasting and bathing. For this reason she was not afraid of a wolf.

      The grandmother herself told this story to Mrs. Leclair. Mrs. Leclair obviously believed it herself.

Appendix D: Note 25 Pheasant

#25   Book 8 p. 22 et. Seq [p22-30] diagram and description of a pheasant trap from Mr. & Mrs. Little Sam (Annie). See specimen #53, pheasant story. See Appendix D.

pheasant trap Little Sam and his wife   see specimen # 53

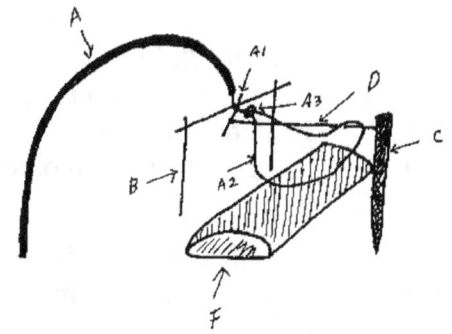

A is a pliable stick with the string A2 and the loop A3 of cherry bark. A was held down to the arch B by means of the little stick A1 attached to the string of A. The little stick was again held in place by means of stick D which was set against C. F represents a [p23] rotten log covered with moss. The string was made to lie over this log and the stick D. The pheasant laid its eggs on moss as on that of log. When the pheasant flew down upon the log, the stick D would come out of place and cause A to snap up and this in turn would close the sling catching the pheasant.

The Sams both assured me that the Snohomish did not use this trap, but that it was characteristic of the Snuqualmi.

The model obtained from Little Sam (specimen # 53) is smaller than the actual trap used.

Besides pheasants, loons and ducks were also caught with this trap. When [p24] loons were caught salmon was put on the log. When ducks were caught rotten salmon was the bait.

When pheasants were caught, two sticks wrapped with moss (see #53E) were stuck into the rotten log, one at each end (not shown in diagram). These were the "wives" of rotten log. Without these "wives" on the log, it would be impossible to catch pheasants. When loons or ducks are trapped there are not "wives" on the log. They are only used when pheasants are trapped. This usage is explained by the following story which the Sams told me:

There are five pheasants camping [p25] on a river at a place called Sa'tsqad. They are four brothers and one sister. The girl is a pheasant, the men are Steel-head salmon, but as far as I could make out, are pheasants at the same time. The woman has five children, four boys and one girl. The brothers of the pheasant woman (the steel-head salmon) are married. Wild-cat (= p!etcɛβ) wants to marry pheasant woman, but she does not like him because he has an ugly face.

Pheasant woman has four sisters. She asks them to go to get crab-apples with her. She climbs up a crab-apple tree and begins to sing. Wild-cat sees her, and shoots her in the anus. [p26]

This does not kill her. She simply pulls the arrow out and goes home. Wild-cat runs away because he is afraid of the revenge of the brothers of pheasant woman.

The pheasant has the Old Log as a husband. This husband is the log F in the trap (see diagram). Pheasant is very fond of this husband. Her 5 children are children of this log. The Old Log has two more wives. These are the "wives" of the trap (#53E), namely the two sticks with moss put up on the log of the trap. These two women talk bad about pheasant, so the pheasant comes and fights with them, first with the one, then with the other. [p27]

The Wild-cat (p!etcɛβ) makes trap (#53) for the pheasant over the Old Log. When pheasant is caught in it, the Wild-cat is glad and eats her. The daughter of pheasant goes to the trap and sees the blood of her mother. She knows that her mother has been killed and goes home and cries. She tells her uncles, the Steel-head-salmons, that her mother has been killed.

The youngest brother of the dead pheasant woman goes to a place where wild-cat is want to cross a river on a log. (Log lies over river). On this log he makes a trap for the wild-cat. The wild-cat is caught and falls into the river and dies. (End)

Annie Sam [p27a] (wife of Little Sam) said that the five pheasants are called sdōdōhōmc.

This [p28] is a Snuqualmi story.

Little Sam is a pure Snohomish. He learned the use of the trap from the grandfather of Annie Sam {= Little Sam's wife}. She is partly a Snuqualmi. This old man was very fond of Little Sam, because he was clean and would not wet the bed, as Annie Sam put it. He taught Little Sam to make this pheasant trap. For this the mother of Little Sam gave the grandfather of Mrs. Sam {= Annie Sam} two blankets.

At the time Little Sam learned to use the pheasant trap he also got the sq^{u}lōβ (= pheasant {sg^{w}əlub}) sklaletut. He fasted for a number of days. Then [p29] he finds a white pheasant. The feathers are all white. This pheasant was a woman, said Annie Sam. Little Sam sleeps with the (= pheasant). He sleeps in the bushing right next to the pheasant trap. He sleeps two days and two nights. Then the grandfather of Mrs. Sam (Annie) went out to get Little Sam. He carries him home and lets him sleep five days in the house. Then he makes the boy bathe, smashes up some salmon and makes some soup of it in a basket. Sam tries to eat it 3 times, but vomits it everytime, finally the fourth time the soup stays down.

As far as I could make out, [p30] it was essential for Little Sam to get the sq^{u}lōβ sklālētut in order to catch pheasants with the trap.

Little Sam also has the cau'ł (ground hog) sklālētut …

Appendix E: Notes #30 – #34
Firedrill, Cooking, Fernroots, and Bulbs

16 Book 9, p 28 et seq firedrill

Fire-drill = cō'laktcup, this was made of the root of a tree called xā'q!tī. This tree does not grow in this country, it grows on the upper part of the Snohomish river.

The next day (Nov 4, 1916) Sam made me a model of a firedrill (see specimen #70). Annie now explained to me that only the stick upon which is drilled and the <u>point</u> of the driller is made of xā'q!tī. The rest of the driller is made of black wild cherry. The point is bound to the handle by means of wild cherry bark. If xā'q!tī (root of) can not be obtained, then pussy willow was used for the point of the driller and the wood upon which was drilled. Very dry cedar bark was used as fuse.

Story [p30-32] of how Little Sam was sent out to quest by Annie's own Grandfather, with a dry cedarbark firebrand (like specimen #69) set to burn 10 days, then for 14 days, and, last, for 15 days, when he succeeded. "When I {HKH} insisted upon knowing the name of this sklālītut, Little Sam suddenly burst out in tears and sobbed. On asking him he said that if he told me that name he would have to die. After appeasing the old man, he proceeded to tell men about this sklālītut."[52]

17 Book 9, p 35 Preparation of the fern-root of specimen # 71.

The root is baked {scorched?} over a fire. Then it is scraped with a stick. Then it is pounded on a rock with a stick called stā'tcōq!ᵘ. This pounding makes it possible to tear the outside fibers of the root from the inside ones.

The outside fibers are eaten with dried salmon eggs. The inside fibers [p36] are dried over the fire, smashed up to powder and eaten with <u>fresh</u> salmon eggs.

{BC suggests #71 is hairy brackenfern, *Pteridium aquilinum* (L.) Kuh var. *pubescens*.}

18 Book 9, p 36 Preparation of the fern-root of specimen # 72.

The ends of the little individual bulbs are cut off (Annie cut a few ends off of the specimen in my collection). Then the roots are cooked in the following way: First stones are heated, then the following layers are put on them: fern leaves, sallal berry twigs, then fern-roots, sallal berry twigs, fern leaves and a layer of sand & ashes ½ to 1 ft deep. On

---

[52] Dr Brian Compton {BC, 7 Dec 03}, in looking at this note, draws a comparison to Twana use of yellow willow for a fire drill (Elmendorf 1960: 219) and wrote "The contemporary nomenclature for this tree would be *Salix lucida* Muhl. ssp. *lasiandra* (Benth.) E. Murr. (pacific willow)."

top of this a fire is made. The roots cook for 24 hours. When cooked the little individual bulbs are broken off from (continued on opposite page !) [p36a] (continued from p 36) the roots and the skin is torn off them. They are eaten with dry salmon eggs.

{BC suggests #72 is common ladyfern, *Athyrium filix-femina* [L.] Roth, or perhaps spreading woodfern, *Dryopteris expansa* (K. Presl) Fraser-Jenkins & Jermy.}

19 Book 9 pp 32-35 bulbs Annie Sam (Nov 4, 1916)

Preparation of the dzā'bēt bulbs (see specimen #73 – 507). It was boiled by means of hot rocks in a basket together with salmon. A soup was made in this way. There was another way of making dzā'bēt, namely as follows:

A hole was made in the ground and a fire made in it. The stones were laid on top of four sticks laid thus # (seen from above) and a fire built underneath. The fire would consume the sticks on which the stones lay and the stones would fall down. On top of the hot rocks would be laid a layer of hemlock twigs, then some wild pea vines, then salal-berry leaves then wild pea vines, the hemlock twigs, then a layer of sand about 1 ft deep. Then a fire was built on top. The bulbs were cooked for 3 days and 2 nights in this way.

[BC links #73 to the Lushootseed term for rooty vegetables and to unattributed plant in Bates, Hess, and Hilbert (1994, 87). The wild pea vines may have been American verch, *Vicia Americana*].

Preparation of tsāgwītc (see specimen #75- 509)

Cooked in basket by means of hot stones together with salmon to make soup.

[BC suggests #75 "is probably Lilium columbanun (Columbian or tiger lily)".]

Tc!ālēq!ᵘ (see specimen #74 – 508) was cooked in the same way, however, with clams, never with salmon.

Tc!ālēq!ᵘ and tsāgwītc are also prepared in the following way:

A fire is built in sand. Then the hot sand and ashes are pushed aside and maple leaves are laid on the sand, then the bulbs are put on the leaves, and the bulbs are then again covered with maple leaves. Over this is then put a [p35] layer of hot ashes and sand. The bulbs are allowed to cook 1 to 1 1/2 hours. The sand is brushed away carefully with a duck wing. When tsāgwītc is cooked in this way it is eaten with salmon eggs.

[BC suggests identifications of salal as *Gaultheria shallon* Pursh, western hemlock as *Tsuga heterophylla* [Raf.] Sarg., and maple as perhaps bigleaf maple, *Acer macrophyllum* Pursh.]

Appendix F: Notes #44, #46, #47 Gifts

#22   Book 10 pp 3 & 4 Wealth Power tiōłbaxᵘ, see Appendix F.

#88   522   imitation of the stick $ .25

which stiqāyu sklālētut gave to s-dē'u☉ (see Book 10 pp 3 & 4). The end represents a deer foot [hoof]. This stick is called sq! ōsid which is also the general name for "cane." It is painted red. Little Sam [p32 [31]] said (Nov 8??) that he did not have such a stick. I believe however he only said this so that he would not have to explain the details of the stiqāyu sklālētut.

tiōłbaxᵘ [tiyułbaxad]

s-dē'u☉ fasts 10 days. Then he makes a cedar raft and gets a rock. He goes out on the lake with the raft. When he is in the middle of the lake, he puts water into his ears, take the rock into his hands, and descends into the lake. He comes to the house of stiqāyu. Stiqāyu teaches him to make traps and to catch seal, sturgeon, flounders, smelt, sole, salmon, deer. After coming up out of the water, s-dē'u☉ slept 2 days and 1 night.

stiqāyu gave s-dē'u☉ a stick with a carved deer foot at the end (see specimen # 88)

[p4] The daughter of s-dē'u☉ waved this cane. At once 10 he-elks and 10 she-elks dropped dead by themselves.

Sam has the stiqāyu sklālētut and can hunt deer. I reminded him of the fact that the preceding day he had told me that no Snohomish ever hunted the deer. He said that he had just said that to me the preceding day, because he did not want to talk about his sklālētut. (He always began to cry when I urged him to tell me about one of his sklālētuts.) To-day he said that a Snohomish with a stiqāyu sklālētut could hunt deer and also the bear.   Stiqāyu   s-dē'u☉

23   Book 10 p 7 Coiled Basketry (Sam and Annie) Nov 19, 1916, see Appendix F.

24   Book 10 p 7 Coiled Basketry (Sam and Annie) Nov 19, 1916, see Appendix F.

The Snohomish did not make any coiled baskets. Sam & Annie never positive on this point. But the Snuqualmi make these baskets. The foundation was made of dried cedar roots (= ts! āpx).

The material for the black imbrication is called dābts. It is the root of the plant of specimen # 89. The material for the white imbrication is called tcatōlbixᵘ. This is a mountain grass which the Indians get in the Cascade Mountains. For samples of this grass see specimen # 90.

ts!āpx, dābts, and tcatōlbix^u are all dried. Before using these materials the women soak them in water to [p8] make them pliable. They would break otherwise.[53]

Twined baskets (= xalā'yōtsid)were made by the Snohomish, Snuqualmi, Sdodohomc [Pilchucks], and Skykomish. When these twined baskets were finished the woman fills them with dry sand and leaves them that way for a few hours. This is done "to straighten them out."

---

[53] BC suggests cedar is *Thuja plicata*, the black is *Equisetum*, and the grass is *Xerophyllum tenas* ~ bear grass.

Appendix G: Mountain Beavers (Note #23)

HKH recorded the most complete information on this species, whose past ethnographic record is confused. Not only did he collect stories in which it figured and ethnographic details of its use, but he also collected a pelt and trap now at AMNH. In the Northwest, mountain beaver (now *Aplodontia rufa* (Rafinesque)) has two subspecies of *A. rufa rufa* around Mt Hood and the Puget lowlands, which is smaller, and of *A. rufa rainieri* (Merriam), found in the higher Cascades. Distinguished by long whiskers and claws, it eats any and all vegetation, including fir and hemlock twigs in winter. It sometimes diverts streams into tunnels, and occasionally gnaws bark and trims trees.[54] It is a most curious animal.

The mountain beaver is not a beaver, nor does it live in the mountains. It inhabits the damp, forested foothills of the Cascade Range of Washington, Oregon, and California. Commonly known in Oregon as a boomer, it does not boom; in some sections called a whistler, it does not whistle. This much misnamed rodent and its eight subspecies have been set apart in a family of their own. They are found nowhere outside of North America.[55]

It often plays the role of heroine in epics, such as the War of the Winds set in the Duwamish Valley. Industry, year around activity, tunnel engineering, and plant care are hallmarks of this chubby, bobtailed rodent, which is usually about a foot long and weighs a few pounds. Such strongly female, domestic associations make it an ideal wife in folklore.

From entrances usually behind a bush or stump, it digs shallow burrows through soft, moist ground; emerges mostly at night due to poor eyesight, and is remarkably guileless. These rambling tunnels, with a roof plastered with packed clay and a floor of dry leaves and grass, include a nest chamber. Active all year, it continues to tunnel through deep snow. During a flood, however, it swims out to find refuge at the highest elevations.[56]

An intensive herbivore, it delights in young fruit trees and fresh farm crops in new fields so that it quickly becomes a nuisance near human cultivation. It will scout for food by climbing saplings as much as 15 feet tall, trimming back side branches with its teeth to leave gripping stubs. Later, it will cut down the tree itself for food.

---

[54] Walter Dalquist, *Mammals of Washington* 1948: 367-369; Arthur Kruckeberg, The Natural History of Puget Sound 1991: 213-215; Ian Cowan and Charles Guiguet, *The Mammals of British Columbia* 1978.

[55] Ralph DeSola, *American Wild Life Illustrated* 1946: 57-60.

[56] Ralph DeSola, *American Wild Life Illustrated* 1946: 57-60.

Members live dispersed, sometimes in scattered neighborhoods but never in colonies. Such habitat spacing is encouraged by a strong musky odor. They mate February to March. Females gestate a month, and have a litter of two to five pups, which are grey with large heads and closed eyes. They can be made into pets if confined outside in large enough enclosures to permit burrows, but they quickly die when held captive inside.[57]

The head is large, wide and low with small eyes, small ears and long vibrissae. The legs are short and heavy, but the forefeet are small and handlike; the hindfeet are large and powerful. The claws of both forefeet and hindfeet are long and strong. ... The feet are pink. [58]

The animals are most abundant near springs, streams and damp places, although they are not aquatic. The tangled jungles of deciduous trees and shrubs that grow in ravines and stream valleys of the Puget Sound area present optimum habitat. ... Small streams flow through some burrows. ... [One] nest was composed of the leaves and stems of bracken [ferns] laced together with grass and fine twigs. [59]

Although principally nocturnal, mountain beavers are not infrequently active by day, especially in the fall. At this season they harvest food and spread it on logs to dry. The cured hay is removed to their burrows for nesting material and food. ... In winter they eat such evergreen shrubs as salal (*Gaultheria shallon*) and Oregon grape (*Berberis nervosa*). They also eat the bark of trees, especially that of the willow (*Salix*). Under cover of snow, in the mountains, they burrow to some extent and pack excavated earth in snow burrows. The melting of the snow in the spring reveals the earth core, six to eight inches in diameter and two to four feet long. Several such earth cores were forked, showing that part of the earth had been pushed into a branching burrow.[60]

The mountain beaver holds its food in its forefeet, squirrellike, when it eats. Its food consists of the leaves and bark of woody plants and entire herbs, including roots. The mountain beaver is the only mammal so far as known that eats the bracken fern. It feeds on the branches of coniferous trees, including Douglas fir, red cedar, and hemlock. Such thorny species as blackberry, black-cap and devil's club are eaten. The odiferous skunk cabbage and the stinging

---

[57] Walter Dalquist, *Mammals of Washington* 1948: 367-369.

[58] Dalquist 1948: 367-69.

[59] Dalquist 1948: 367-369.

[60] Dalquist 1948: 367-369.

nettle are on its bill of fare. A list of its food would include most plants found in its habitat, and we know of no species that it refuses as food. ...[61]

It undermines roads and trails and defiles springs and streams. Control is simple for the animals readily enter steel traps set in their burrows.[62]

Its burrows can have up to a 19 inch diameter, with separate chambers for nest, offal, and food,

… surrounded by fan-shaped earth mounds and pathways; in very wet areas, a "tent" of sticks covered with leaves and fern fronds erected over burrow entrances; in late summer, "hay piles" of ferns and other vegetations up to 2 feet high on logs or ground.[63]

Baseball-size balls of stone or clay [they] encountered in digging, which the animal occasionally gnaws upon to sharpen its teeth and used to close off nesting or feeding areas when vacated.[64]

In all, mountain beavers eat and act much like humans. Natives relied on bracken fern roots as a major food, along with other roots and berries. Nettles, willows, and devil's club are important medicines, and nettle fiber was once woven into nets. Evergreen wood was carved into a variety of tools. As competitors for the same resources, natives and mountain beavers would have frequently observed each other and recognized their common bonds.

---

[61] Dalquist 1948: 367-369.

[62] Dalquist 1948: 367-369.

[63] John Whitaker, *The Audubon Society Field Guide to North American Mammals* 1980: 367.

[64] Whitaker, *Audubon Guild to Mammals* 1980: 368.

Notebook 32 [HKH]

Specimens   1917   Puyallup

July 6 large basket $8.00   no 1   502/841

      Brought from Joe Swayle. "Fly" diagram around rim. Joe did not know what the main design was. It was made on the "White River" by the Renton band (or a Puyallup people). (Renton Indians = Dwamish)

July 2 twined basket $2.50   no 2   /842

      Bought from Joe Swayle. Made by Chehalis woman

                                                                                   2

#3 brought from white woman in Tacoma. It is from East of mts $2.00   /843

#4 brought from white woman in Tacoma. Made by a young Cowlitz girl .50   /844

#5-23 inclusively were brought on the Muckleshoot reservation

                                                                                     3

cabEdoltc[65]

#8 and #14 have the design *cabed* according to Old Anne, who made no 14 (not no 8) *ca'bid* is a net for catching ducks according to Annie? But the man who sold me net no 20 also called this *ca'bEd*. He said it was used for catching fish in a creek.[66] A basket with a *ca'bed* design was called *cabEdoltc* by old Anne.

#10 old bag of hide used in Indian?? [Treaty] War in Governor Steven's time. Morris Lobehan said that it used to be higher. It has been trimmed down, he said.

---

[65] Called a trawl net, it had a pocket and was hauled between paired canoes, this term šəbidulc means 'net + design' (literally 'basket, container') ZZ. The diagram of this net use was left out of the English version of Haeberlin and Gunther.

[66] Such nets, of course, were efficiently deployed on land, air, and water to catch deer, ducks, and fish. Certain habitats and local conditions called for distinctive coloring and design of the net, but it had many generic usages.

E

#5 made by Snuqualmi woman (basket) $2 /845

#6 made by Muckleshoot (basket) .50 /846

#7 (basket) 4.00 /847

#8 Muckleshoot (basket) ca'bEd (net for ducks) 1.00 /848

#9 Muckleshoot (basket) 1.00 /849

#10 buckskin bag used in war of Gov Stevens .75 /850

#11 Muckleshoot (basket) 4.00 /851

#12 made by Snuqualmi (basket) 4.00 /852

#13 " " " " (basket) 3.00 /853

4

#16 and #17 have the design ts!aut?? "gills of salmon" according to Old Annie who made the basket.[67] Anne is a Muckleshoot. A basket with this design is called ts!aitolitz

[taɬ = spear head for catching salmon]

4 ?

kwaux^u Klickitat Snuqualmi ts!aitolitz[68]

14 made by old Anne (Muckleshoot) 2.00 50.2/854
        ca'bEd (basket)

15 Klickitat bag 1.00 /855

16 made by Old Anne (ts!ait) (basket) 1.50 /856

17 " " " 4.00 /857

18 bow and arrows 4.00 /858 A to U [A, B-U]

19 net for salmon (with string) 1.50 /859
        kwaux^u

20 net for little fish .75 /860
        ca'bEd

21 Snuqualmi moccasins for men & woman 2.00 /861 AB 16.75

---

[67] Gills is sċay?t ZZ.

[68] ts!aitolitz may be sċay?tulc = 'gill + basket' ('design').

5

#20 is a net for catching little fish like trout in creek. A hoop of wood was fastened to mouth & attached to pole. It is called ca'bɛd.

#19 is a net for catching salmon. It is called kwaix^u. A hoop was fastened to two cross-wise poles . It was dipped into the water from a platform. A string ran in some way from the end to the finger of the fisher. When a fish got into the trap the fisher would know it by the jerking of the string.

[6] 5

woman's skirt, made by Muckleshoot woman 10.00 /862

mat ~~basket~~ making implement .25 /863

July 11, 1917 I sent Goddard the first shipment of specimens from Auburn, Wash. They were specimens #5-23. The cost of this shipment was as follows:

$47.25 for specimens

   .85 for boxing

$48.10 total

7

parfleches like #27 were <u>not</u> made by Squalli.

Pete Kalama said that Squalli never made mats like those of nos 32 & 33. These mats the Squalli got from Sound Indians in British Columbia.

He also said that Squalli only made stiff baskets. (This contradicts what Henry Martin said). Basket #31 also came from British Columbia Indians.

Squalli only make soft baskets

8 [6]

Nisqually Sq [Squally] Skokomish

24 basket .50 50.2/864

25 " 1.00 /865

26 Skokomish basket 6.00 /866

27 Yakima parfleche, traded to Squalli 5.00 /867

28 basket (Skokomish) 3.50 /868

29 spoon of horn .25 X

30 Skokomish basket 3.50 /869

31 basket from BC Indians, not made by Squally .25 /870

32 mat from BC Indians not made by Squally 1.00 /871

 21.00

#34 is an old Cowlitz basket. An old Cowlitz woman sold it to me. She said it had been made before she was born.

#38 This is the oldest basket that the Indians know about. They prized it very highly & all agreed upon the great age. They said it was 200 years old. This is very likely exaggerated. They were positive in asserting that it was made by the great grandmother of an old woman who died about 2 year ago at the age of 75 years. The maker of the basket was a Squalli woman. The basket was made among the Squalli.

 Quinault

33 mat from BC Indians   1.00 /872

 not made by Squalli

34 Cowlitz basket, old   8.00 /873

35 wooden spoon   .75   /874

36 Quinault basket   1.24 /875

37 Chehalis basket (Chehalis)   2.00 /876

38 very old Squalli basket   8.00 /877

 200 years old

 $24.00

#24-38 were bought on the Nisqualli reservation.

 X

 13.65

 6.65

 4.50

 24.89

 57

 48.10

$ 129.90

8

Second shipment of specimens from Tacoma in two boxes on July 21, 1917. Pieces were marked #1-4 and ?-38. The cost was as follows:

Specimens	$55.00
Boxing	1.00
Cartage	1.00
	$ 57.00 total

    57.00
    48.10
    52.30
$157.40

9

Tulalip

tamanuwus   Snuqualmi

#39 paddle .75 /891

#40 twined basket, made on Tulalip reservation .50 /879

#41 basket made by woman partly Snuqualmi, partly Yakima

     2.00 /880

#42 basket from Quinault 4.00 /881

#43 basket 1.00 /882

#44 new? Basket 4.00 /883

#45 tamanawus stick (tŏstEd) .40 /884[69]

#46 basket (wicker weave) 1.00 /885

x

#47 was a type of canoe called sdŭx̌ʷwiɫ.[70] It was used on saltwater for catching seal, sturgeon, etc??

#50 & #51 both have the gill-net design (= L!ots!Lots!itoib).[71] The design is not quite finished on #50. Mrs Jules said it might to go higher up. I saw another basket much larger, thus

---

[69] These poles are təstəd, related to sgʷədilič Bates, Hess, and Hilbert 1994: 100.

[70] Hunting canoe is sdəxʷiɫ.

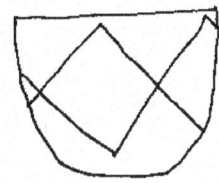 The design was also called *L!ots! L!ots!itub* by Mrs Jules??

X

Snohomish sduxwił

47 model of canoe .50 /886

48 unfinished basket, made by girl .25 /887

49 ditto .25 /888

50 made by Skagit woman for children 1.50 /889

     (mother-in-law of Charlie Jules)

51 ditto 1.00 /890

52 spoon .15 X??

53 man's paddle 1.50 50.2/878

54 basket 1.50 /890

11

55 basket, design called "fern leaf" 3.00 /893

56 model of water bucket .50 50.2/894

    Larger bucket of this kind were made. Four sides were made of one piece of wood, which was soaked in water & heated & bent at grooves. The old type of bucket also had handle of twigs. These buckets were said to keep water. Fern leaves were put over bucket to keep water clean. The ends of the piece of wood used for 4 sides was joined together by pegs of cedar. Bottom was fastened to sides by the same means. The seams were made water-tight by means of pitch. Bucket was made of cedar.

12

sgudeletc sklaletut

#57 model of board of swudeletch .25 /895

    (see other notebooks)

#58 model of tamanuwas pole (tostEd) .25 /896

    of sgudeletc sklaletut. Real pole was about 10 feet long

#59 model of Snohomish instrument .50 /897

---

[71] This seems to refer to λucλučitəb = 'the webbing of a net' ZZ.

for killing shark when boy dove into water to get spirit (See book #34).[72] Original somewhat longer. Two pieces tied together with cedar twigs.

#60 model of stick to scare up flounder gratis /897

Original much longer (See book #34)[73]

#76 pin for holding blanket together gratis / [page total =] 1.00

(numbered #60 by mistake, two no 60 in my collection)

13

stone celt   taɬ

#61 stone chisel found by Annie Sam near her house gratis /899

#62 basket made on Tulalip reserv[ation] 3.00 /900

#63 harpoon for catching seal & sturgeon (called taɬ) 3.00 /901 A-D

This model was made by Little Sam. The original was longer. The parts of the original were made of the following material:

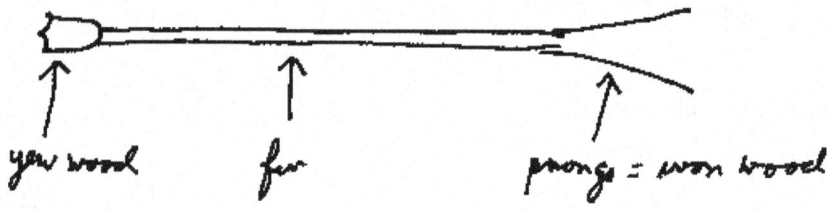

Duck float was made [of] cedar. The point of detachable heads was made of seasoned yew wood (also horn?). The two "ears"

[page total =] 6.00

x

of the head were made of elk-horn. The rope was made of bark. The rope was fastened to shaft of harpoon by means of a slip-knot. They would open as soon as animal was hit. The harpooned animal would drag float along. When it was tired out, the hunter grabbed hold of float by projection at its tail. Then the hunter killed the animal by thrusting a sharp spear made of seasoned yew-wood several times into the back of the head of the animal.

---

[72] Haeberlin and Gunther 1930: 69.

[73] Book #34, devoted to clothing and tools, mentions [p3] "Men in canoe came from shore & scared flounder {into net} by splashing a long pole (= pŏx^{u}tɛd) in water. This pole was 2½ the distance of outstretched arms and was wider at end. Made of one piece."

A harpoon for catching salmon was made similarly. It also had {iron wood} two prongs, the spear heads were detachable, but were tied to spear-shaft by means of rope. If spear head were not detachable, the fish would break off prongs of harpoon.

32-14b

Lillooet Klickitat

#69 This basket is interesting because it is a mixture of the Lillooet & the Klickitat type. The woman from whom I brought it was sure that it was made by a Skagit woman. She proclaimed it to be a basket of the typical Skagit type. The designs are "combs" (= cɛpcɛpa's)[74]

#70 The design is that of "flounders."

#71 Mrs Johnson said that the head dress was used in treaty-day for qwaxq sklalitut. But she says it might properly be used for any kind of sklalitut. When it is used, duck feathers are put on the cedar bark.

x

Suquamish Skag[it]'s qwoxq – sklalitut[75]

#64 basket 2.50 /902

#65 clam basket .50 /903

#66 basket made by Suquamish (?) 1.50 /904

woman from whom I brought this basket thought that [a] Suquamish woman made it

#67 paddle (man's) .25 /905

#68 needle for making mats .25 /906

#69 Skagit basket, "combs" [design] 6.00 /907

#70 basket made by wife of Tommy Johnson, flounder-pattern 4.00 /908

#71 cedar headdress .25 /910

used on treaty day with qwoxq – sklalitut (used with duck feathers)

x

#72 This is a storage basket. Mrs Johnson claims that in olden times they had the same kind of basket with a lid just like this one.

---

[74] Comb is šəpšəpac ZZ.

[75] Probably = q̓ʷuxq̓ʷ(əd).

#74 The designs on this basket are Lek!Luk!ola, which are the gamb{ril ??} poles of a mat house to which the mats are tied. Or more correctly I believed the Lek!Luk!ola are notched & hold the horizontal poles of roof to which the mats are tied.

x

     added up numbers

#72 basket used in old times .25 /909

     Old time basket also lid like this one.

#73 basket 1.00 /911

#74 basket with Lek!Luk!ola design 2.00 /912

#75 gambling set 3.00 /913 A-U

#76 pin for holding blanket together 50.2/914

     numbered #60 by mistake, see p 12

On Aug 4 1917, I sent Goddard a third shipment of specimens in 3 boxes from Marysville, Wash. The specimens were numbered from #39-#76.

For specimens	$52.30
Boxing & cartage	1.25
Total	$53.55

x

random note:

     golatc = a fish net manipulated by one man in a river to catch salmon.[76] It is attached to pole & dipped into water. It is cone-shaped. Tommy Johnson said that it is not the same as ca'bɛd. The later is manipulated by four men, two in each canoe.

$48.10 1st shipment	July 11, 1917
57.00 2nd "	July 21, 1917
53.00 3rd "	Aug 4, 1917
$158.65	

$ 175.00
− 158.65 =
$ 16.35 = remainder

---

[76] Dip net is qʷuləc ZZ.

x

svastika Swinomish

#77 blanket of mountain goat wool 1/50 50.2/915

Made by Swinomish woman. Originally white but dyed brown by woman from whom I brought it.

This blanket I sent to Goddard by insured parcel post on Aug. [13, 1917]

#78-82 plant specimens

#83 basket 4.50 /915

design "lakes running into one another"

#84 Yakima bag 1/50 /916

#85 basket with svastika design 2.00 /917

31 –19 x

#86 bead[ed] belt, native string $1.50 /918

(beads strung on native string)

#87 belt with beadwork, of leather 2.00 /919

#88 basket with "box" design 3.00 /920

On Aug 17, 1917 I sent Goddard # 1 box of specimens (nos 83-88) from Auburn, Wash.[77] The charges of this shipment were:

specimens $ 14.50
boxing-cartage   .50 =
                   $ 15.00

---

[77] Auburn, in King County, was platted by Levi Ballard, father of Arthur, as Slaughter in memory of Lt William Slaughter, slain in the Treaty War. The Muckleshoot reservation is nearby. It is unclear if Arthur and Herman ever met, though ACB once mentioned seeing plant or root specimens drying in a Muckleshoot home for HKH to add to his collection.

Complete list of shipments of specimens

$ 48.10 (1 box) 1st shipment July 11, 1917
    57.00 (2 boxes) 2nd "   July 21, 1917
    53.55 (3 boxes) 3rd "   Aug 4, 1917
     1.50 (parcel post)   Aug 13, 1917
    <u>15.00</u> 1 box (express   Aug 17, 1917)
$<u>175.15</u> total

=====

=====

Letters / Correspondence[78]

Philadelphia, American Philosophical Society [APS] # 986

New York, April 27, 1913

Dear Professor Boas !

I hope you remember that once before I asked you to give me your advice regarding Dr. Haeberlin's Indian boards. [??]

As you hear Dr. Seligman has decided to show them next month. He wants me to suggest the right expert willing to take on the demonstration in New York. - Not only as historical documents will it create a certain interest, but also because of its unique character of imagination.

I send you also the letters of Mrs. Mestor the biologist and would be happy to hear from you.

> Yours sincerely Herman Haeberlin
> 615 W. 143
> N.Y. 27/ 4/ 13

Nov 1 1913 Leipsig at APS <paraphrased>

HKH writes to Boas summarizing their talk at Café Josti in Berlin during the prior summer. While he was encouraged to apply for a fellowship at Columbia, receiving any stipend would depend on his not having a PhD but being a candidate for that degree. So instead of taking his degree that winter, based on his Berlin study of "ornaments of the ancient Pueblo," he would postpone his degree until he had a chance to take it in the US. He was in Leipsig for the winter term to "deal with a certain phase of the social organization of the Pueblo Indians." He wonders if the application can be general instead of specific to ethnology.

Nov 24 1913 NY at APS <paraphrased>

Boas to HKH sending along the blank forms for application, with the stipulation that it has to be in anthropology.

---

[78] Translations from the German were done by Ulrich Fritzsche M.D, of Seattle WA, and finished on March 10, 2001. As a native German speaker with a medical degree and background, Dr Fritzsche was unusually qualified to undertake this task at my request, providing his usual enthusiasm, and deserves great thanks. Astrida Blukis Onat and I made preliminary translations lacking his expertise.

Dec 9 1913 Leipsig at APS <paraphrased>

HKH confirms that a letter of support was send by Prof K Weule, director of the Leipsig Museum of Ethnology, asking that a stipend be included. "It would give me a possibility of attaining an American Ph.D.-degree which, as you know, would be of much greater service to me in my future career in America than a German degree."

Dec 20 1913 NY at APS <paraphrased>

FB asks HKH to send as many endorsements from Professors in Leipzig and Berlin as possible, as well as "state also in what particular work you are engaged and what you want to do here."

[HKH goes to Columbia in 1914, takes his PhD based on library research of Pueblo cosmic genders ("fertility"), engages in various museum and archaeological research projects, and then begins fieldwork on Puget Sound.]

Jan 7 1916 NY at APS <paraphrased>

FB writes HKH in DC, giving price estimates from Weber for photographs and pen and ink drawings of baskets for a total of $8. FB indicates "a total expenditure of $75 for Washington specimens".

?? at APS <paraphrased>

HKH writes De Lancey Gill of the BAE (see Appendix I) about "making illustrations for my paper on types of pottery from the Valley of Mexico" using 114 sherds from Cambridge (Ma) and 24 from Philadelphia (Pa). Of the Harvard sherds, 104 have been marked in pencil so their portrayal can be specified in some detail and color.

Sept 12 1916 Chicago in German at APS # 372 A

Chicago, September 12. 1916

Dear Professor Boas,

As you can see I'm now in Chicago. I arrived 5 PM yesterday. I haven't seen Laufer [*] yet, but I'll see him this morning.

I sent to you the letter you had mentioned. I've given your daughter two keys to the two cabinets in the seminar room, where I locked up my manuscripts. It's the second and third cabinet from the window behind the large cabinet. There you'll find everything in case you are interested. I've also given Helen a small package with pieces of broken pottery from Puerto Rico. They are pieces from the jungle and from the cave. Nelson mentioned to me that the texture of the two kinds is different. The pieces from the cave have a dark gray color while those coming from the jungle are red. Maybe you know somebody who can analyze them. That's the only item regarding my Puerto Rico work that needs to be finished. The remaining transcriptions and additions I have finished last week in New York.

Concerning the color plates for the basketry it would be desirable to have at least the following five baskets reproduced in colors:

50 – 2473	(Klickitat)
50 – 1413	same
16 – 8731	Thompson
16 – 4637	same
16 – 5906	Lill [ooet]

In case you would like to add more color plates, I would propose the following ones. I put them in the desirable order:

16 - 4611
16 - 4645
16 - 8835
16 - 5907
16 - 9540

In regards to the rectangular baskets I definitely would prefer the long side to be shown. In case you should reproduce only four baskets in color, I would prefer you chose the larger one of the above mentioned Klickitat baskets, as it is more desirable than the smaller one. Even though I have the images of both baskets clearly in my head, I don't know at the moment whether 50-2473 or 50-1413 is the larger one.

My address remains: General Delivery, Seattle. I'll leave here tomorrow or the day after. I have asked [Pliny Earle] Goddard [*] to have Sargent's baskets wrapped. Lowdermilk informed me the day before my departure that he could provide me with Eells and Swan, each for $ 1.50. I can have the two books sent west for me. You had recently written to Hodge regarding these books. I don't know whether you had asked him whether he could lend them separately to me, or whether you had just inquired where I could get them. Mr. Liebowitz has informed me that he sent you Phillip's "Totem Tales." The museum wasn't able to provide me with or lend me [Harlan] Smith "Archaeology of Puget Sound." You have but one copy yourself. The reason being that it is published in Holland. It would be easy to get in Leiden. I have taken with me Smith "Cairns of B.C. and Washington" and "Archaeology of the Lower Fraser".

I hope all is very well with you and your dear family. Give my regards to everyone, especially to your wife. Yours sincerely, Herman Haeberlin.

P.S. Aitken's and Mason's Puerto Rico things which I had put out to be drawn are either with Robert or Sabine. Everything is labeled and matches the list I sent you last June. {HKH's undiagnosed diabetes so sapped his strength he left Puerto Rico early.}

Sept 18 1916 Seattle in German at APS # 583

September 18, 1916

Dear Professor Boas,

I arrived last evening in Seattle. I have received the two publications by Eells and Swan. Thank you for your efforts. Philipps "Totem Tales" did also get here. You didn't annotate some of the tales. Does that mean they are Salish?

I remained for three days in Chicago, and did get to see a lot of Laufer. He is an extremely sympathetic person. I would like to get to know him better. I'll have the opportunity on my way back. He talked to me about the position now open at the museum, and told me to think about taking it. He asked me not to talk with anyone else about it except with you. The whole thing appears not very promising and desirable. Even Dr. Laufer admitted that he wouldn't recommend the position to a friend. Present conditions at the Chicago Museum seem to be rather unsettled. The trustees insist that no research project can be undertaken until the collections are in the new building, and that may be two or three years down the road. Until then work for museum people will be limited to cataloguing and decorating their display cases. If possible I would like to avoid this exclusively 'museological' work. I would like to work with Dr. Laufer. He gives the impression of being a very stimulating person, but otherwise the whole milieu is not very energizing. I have told Dr. Laufer that I would think about it during the coming weeks. Actually I have already made up my mind not to accept. I do hope to work again next year with you and for you - work far more appealing than cataloguing.

This afternoon I left Seattle for Everett, a town north of Seattle and only a few miles south of the Tulalip Reservation. Tomorrow morning I'll take the boat for the reservation to see what can be done there.

Today I received a letter from [James] Teit [*]. He had some suggestions regarding the Indian villages we are about to visit. I have written to you from Chicago in regards to the color plates. I hope everything is clear. The basket collection in Chicago is good and offers some interesting things. The catalogue is rich in information about design-names. Newcombe collected them. Is this information still reliable?

Please give my regards to your family and especially to your wife. Yours sincerely, Herman Haeberlin

P.S. My address remains General Delivery, Seattle, Washington

Sept 21 1916 Tulalip in German at APS # 387

Tulalip, Washington, September 21, 1916

Dear Professor Boas,

Since yesterday I have settled here on the Tulalip Reservation. My address is simply Tulalip, Washington. I did my first work last evening. I had someone describe to me the s t a ha 'lem' game. What makes it so complicated is the way it is told. A 47 year old man described it to me. He speaks good English and was recommended to me by everyone as the most reliable and intelligent Indian. He also is considered as the most knowledgeable of the old customs and the most energetic in sustaining them. He seems to be very enthusiastic about the idea that the old things be published before they are lost for ever. He doesn't want to have any money for it. When he accepts it he wants it to be seen just as a gift from me. He says he doesn't want any " pay." His attitude embarrassed me somewhat yesterday. He wants to sacrifice as much time for me as possible, but unfortunately he doesn't always have the time, because he has all kinds of work to do for the school. This morning another man will visit with me. He is in his seventies and lives nearby. Again, he also doesn't have much time, because he has much work to do on his fields. Under these circumstances much time is being lost. Also, all Indians live by themselves and in single family units all over the reservation. The school is still the most centrally located. Fortunately there are quite a few Indians houses which can be reached by foot.

I hope all is well with you and your family. Please extend my greetings to your wife. Yours Sincerely, Herman Haeberlin

Sept 25 1916 Tulalip in German at APS # 590

Tulalip, Washington, September 25, 1916

Dear Professor Boas,

It's almost a week I'm on this reservation. I've been quite busy. I've recorded several stories in English. I had two different people tell me about the smet'na'g ceremonial, the boards to which are in the museum. Then I heard quite a bit about games, ghosts, shamans, and many other things. I haven't done much language wise except familiarize myself with phonetics. I could have done so much more if I didn't loose so much time. The big problem is that all the most capable people have all so much work to do. On occasion they are more than willing to work for me, but then I find out that they have to work all day and are only free in the evening. The same goes for the women. I do hope that in time I can come to an arrangement with my informants so that I lose less time.

Racially people are strongly mixed here. However it is considered a Snohomish reservation. Now the old culture has strongly disintegrated. You hardly can find baskets any longer. It's hightime that someone does work here. Many subtleties, I feel, can no longer be noticed. To get many stories is even difficult. The younger people don't speak Snohomish any longer and if they do, not very well. I had no idea to which extent Indian life has come apart.

After learning here as much as possible I shall try to look around other reservations, especially on the former Puyallup reservation. But I will still remain a few weeks on the Tulalip. Not much can be done any longer, I believe, with school children. The older children don't return any longer.

I hope all is well with you and your family. Greetings to everyone, especially to your wife. Yours Sincerely, Herman Haeberlin

Sept 27 1916 NY at APS <paraphrased>

FB writes HKH at Tulalip, thanking him for letters from Everett and Tulalip showing he has made a "good start." FB forwarded relevant books from his summer retreat on Lake George. The Smithsonian also sent books HKH had tried to get through Lowdermilk. Alfred Kroeber wrote FB asking him to ask HKH to go to San Francisco and Berkeley for Thanksgiving because they are planning a meeting at that time.[79] FB tells HKH he thinks this would "be wise on your part". "I read between the lines of Kroeber's letter that he is thinking of the possibility of a university position for you in California; and I think that is of sufficient importance to justify your going there." HKH met Berhold Laufer at Chicago on his way west and apparently was considering a job, thankless it seems, at the Field Museum.

Oct 7 1916 Tulalip in German at APS # 445

Tulalip, Wash., October 7, 1916

Dear Professor Boas,

I received your much valued letter of September 27, as well as the extract from BAAS for 1902. Philipps "Totem Tales" already had arrived two weeks ago. I thank you for all. The Smithsonian Institution did send me Swan as well as two publications by Eells. The last few days weren't very productive for me. There is an "Indian Fair " going on and no Indian is willing to work for me. They all want to go to the Fair. I'm glad it's all over tomorrow. I'm now already working for 2 1/2 weeks here. During that time I collected quite a bit of ethnographic material about the Snohomish. In addition I have recorded a number of stories in English. Some are quite long. A 'coyote' story is almost 75 pages. I haven't done much in regards to the language. I thought it would be best, first to get some general impression about this culture, and collect as many stories in English as possible, in order to get an idea what the mythology in general may look like.

Obviously I familiarized myself with phonetics, while collecting a mixed vocabulary. Then I also collected a number of "noun-reduplications." I thought I would really get into the language, as soon as I had gotten a general overview of the ethnography and mythology. In time I should be able to judge which informants are best used for language work. For that type of work you definitely look for the most intelligent ones. Finally I bought specimens for $ 46- So far I have 22 pieces, among them several types of baskets, an oar, a mat, a mountain goat blanket, a spindle and similar things. I will buy the other things for Goddard as soon as he sends me the money. In case you should see him, please tell him that he should send the money as soon as possible. In case I should travel to San Francisco next month, I would prefer to send the whole collection before my departure, because I don't know where to leave all these things.

---

[79] After HKH died, Kroeber wrote Edward Sapir, 3 March 1924, that Gladys Reichard had taken on HKH's Boasian mantle: "She is hard and efficient and charmless – the opposite of Haeberlin; but equally saturated with the old man; and Haeberlin's successor, almost, in his devotion" (Golla 1984: 410).

When I finally have the funds I can easily buy with the rest of the money.

If you think it's a good idea I will travel Thanksgiving to San Francisco. It might be worthwhile. Perhaps Kroeber can make me some kind of offer. As I have written to you already, I don't want to accept the position in Chicago. It doesn't appear very enticing. What it means is two or three years of nothing else but filling up museum display cabinets. On top of that the material is just collected blindly without any scientific data. All these trustees are interested in is to see as many display cabinets as possible being filled. I would feel most unhappy with such a quantitative assessment of scientific work.

The phonetic of the Snohomish language isn't easy. The consonants vary quite a bit. A certain difficulty exists due to the fact that I don't know whether I should distinguish between a *d* and *n* with half-shut nasal opening, or whether it's always one and the same sound. It's the same story naturally with *b* and *m.* One particular sound is new to me. It is a frontal strong spoken with *n* timbre. A voiced *l* doesn't seem to exist. But I'm not quite sure yet.

This summer you had repeatedly asked me to inquire into hunting and fishing privileges. As I understood it you were questioning whether certain families or certain tribes possess the sole right to use certain hunting and fishing grounds. I have repeatedly inquired into this, but always with the same result, not to hear what you seemingly expected to hear. The answers always were: the Snohomish hunted and fished north and south of the Snohomish river, and that all Snohomish families somehow were allowed to hunt and fish in this area. In addition, that the borders between the hunting grounds of different tribes were fluid and undetermined. When I ask then whether an Indian from another tribe, let's say a Lummi, could hunt in the Snohomish territory, I would receive for an answer that he could well do that, if he had friends or relatives. But if he were to be a total stranger, it certainly could cause problems. But my informants thought it very unlikely that a stranger would hunt on Snohomish grounds. Why shouldn't he hunt at home. Their answers are not much to the point. Please let me know immediately what do you mean by 'privileges', and what do you think about their answers.

There is something else I would like to get your opinion about. You once told me that Puget Sound Salish made no imbricated baskets with imbrication. But now I find that the women here for the most part make 'Klickitat' baskets, which means coiled oval baskets with imbrication. Do you think that's a late introduction from the Klickitat and Yakima. I have seen here such baskets, made only 30 or more years ago, by Snohomish women. I don't get to see much of twined baskets. The women say it's not practical any more to make those baskets, because they are too soft for berry picking. In earlier times the twined baskets supposedly were exclusively used to store things at the houses. Please write to me what in your opinion the status is of basket weaving in Puget Sound.

I hope you feeling well. Please give my cordial regards to your wife.

Yours Sincerely,   Herman Haeberlin

Oct 13, 1916 NY at APS <paraphrased>

FB thanks HKH for his letter of Oct 7 about the Indian Fair, which took up everyone's time and must have frustrated him since FB adds, "There is ample opportunity for learning patience on a trip like yours". FB has asked HKH to look into "privileges", a feature of the North Pacific (naming Nootka, Kwakiutl)[80] that characterized elite families. FB was interested if these were held by certain families or by certain ranks, such as a chief. FB also notes that key resource sites in the water, such as fishing banks, were owned and claimed by a means of triangulating off landmarks along the horizon. FB will write to Goddard about money, and Mr Sargent wrote to offer more money in January, presumably for Teit's work. FB is "not surprised to hear that the Snohomish women make imbricated basketry" as Teit had noted the distribution reached Puget Sound and Boas himself saw such baskets about 1890. FB urged HKH to go to Berkeley and forget about any Chicago job because "it is annoying to work for trustees who do not appreciate the scientific character of the work". Still, HKH should have the experience of museum routine. FB and Laufer will talk over Christmas, when the annual meeting is held.

Oct 17 1916 NY at APS <paraphrased>

FB recommends HKH try "to study the personal distribution of designs among the women of Puget Sound". This work would help when he joined Teit. FB was interested in the designs made by each woman, how designs are criticized, and how they are taught to young girls. HKH should also observe the regularity and speed of movement of a expert basket weaver so as to judge the connection between regularity of effort and appearance of the finished work. FB has marked only those stories in Phillips's *Totem Tales* he could place based on his own work in Puget Sound.

Oct 22 1916 Tulalip in German at APS # 499

Tulalip, Washington, Oct. 22, 1916

Dear Professor Boas,

Frachtenberg [Leo J] and I are working together for almost a week. He wants to work another week with me. I think I have gained quite a bit during his presence. I had great difficulties with phonetics before he came, and it was impossible for me to record any texts. Now, after having worked together almost every day with the language, everything goes much better, and Frachtenberg wants to stay until I'm capable to record texts by myself. In short, I'm very grateful to you for the arrangement of us being able to work together for a while. Unfortunately I have very little to offer to Frachtenberg. He has been working already for three months on the ethnography of the Quilleyute and knows the ethnologic conditions in this area better that I do. But he seems to have an interest in the work on the Tulalip and has no regrets to be here.

I have received your much valued letter of October 17. I will try to learn as much as possible about the special problems in regards to basket weaving, but the conditions

---

[80] Now known as Nuchalnuth and Kwakwaka'wakw.

for such studies are not very favorable here. Almost no baskets are being made any longer here. The women always say that they don't have time to make such baskets. I haven't heard of any case where a young girl was taught by a woman how to weave baskets. The new baskets are all 'decadent' and are made with a sewing needle. There are only a few old women who still know the design patterns. Women under forty just don't know them any more.

This Tuesday Frachtenberg and I will move to Marysville, a small town on the border of the Tulalip reservation. Conditions are much better there compared to here, where I live. A number of people live there and are easier to reach from Marysville, while here the Indians live far apart from each other. The Indians in Marysville have more free time compared to the ones I've worked with until now.

Please extend my sincere regards to your family.

Yours Sincerely, Herman Haeberlin

My future address: General Delivery, Marysville, Washington.

Oct 29, 1916 Hotel Currie, Marysville at AMNH Anthro Archives <paraphrased>

HKH to PEG [Goddard] about express and collect shipment of the 27th, with list to follow.

Oct 30 1916 ?? [Tulalip] in German Frachtenberg at APS # 531

October 30, 1916

Dear Professor Boas,

Frachtenberg left this Sunday for Portland to see his family. His presence was extremely helpful to me. I'm making good progress with phonetics. Unfortunately I couldn't offer anything in return, but he seemed to be interested in the work here and enjoyed working with me.

Frachtenberg informed you that I'm having trouble with my health, as I have too much sugar. It hit me out of the blue. I never expected such a thing. Shortly after my arrival here the first symptoms appeared. I didn't pay much attention to it until Frachtenberg urged me to consult a doctor. The first advised me to return home, which unsettled me somewhat. The same day Frachtenberg and I went to Seattle and I consulted a doctor there, who confirmed the diagnosis. My blood sugar is very high at 6.6 %. Immediately I had to go on a diet and swallow a lot of medicine. Today I returned to the doctor in Seattle. The sugar is still high, but I don't have any longer the dry thirst, which I had last week. The diabetes also affected my eye sight badly, which was the most unsettling for me. Since I'm sticking to a diet my eye sight is normal again. The doctor said that diabetes often involves the eyes. Staying on a diet is the main thing. Fortunately I can do this very well in Marysville. I couldn't have done it in Tulalip, because there I had to eat whatever I received. I have to travel twice a week to Seattle. At the moment there is no reason why I couldn't continue with my work, even though I don't have all my energy back. Today the doctor was satisfied with my progress, but the sugar was still high. He thinks that my diabetes is not of recent origin, but has been there for a year or more, without me being aware of it.

During last week I collected a number of texts with translations. In the future I will involve myself again more with ethnology.

Hopefully all is very well with you and your dear family. My warmest regards to your wife. Yours Sincerely, Herman Haeberlin.

Nov 1 1916 AMNH Antho Archives <paraphrased>

HKH to PEG enclosing a list of Oct 27 shipment with value of $87.05.

[1-47, divided 1-18 = $35.55, 19-39 = 67.30, 40-47 = $87.05]

Nov 3 1916 Marysville in German at APS

Marysville, Washington, November 3, 1916

Dear Professor Boas,

I don't want to bother you with the history of my illness, and I wouldn't have brought it up again if Frachtenberg hadn't mentioned me in his letter to you. Yesterday I saw the doctor again in Seattle. He was generally satisfied with my improvement. The sugar level hasn't really dropped that much, but he feels that in time it will happen. The best sign is that the treatment with the diet is beginning to work: I gained weight during the last week. Also the dry thirst that had bothered me for weeks is almost gone. This illness had a strange effect on my eyes. The doctor says that's not unusual with diabetes. Shortly after I arrived at Tulalip my eyes became weaker and weaker with frightening speed. First I thought that I was dealing with an increasing nearsightedness. Already during the summer of 1914 a doctor prescribed some glasses for it. Now, on a strict diet, suddenly my eyes have markedly improved. I can see well again with or without glasses. This confirms the doctor in his opinion that I might have had a case of unknown diabetes for a long time, manifesting itself first in my eyes.

I keep now a very strict diet. Luckily I can do this in Marysville. In Tulalip, where I spent the first five weeks, I couldn't have done this. There I had to eat whatever I was given. Marysville borders the same reservation from which I can easily be in Seattle in 2 1/4 hours. I have to be twice weekly in Seattle. I'm being treated by a German doctor who comes across as very trustworthy and who takes my case seriously. Frachtenberg knew him by name.

My work is slowly progressing. In this kind of work so much time is being lost due to lack of punctuality on the Indians' part. Now I'm working with a pair of very old people. They are very difficult to understand but know a lot. Dealing with younger people is a complete waste of time because they don't know anything. On October 27 I sent $ 87 worth of specimens to Goddard. Soon I will send some more. Just recently I received the photographs of the Lillooet and Thompson baskets. These are most likely the photographs [Edward] Sapir [*] sent to you. If in the near future you should write to Sapir please ask him to provide me with an official letter from the Geological Survey, similar to the one I have from Washington D.C. I really don't want to have any troubles in Canada. I would be most grateful for it. Various sources tell me, and I'm glad to hear it, that in general things are going well for you since you returned to New York.

Please give my regards to your family and especially to your wife. My mother informs me that she was very happy about the letter your wife sent to her. Yours Sincerely, Herman Haeberlin

My address is simply Marysville, Washington.

Nov 6 1916 ?? in German at APS # 546 [Cf Dr George F Warmburg]

November 6, 1916

Dear Professor Boas,

I just returned from Seattle where I saw again Dr. [George F] Warmburg. He showed me the telegram you sent to him. He also informed me what he told you. I really would like to thank you for this new sign of your kindness and consideration. As I have written to you and as Dr. Warmburg telegraphed, my condition improved as soon as I started to stay on my diet. This improvement mainly benefited my eyes, which had been considerably weakened. So, that's much better. My condition actually was the same today as four days ago when I saw Dr. Warmburg. Unfortunately the sugar level isn't dropping. It's still as high as in the beginning. Dr. Warmburg was less optimistic about that today. He advised me to return Thursday, November 9. In case the sugar still hasn't dropped, he thinks the best might be to return to New York and seek consultation with a specialist. This really is beginning to affect me. All my beautiful plans go up in smoke. The worst part for me is that if I return to New York now I have to tell my parents about it, and right now they have their own worries. On the other hand I don't want to do anything that would be harmful to my health. A full recovery is probably unlikely. Over time I have to learn how to live with my condition, but for an ethnologist it's hardly something to look for.

I work every day with my informants. I have two wonderful old people who make all kinds of models for me. They are the only ones I could motivate to do this for me. If I were to be in good health now I would look with great confidence at my work. I'm doing quite all right now with phonetics due to the fact that Frachtenberg was here. He was a big help to me. I really enjoyed being with him. The two weeks passed all too fast. The biggest obstacle still remains for me to hear the glottal stops within a word especially if they come before a fortis.

I'm so happy to hear that all in all you doing well. Don't exert yourself too much. I will immediately inform you about the results of my doctor's visit on Thursday, obviously by telegram. Give my regards to your wife.

Yours Sincerely, Herman Haeberlin

Nov 7? 1916 AMNH Anthro Archives

Accession Record for expedition, 1 box 19753, Marysville, Wash.

Nov 10 1916 Marysville in German at APS # 653

Marysville, Washington, November 10, 1916.

Dear Professor Boas,

I just received your much valued letter of November 5, where you asked me to return to New York. First I would like to say that I value your advice more than from anyone else except from my parents. However, permit me that I write to you again before I make the decision whether I should return right now. This is going to be a difficult decision for me. I don't want you to imagine the situation being worse than it really is.

As I have written to you yesterday evening from Everett, my condition has improved further. I have gained weight and the blood sugar stood yesterday afternoon at only 2%. Dr. Warmburg says that falling sugar levels are often associated with other adverse symptoms. But this is presently not the case with me. Twice weekly I travel to Seattle.

When you telegraphed Dr. Warmburg, he suggested not yet to call me back because my condition had improved. Had you already received Dr. Warmburg's answer when you wrote me the letter I just received? I don't want to act precipitously, since it's at all possible that you might have come to a different conclusion because of the telegram and my later letter?

Under the present condition I obviously would prefer being in New York rather than way out here. But so much is at stake. Since my trip to Puerto Rico wasn't a success {due to undiagnosed diabetes}, I'm afraid I'll never again receive funds for field work, especially if this trip also ends with a fiasco. I'm doing quite all right now with my work. I have a good working relationship with several good informants. There is one more reason why it is so difficult for me to decide at this moment to return. My parents expect that I will stay at least until Christmas. If I leave now they will worry a lot. It is also my deepest wish to stay until Christmas, and that's just barely six weeks.

Don't assume that I'm living out here in the wilderness. Any time of the day it takes me just 2 1/2 hours to be in Seattle. I'm living in a nice small hotel. The owner feeds me only such food that goes along with my diet. In addition I'm exposed to much fresh air which Dr. Warmburg thinks is important. He doesn't see yet any reason for me to leave in view of the falling sugar. If it wasn't for this improvement I wouldn't hesitate one moment and return immediately.

Please give it some more consideration, and don't be upset about me hesitating. If despite this letter you still feel I should return I will do so without hesitation. Please let me know your decision as soon as possible. If I can remain here until Christmas, I will be able to present a very good description of the ethnography of the Snohomish and Snoqualmi. Please let me know what I should do in regards to Teit and the Chicago baskets. It would be extremely painful for me if I couldn't write any more on this paper about Salish baskets.

I put in more effort into it than in any of my other works. Here I see a wonderful opportunity to clearly demonstrate the methodological relationships of art history to ethnology.

I'm looking forward to your decision. Please give my warmest regards to your wife.   Yours Sincerely, Herman Haeberlin

Nov 10 1916 Marysville at AMNH Anthro Archives <paraphrased>

HKH to PEG noting a second box was sent Nov 8th by express, and enclosing a list of accession numbers and prices. [6,48,49,50,79,81,64,85 $9.00, boxing .75 = $9.75]

Nov 16, 1916

Accession Record for expedition, 1 box 1916-82, Marysville, Wash.

Nov 20 1916

Accession Record for expedition, 1 box 1916-82, Marysville, Wash.

Nov 26, 1916 at AMNH Anthro Archives

HKH writes from NYC to PE Goddard "Enclosed find a list of the specimens I sent you in a [third] box on Nov 14."

Dec 14 1916 at AMNH Anthro Archives <paraphrased>

HKH to Clark Wissler [CW], noting of the grant of $250, as $75 for collecting expenses and $175 for specimen purchases. HKH spent $131.30 purchases + $56.38 expenses = $187.58 leaving $62.42

Dec 21 1916 at AMNH Anthro Archives

CW to Dr FA Lucas sending on HKH refund check. "Dr Haeberlin has a traveling fellowship from Columbia University and offered to make some collections for us among the Salish Indians of Washington... As the money was used entirely for the purchase of specimens from Indians, there are no vouchers."

Dec 21 1916 at AMNH Anthro Archives

Dear Dr Wissler,

I beg to acknowledge receipt of check from Dr Haeberlin for $62.42 balance, unexpended, of funds advanced for purchase of specimens.

Cordially, FA Lucas

25th Jany /17 Spences Bridge at APS <paraphrased>

James Teit responds to questions sent by Boas, but suggests that the local band only has 5-6 women making baskets and only one does it constantly. Basketry was mostly done until April, and Spuzzum would be a better place for the study, with comparative work at Lytton and Nicola Valley. He has also heard from Dr HKH.

Sept 5 1917 Chicago in German at APS

Chicago, September 5, 1917

Dear Professor Boas,

I just arrived in Chicago. Your telegram surprised me somewhat, I hadn't thought about such an offer. I received it after I had left Marysville and while I was working with a Squali woman on the Nisqualli Reservation. Your letter reached me only in Denver, where last Sunday and Labor Day I spent with some old acquaintances from Leipzig. My round trip ticket led me via Union Pacific through Denver. Your letter arrived late because it had been addressed to Marysville. I didn't wait any longer for it in Tacoma because I had already decided that I wouldn't accept Kroeber's offer. Even though I wouldn't have minded to be together with Kroeber and Lowie many reasons spoke against it. It wouldn't be the right thing to study right now a Californian tribe. The proper thing to do is to concentrate on my Salish things and do a thorough comparative analysis of Snohomish and Squalli tribes with other North Pacific tribes. Naturally for such a comparative analysis the place is New York with you. Also I feel that next year's upcoming connection with the NY Museum is important, especially since I hope to get the Pawnee project[81] next spring. If I had in mind to acquire permanent employment in America, the Californian offer might be desirable. But you know what my intentions are. Under these circumstances I think a closer affiliation with the New York Museum might be more helpful to me for the future than a position at Berkeley. I really appreciate your friendly advice. My decision is completely independent because I made it right then when your telegram arrived. I'm wondering why I haven't heard a word from Kroeber himself.

Up to now I have spent exactly $ 514.85 (without specimens).[82] We figured $ 600.00- That leaves me with $ 85.15. It has to cover my stay in Chicago, the trip to New York from here (not included in my round trip) and possibly a few days in Ottawa. If you agree I would like to stay for 10 days in Chicago. I think that's about what you had

---

[81] Pawnee project may refer to follow-up work after George Dorsey left the Field Museum in 1915. He had done Pawnee and comparative Caddoan studies, working with Skiri speakers James Murie and Roaming Scout, until 1907. Alfred Cort Haddon, the early British anthropologist, joined Dorsey among the Pawnee in 1901.

[82] These funds for a fellowship devoted to travel, museum research, and fieldwork were provided by Howard Sargent.

in mind. I would like to study the art collection, especially [George] Dorsey's things from the Puget Sound area, and if possible to see a bit of Laufer. He's supposed to be so busy. It might not come to that. Teit promised to send me his field notes on basketry at the end of the month. Please let me know as soon as possible whether I could have a look at the art collection in Ottawa before I return to New York. I would also like to know whether I can have photographs made of specimens in Chicago I can use for my Snohomish ethnography.

All in all I'm satisfied with the results of my trip. I hope that you'll agree. I'm happy that I left again this summer and nothing interfered with it.

With warmest regards to you and your family I remain sincerely,

Herman Haeberlin

Sept 12 1917 Chicago in German at APS

Chicago, Ill. September 12, 1917

Dear Professor Boas,

Many thanks for your {birthday} congratulations. I was delighted to receive your letter and the cards from your family. I accept with gratitude your invitation to come for a few days to Lake George. I decided to visit you before I depart for Ottawa. I feel it's important to discuss a few points about basketry with you before I study the collection in Ottawa. I had to promise my relatives in Akron that I would spend coming Sunday with them. Thus I will leave here Saturday. On Monday I shall leave Akron and Tuesday morning (September 18) arrive at yours. The boat arrives at 10:50 in Bolton. Would you please be so kind to have someone call Meranville that he sends a car to the boat.

I made very good use of my time in Chicago. Dr. Laufer is extremely kind and gives me plenty of his time. There is a lot we have to discuss. My stay in Chicago is not expensive at all. I'm looking forward to see you and your family soon.

Best regards, Herman Haeberlin

Nov ? 1917

Ye Old Curiosity Shop
        Colman Dock
                Seattle, Wash

This store has an old cedar-bark skirt from the Fort Madison {Suquamish} Reservation. It was offered to me for $8. I also saw a smelt-rake in this store.   [unsigned HKH]

Nov 12 1917 <paraphrased>

PE Goddard writes Ye Old Curiosity Shop, seeking to buy for $8 a cedar bark skirt seen there by Dr HK Haeberlin. {This rain cape has painted whales facing each other}

Ye Old Curiosity Shop, on the Colman Dock Front, JE Standley, Prop; EV Standley, Mgr, responded with a carefully handprinted statement

DRESS <u>MADE OF WOOD</u> INDIANS OF PUGET SOUND COUNTRY MADE CRUDE SKIRTS AND BLANKETS OUT OF BEATEN CEDAR BARK OR SKIN OF THE TREE.

THIS SKIRT WAS SECURED AT "Old Man's house" THE TOTEM POLE HOUSE AT PORT MADISON

THE HOME OF CHIEF SEATTLE AND THE DRESS WAS CLAIMED AS THE ONE ANGELINE WORE.

Jan 9th 1918 Cambridge at APS <paraphrased>

HKH to Boas about his getting stronger but needing a long convalescence. He is discouraged to upset the plans of both FB and himself with "so many hot irons I have in the fire". He has not told his parents and asks advice from FB. HKH dictated this letter to his nurse, V Gustafson.

Jan 11 1918 NY at APS <paraphrased>

FB to HKH at home of Mr P Peaselee, 64 Kirkland St, Cambridge, Massachusetts. FB is exceedingly glad at the progress of HKH and asks him not to worry. He must tell his parents he is sick. FB will send his own letter to them, saying he has been to visit. HKH's classes have been sent to the museum by Goldenweiser and Boas, though "I presume they will be glad when they have you back."

Jan 15 1918 Cambridge in German at APS

Cambridge, Mass
64 Kirkland Str.
Jan 15, 1918

Dear Professor Boas,

I'm most thankful for your friendly letter! I have written to my parents about my illness following your friendly advice. I would be much obliged if you would also tell them how this came about. You know the address:

c/o Mr. W. Knipers
Sophia Plein 2
Amsterdam

I'm getting better everyday. But the slow progress is so discouraging. I still feel very weak, and I would like to do something but I'm just not ready yet.

Yours sincerely HH

P.S. Please be optimistic when you write to my parents

Jan 19 1918 Cambridge in German at APS

Cambridge, Mass. Jan 19, 1918
64 Kirkland Str.

Dear Professor Boas,

I want to thank you belatedly from the bottom of my heart for having visited me during my illness. It was very kind of you. At the time I have struggled with hands and feet against it, but no one really bothered to ask for my opinion. I was very surprised when I saw you.

I'm doing as well as expected, at least that's what the doctor says. For me things are progressing so slowly. I still have the nurse. The worst of all, my legs are still so wobbled. I just don't know what to do with these silly beasts. As soon as I can walk again I shall return to New York. I'm anxious to see you again.

In the meantime the longing for my parents has gotten stronger than ever. I have discussed it with my doctor. He also feels I should make every effort to see them. One just can't continue living in boarding houses and reconvalescent homes. So if at all possible, I hope to take off at the end of this term.

What's the status of Teit's material? Has it finally arrived?

Please give my most heartfelt regards to your family. Yours sincerely HH

Jan 22 1918 at APS <paraphrased>

FB asks HKH not to be impatient. Teit has sent two bundles "but very little of what we want." Frachtenberg is finally going to be confronted with his accusers?? because a senator made Walcott give in.[83] Dr Wolf sends greetings from a detention camp in Canada.

Jan 23 1918 Cambridge in German at APS

Cambridge, Mass. Jan 23, 1918
64 Kirkland Str.

Dear Professor Boas,

Many thanks for your letter of January 22! My health has not progressed at all during the last week. My strength just doesn't want to come back. For that reason we consulted a specialist yesterday. He insists that I'm in relative good condition. He follows a different principle. Instead of feeding me he systematically starves me to determine accurately how many carbohydrates and fat etc. I can tolerate. My diet has to be strictly regulated. The crux of the matter is that Dwyer never did this. He appeared to overlook completely the complexity of the situation.

---

[83] The BAE fired Leo Frachtenberg on 1 October 1917 for being Austrian-born, Jewish, and Boasian. Boas himself was condemned by Wasp American Anthropologists in December 1919 (Golla 1984: 262 note 1).

I have to say that often I get so depressed. To lay around with nothing to do except to hunt after crickets is unbearable. My sole consolation is that may be this May or June I can go to Europe. My doctor strongly advised me to do so. I would be very grateful if you could assist me with this.

I'm happy to hear that Dr. Wolfe is the same one I had in mind. I would love to correspond with him. Please extend my regards to him. HH

Jan 25 1918 at APS <paraphrased>

FB urges HKH to take proper care of his diet and avoid worrying. "Amuse yourself with reading, and don't think of your work, which can wait." Once his health improves, they will quickly get him a pass from DC.

Feb 4, 1918 Cambridge in German at APS

Cambridge, Mass. February 4, 1918

Dear Professor Boas,

I would be very happy to hear something from you. For the past 2 weeks I'm undergoing Allen's starvation diet.[84] Obviously I'm very weak. On occasion I'm close to despair, and I doubt whether I'll ever leave this sick bed. Two things I dread the most, an endless and useless protracted illness, and second that I will never see my parents again. Do you think I will get a passport and do you hear occasionally from Mr. Leach? The doctor isn't without hope, on the contrary, but you know how doctors are. Please be so kind and write to me. HH

HKH dies 12 February & his body is sent to Akron for family burial.

March 12 1918 Amsterdam at APS <paraphrased>

Herman senior (the father) thanks FB for his report on his son's condition, sending FB $300 in February to help his son and the same amount in March. Their wives send greetings.

---

[84] Frederick Madison Allen's methods seem to have been universally accepted in medical schools and among up-to-date practitioners as the best therapy available at the time. James Havens Jr. was the first person in the United States to receive insulin on May 21, 1922. Decades after the discovery of insulin, doctors were reminded of the pre-insulin diabetics when they saw the emaciated pictures of the survivors of Belsen and Buchenwald, according to Michael Bliss, "The Discovery of Insulin", consulted by Ulrich Fritzsche, MD, the translator of these HKH letters.

March 27 1918 Amsterdam at APS <paraphrased>

FB wrote Herman senior on the 17th. The parents heard the sad news first from Laufer, then "our folks in Akron", Miss Peaslee and Miss Gustavson, and Mrs Boas. "Fate was cruel to us," after his mother's work and love made a man of him, in the fullest sense of the word. Miss Peaslee [apparently Herman's fiancé] told the parents HKH had been homesick and depressed for much of the past year, immersing himself in hard work. After he left Germany in 1914, he wrote his mother twice a week. They had a cheerful tone until spring of 1917, and always mentioned FB and his family members. HKH was to return home in 1915 but that seemed unwise. When "diabetes first attacked him", he made a full report to his mother. His liberal diet and return to the field suggested all was well. In spring 1917 he planned to work at Leyden University, but conditions were getting worse in Europe. Physicians they consulted advised HKH to stay in the US. In the spring of 1918, HKH planned to be in Stockholm and his parents made no objection. In the fall of 1917, the Akron relatives saw HKH and reported him "the perfect picture of health". The parents are greatly troubled that HKH did not report to them as fully about his health as he did to those in the US. FB and family are greatly thanked for every kindness, with a request to make sure that all expenses are settled and they make up for anything outstanding.

May 28th 1918 Amsterdam hand written, at APS <paraphrased>

Herman senior offers his US investments ($10,000) to fund, with its annual interest, the Herman Haeberlin Research Fellowship in anthropology, irrespective of nationality or religious faith as that the name of "our poor boy" will live on.

July 8, 1918 Lake George ?? at APS <paraphrased>

FB assures Herman senior that son HKH had mood swings but was not overly depressed, knowing "the only salvation is in work in order to distract our thought from the troubles that beset us on all sides". HKH was always truthful, never suspecting the worst. He returned to Puget Sound with a stricter diet but seemed well. After his return, his physician was drafted so he had to change doctors as his condition worsened. FB wanted HKH to spend Christmas with his family, but instead he went to Cambridge to be with the Peeslees and there his final illness overtook him. FB received the money send by the father and used it to pay HKH's board bill and nurse of about $170. All the rest of the money he sent on to the Kuno Feddersons in Akron, who had paid all the other expenses.

Your son completed a very large amount of work in the few years that were given to him for productive work. Comparatively speaking, little of it has been printed, and I have been trying since that time to have his manuscripts completed and published. About two weeks ago a long paper of his on the results of his journey to Puget Sound appeared. I have sent you a copy, and shall send another one when I get back to New York, because printed matter is so often lost nowadays. I also prepared another paper of his on Mexican pottery, and one on certain customs of the Indians of Puget Sound, which I expect will appear during the summer and fall; but besides this there are a number of larger pieces of work which will require time to complete. The book on one group of western tribes, in the preparation of which he assisted me and to which he write [wrote] an important chapter, will probably not appear until a couple of years hence. Another one on basketry of British Columbia was well advanced, and I hope will be finished during the coming winter. I shall, of course, see to it that you receive copies of all these as they appear.

I feel his death as a great personal loss ...

July 22, 1918 NY at APS <paraphrased>

FB writes Herman senior to follow up on his letters of April and June, much touched by the decision to set up a fellowship to commemorate HKH. He asks that it be at Columbia because of its connection to HKH and the prospect that it "will remain a center of anthropological activity." Further, the collections made by HKH reside at AMNH "and the two support each other. From this point of view, it seems to my mind that Columbia would be a perfectly safe place in which adequate returns of such a foundation might be expected." The fellowship should depend on having "a certain definite research task" that should be published.

August 7 1918 Lake George ?? at APS <paraphrased>

FB sends another copy of the July 22 letter and reports on discussions, without using names or amounts, with "a few other anthropologists of good judgement" to set up the fellowship for "productive work" that results in publication. A large fund at Columbia pays the salary of a Professor of American Archaeology, but a few hundred dollars is left over every year that Boas wants to apply to a publications fund, augmented with sales. Any collections made would go to AMNH "to express the wish that the fellowship may draw together more closely the anthropological work of different institutions." Making it the exclusive means of support would guard against redirecting the fund "for the support of work of older men". Instead it should support young men like HKH. These remarks, of course, are only suggestions and the parents can take any direction they desire. Over the years, HKH had mood swings, but FB saw him every day and saw no cause for alarm. His parents are not to reproach themselves for what had to do with the state of the world at war.

October 19th 1918 Amsterdam at APS <paraphrased>

Herman senior lists all the FB letters he has received. The parents are confirmed in turning over their $10,000 US investments to fund a Herman Haeberlin Research Fellowship at an American institution entirely in the judgment of FB. The investment consists of US insurance policies from 15-34 years old. The Feddersons paid the premiums during the war years, and the remainder of the funds will be secured to him. Herman senior hopes to visit the US to set all this up. Meanwhile he asks FB to have an enabling document drawn up. Herman senior has had letters of assignment deposited in the safe at his bank.

Oct 6 1919 at APS <paraphrased>

FB has received the Dusseldorf address of Herman senior from Fedderson in Akron. He includes another HKH paper and a copy of the HKH obituary read at the annual meeting in later published. The wives have exchanged letters of deep feeling.

Nov 2 1919 Dusseldorf in German at APS # 863

Duesseldorf, November 2, 1919

Dear Professor,

I received your letters, dated July 11 and October 6, within three weeks after they were mailed off. The printed material has yet to reach me. Throughout the war years I did not receive any such material, which I really missed. My wife received a letter from your wife. She wrote three times. Her last letter probably is on its way. I also received your letters, dated July 8, 22, and August 7, 1918, which I answered from here, and on occasion, while here in Amsterdam. It appears that everything from the States with the exception of printed matter arrived.

I have repeatedly and in great detail written to my brother-in-law Fedderson about the difficulties my wife and I have to face regards a possible re-entry into the United States. I assume he has informed you about this. I asked Fedderson to do this, since the main purpose of our trip will be to settle the affairs of our late son Herman. In order to get a passport I visited the American consulate in Koblenz, the Spanish general consul in Berlin, and the American consulate in Holland. In De Haag one insisted that I should live first for some time in Holland, because the peace treaty hasn't been ratified in Washington. Present and somewhat urgent business affairs however do not allow me to do this. Everywhere I'm being told to await ratification, because then the American consulate would resume its service in Germany. As far as we can tell that might be still a long time away. This is especially hard on my poor wife. She'll rest only when she can see and talk to everyone who knew our son in the USA, and can report to her details about the last year of his life. Things he couldn't write directly to us during the war years.

I think that it might be possible with your kind assistance to get the permission in Washington to finally reach this goal and enter the States. The reasons I feel that this might be possible, I heard of cases where through the good services of distinguished American citizens the permission to enter the States was given by the general consulate in Amsterdam. I have no doubts that you will be helpful to me in this matter, assuming you are in a position to do so and expect some success to come out of it. In case you feel you are in a position to do something, I have written a short summary of my present and personal situation. I have not included any explanatory documents, which at present might not be safe to sent.

In the spring of 1883 I emigrated to the United States, after finishing an academic - technical education. I received my US citizenship in 1888. My papers were issued February 6, 1888 by probate judge C. R. Grant, Akron, Ohio. I married my wife, born Alma Fedderson, in 1885. My two children, Elsa and Herman, were born 1886 and 1890 in Akron. In December of 1906 I left Akron for Duesseldorf, where I entered into the service of large machine producing factory. My return to Germany was mainly guided by my desire to give my children a superb scientific education. My daughter studied music. You know about my son. I was neither in Germany nor in America politically active.

Since this spring I work as a consultant engineer in Duesseldorf, and as such have a large practice. During the war I worked mainly for a large Dutch company, which also did business in Dutch East India. I'm still working for this company as an expert in large purchases for Holland and its colonies.

I'm well aware that it would have been my patriotic duty to return at the beginning of the war to the States. However, due to the fact that my daughter was married to a German on the battlefield, I preferred staying here. I don't think anyone can blame me for this. That's why I'm asking only for a three months' stay. I don't want to separate from the only child left.

Dear Sir, let me assure you in advance of my deepest gratitude in case you can be of any help. I will cease any further steps in regards to a passport until I hear from you.

HH sen.

Nov 5 1919 NY at APS <paraphrased>

FB sends 10 copies of the obituary, along with a paper HKH finished and FB had published.

Nov 25 1919 NY at APS <paraphrased>

FB will ask friends of influence for help and advice on getting passports for the parents into the US. He is anxious to meet in person to discuss plans for the memorial fellowship. The wives had written.

Nov 29 1919 Dusseldorf at APS <paraphrased>

The US reprints have arrived and the couple is touched by the memoriam words. The father sends a reprint of HKH's first publication, "Das Flachernornament in der Keramick der alten Pueblo Kultur" [Feather Designs on Ancient Pueblo Pottery]. Going through the list of publications, Herman senior mentioned what he does and does not have, hoping that FB can complete the set.

Dec 11 1919 NY at APS <paraphrased>

FB regrets enclosing an "unsatisfactory reply" from the State department, despite the best efforts of a lady [EC Parsons] he asked to help.[85] FB is writing the Feddersons about permission for a visit by HKH mother. All of these difficulties will go away once peace is declared, and the parents can come together.

Dec 19 1919 NY at APS <paraphrased>

FB responds to letter of Nov 29 with regret. Fedderson has confirmed that HKH's mother was born abroad. FB hopes conditions will improve in January. He is glad that the first paper by HKH was indeed printed in the Baessler Archives, though FB has not seen any copies of the journal since 1914. He will assemble and send copies of all of the published works of HKH.

Sept 12 1921 Dusseldorf in German at APS # 327

Duesseldorf, September 12, 1921

Dear Professor,

I still owe you an answer to your last letter of November 22. I'm grateful for your advice to make payments now for publication of my late son's papers. I assume you had the printing of his papers in German scientific journals in mind. If you would be so kind as to provide me with details, because I hope to be able to pay for it from my own income, assuming there are no unforeseen circumstances such as the requirement of very large sums. This way it might be possible to keep the main fund intact.

Please give my regards to your wife and daughter   HH sen.

Oct 18, 1921 NY at APS <paraphrased>

FB went to New Mexico as soon as he arrived from Europe. HKH father sent a letter of Sept 12th. FB has asked the help of Prof John Bassett Moore in getting the parents to the US. While plans continued for the fellowship, the parents were willing to produce money to defray the publication of some of their son's work in Germany, as discussed with Prof Von den Steinen in Berlin. He ends with greetings from his wife and daughter.

---

[85] The connection to Elsie Clews Parson is confirmed in an inscription of a typed page labeled Notes in re Mr H Haeberlin. Handwritten in four lines are "Return to/ Mrs. Herbert Parsons/ 7 East 76/ New York City". When Herman senior and family returned to Germany in 1906 he again became a German citizen. "The parents are exceedingly anxious to come to the US, where the wife's brother and mother live in Akron".

Sept 23 1924 Dusseldorf in German at APS # 349

Duesseldorf, September 23, 1924

Dear Professor,

Your friendly letter of September 4 was sent after us to Switzerland, where I've been staying for five weeks with my wife.

Many thanks for the information regarding Herman's work. I will heed your advice and contact Dr. Ackerman in Berlin. You know that in the meantime Dr. Danzel received a leading position at the Voelkermuseum in Hamburg. He refused any assistance, but wrote at the same time that you knew of a young German anthropologist, very industrious, who could be of help. He does not give his address. That's why I ask you to give it to me.

We all are in good health, but business wise things are still bad. We haven't felt yet any benefits of the Dawes plan.[86] Personally I believe with many others that in the long run nothing good will come out of it. The productivity of this totally impoverished land appears to be greatly exaggerated.

Our long planned trip to America had to be put on hold because under the present conditions we could not have secured our flat until our return. We hope that this might be possible this coming year, as we also had to postpone seeing again our brother-in-law Kuno Feddersen.

My wife and I regretted very much that we couldn't greet you and your family here in Germany. Probably you were too busy with all the work at the congress. My wife extends her greetings and I close with my hope that in the not too distant future there will be an opportunity to meet again. HH sen.

Dec 5 1924 NY at APS <paraphrased>

FB recommends that Mr Erich Schmidt receive the HKH Fellowship as successor to Dr Danzel.[87] "He is an earnest student and I feel sure that he will make good. At the present time he is very much handicapped by lack of means."

---

[86] Charles Gates Dawes had drawn up a plan which temporarily solved the problems of Germany's inability to pay war reparations by providing a reorganization of German finances through loans from mainly U.S. private investors. UF

[87] With funding from Mrs William Boyce Thompson, Schmidt (1928) surveyed the Gila-Salt river region of Arizona in 1927.

Appendix H: Insulin[88]

The importance of insulin for saving the life of diabetics was discovered by Canadians. After being rushed through University of Toronto medical school and service in WWI, Frederick Banting, an orthopedic surgeon with few patients, began teaching physiology at the University of Western Ontario to support himself. Though he was not a specialist, he became intrigued with diabetes, which was a fatal disease at that time. Symptoms were rapid weight loss, excessive fluid output, constant thirst, and increasing exhaustion. The usual treatment was a near-starvation diet and rest.

Prior research in Germany had shown a link with the pancreas. In the 1860s, Paul Langerhans had shown that the inner cells of the this organ, since known as islets of Landerhans, secrete directly into the blood stream. In 1888, [] Naunyn found the outer cells sent three enzymes (trypsin, amnylopsin, lipase) through ducts. Cutting the ducts did not produce obvious medical results, but removing the entire pancreas resulted in diabetes. Thus the connection was made between the illness and the inner cells. Trying to work with the whole pancreas was futile because the outer digestive juices destroyed whatever was provided by the inner cells.

The ducts kept these secretions apart. Banting decided to tie off the ducts, let the enzymes dissolve the outer cells and then extract the product of the inner ones. Though this had been tried before, the researchers had waited too long to remove the pancreas. The outer fluids had eliminated the inner one.

To find a proper laboratory, Banting had to petition Dr John JR Macleod, a Scots specialist in carbohydrate metabolism and Physiologist at the University of Toronto. Macleod turned him down three times, then set a strict two month deadline for the use of a lab while he was abroad. Charles Best, an undergraduate served as assistant. They experimented on ten dogs. The first surgery was a failure because they used gut to tie off the ducts. For the second attempt, they used silk and the dogs developed diabetes. Extracting fluid from the inner cells of the pancreases of the other dogs, they were able to keep one of them alive for some time. The difficulty was the minute amount of fluid produced by each animal.

Attempts to revive children dying of diabetes showed promise but there was never enough fluid. Finally, a fellow physician Joseph Gilchrist came down with diabetes and offered to serve as their test case. As an MD, Gilchrist kept a full record of his own symptoms and reactions, while Banting and Best researched what they started to call "isletsin." Macleod insisted on using its earlier name of insulin.

In 1923, three related events occurred. The Nobel Prize in Medicine was awarded for insulin, but the twin discoverers cited were Banting and Macleod. Banting, to his credit, split his prize money with Best. The Banting and Best Department of Medical

---

[88] Ruth Fox, *Milestones of Medicine*, The Discovery of Insulin 7: 185-221, 1950.

Research was founded at the University of Toronto, headed by Banting. Commercial production of insulin began using cattle pancreases from slaughter houses.

Macleod, who died in 1935, stayed at Toronto until he returned to Scotland in 1928. In time, Best replaced him as Professor of Physiology. Banting was killed in a plane crash on 21 February 1941.

Appendix I: Brief Biographies

These brief biographies of scholars mentioned in the letters and career of HKH include, where possible, the volume and page of a death notice or obituary in the American Anthropologist (AA).

Arthur **Ballard** (1876-1962) was of an old pioneer family involved in the development of Auburn and of the Ballard neighborhood of Seattle. He learned the native language of Puget Sound as a child and sustained a lifelong interest in the native Lushootseed peoples, especially at Muckleshoot.

Bureau of American Ethnology (**BAE**) was the US government office charged with the collection and publication of massive volumes (in drab green covers) concerned with the native peoples of North America. Founded in 1879 and long directed by John Wesley Powell, it was staffed by dedicated amateurs like James Mooney, by the linguist JP Harrington (below), by natives like JNB Hewitt and Francis LaFleshe, by scientists who had shifted their focus, and by trained Boasians like John Swanton and TT Waterman (below). Before he was ostracized for being a German and a Jew, Boas had a hand in some of its major projects and publications.

Franz **Boas** (1858 - 1942) trained as a physicist in German but changed to native peoples after time in the Canadian Arctic, and especially the Northwest Coast. After working at the Field Museum in Chicago and AMNH in New York City, directing the Jesup North Pacific Expedition, he established academic anthropology at Columbia University, where he recruited Haeberlin from Germany. He was ousted from both museums under painful circumstances beyond his own control, going on to train generations of professional anthropologists to carry his mission forward. AA 45/3/2

George A **Dorsey** (1868 - 1931) took a degree at Harvard, then was based at the Field Museum until he left to become a popular writer on anthropological subjects. His comparative work on Caddoans that he put aside in 1907 and Dorsey left the Field Museum and academic concerns in 1915. AA 33/306, 314

Myron **Eells** (1843 - 1907), of an early missionary family, was long based on Hood Canal among the Twana people resettled on the Skokomish Reservation. His brother Edwin Eells was the federal Indian Agent during some of this time.

George **Gibbs** (1815 - 1873) was from a prominent Northeast family and spent eleven years in the Northwest (1849-61). With a law degree from Harvard, he worked in the customs office at Astoria, Oregon, then joined the California Gold Rush. He served on treaty commissions in Oregon, California, and Washington, as well as the Canadian boundary survey. After he returned East, he oversaw the indemnity payment to HBC for Fort Nisqually. He lived in DC, NY City, and New Haven, marrying his cousin and intending to write up the extensive materials on native languages and ethnography he had assembled during fieldwork in the West and study in the Smithsonian archives. See Jay Miller, George Gibbs Northwest Array 2015.

De Lancey Walker **Gill** (1859 - 1940), born in Camden, South Carolina, was largely self taught with little formal education but in 1887 became assistant draftsman in the supervising Architect's office for the United States Government. Artist-scientist William Henry Holmes noted Gill's artistic ability and recommended his hiring to illustrate for the US Geological Survey and the Bureau of Ethnology, sketching across Indian Territory, Arizona desert, and upper Yellowstone Valley. He turned to photography, producing thousands of portraits of natives calling on the BIA in DC. He married three times, to Rose De Lima Draper (died 1893), Mary Irvin Wright (divorced 1903), a painter, and Katherine Schley, with a total of eight children. Forced to retire at 73, he taught art at the Corcoran Gallery in Washington DC, then retired to Virginia where he died from a fall down his stairs.

Pliny Earle **Goddard** (1869 - 1928), after a Quaker education and missionary work among the Hupa of northern California, turned to anthropology and was at the AMNH until his death. While his invalid wife and children lived in Connecticut, he had a long term relationship with Gladys Reichard (1893 - 1955). She was from a Pennsylvania Dutch family, and taught from 1923 at Barnard College, the female side of Columbia, and assumed HKH's devotion to Boas. AA 31/1

Erna **Gunther** (1896 - 1982) was Alsatian, a mining district fought over by France and Germany. In consequence, her family was bilingual in German and French, as well as fluent in English. She took her BA at Barnard in 1919 and was recruited by Boas for graduate work. She and Leslie Spier had a legal contract instead of a marriage license. Leslie was hired to replace Waterman at UW, but disliked the rain. He joined the faculty at the University of Oklahoma, while Erna worked in New York City on a study of Southwestern folklore. In 1927, both were to return to the museum at UW in Seattle, but only Leslie had the academic job. When he took leave for fieldwork in the Pacific, Erna replaced him and stayed on permanently until she was made unwelcome when the new Burke Museum was build in 1964. She received the Haeberlin notebooks just after he died to extract and publish ethnography and folklore. AA 86/394

John Peabody **Harrington** (1884-1961) was an eccentric genius of languages. The first academicly trained anthropologist to teach at UW, he reported (deposition, Alcea Band of Tillamooks, p202) "In 1910, I was an instructor at summer school at the UW, and during that summer and fall I was at Seattle, and I have done a large amount of field work on the coast before and since 1910." A public lecture he gave inspired Arthur Ballard to pursue his own interest in local fieldwork.

Morris Ketchum **Jesup** (1828 - 1908) as President of AMNH (1880-1906) funded a massive comparative study on both sides of the North Pacific under the direction of Franz Boas, but when it made no grand discovery or conclusion, always anathema to Boasians, there was a falling out that resulted in Boas's move to Columbia University. AA 10/171

Berthold **Laufer** (1874 - 1934) was born in Cologne, took his PhD in Oriental Studies at Leipsig in 1897, and was at AMNH (1903-6) and Columbia (1905-7), before settling at the Field in Chicago (1907-34). He was on Sakhalin Island for the Jesup North Pacific {JNPE}. At his death, his library was divided between two private Chicago libraries, of which only the Newberry's, devoted to the Humanities, survives. AA 36/637, 38/101

Charles **Newcombe** (1849 - 1924) trained as an MD, but devoted his life to building up the collections at what is now the Royal Provincial Museum in Victoria, BC. AA 27/352

Elsie Clews **Parsons** (1975 - 1941) was "free spirited" from a wealthy New York City family, involved in banking and politics. She took graduate degrees and funded substantial fieldwork throughout the Southwest, as well as Mexico and the Caribbean. AA 45/244

George Foster **Peabody** (1852 - 1938), a Georgia banker, who financed a famous media award (Newspapers, radio, TV), appears as the donor of many of the Northwest baskets at AMNH. Correspondence by Franz Boas shows that Peabody provided $5000 at the request of Mrs FN Doubleday to Morris K Jesup and Frederick Ward Putnam at AMNH to purchase the store of CT Briggs in San Francisco. "They asked $6000 for it, but made $1000 a personal donation." On 1 Nov 1901, FB wrote Briggs to ship the 400 baskets "by the Gulf route, Southern Pacific" to AMNH insured at full value.

Frederick Ward **Putnam** (1839 - 1915) trained in zoology under Louis Agassiz, but after 1875 devoted his energies to developing anthropology. Becoming professor at Harvard in 1886, he organized exhibits for the 1894 Chicago World Fair, American Museum of Natural History, and 1903 Berkeley museum. Despite his Ivy League ties, he strongly supported Boas. AA 17/712

Helen Heffron **Roberts** (1888 - 1985) studied music in Chicago, then visited the Southwest, became interested in the Pueblos and studied with Boas (1916-19) for an MA, did fieldwork in Jamaica, the Southwest, California, and Hawaii. She worked at Yale

(1914-36), publishing a study of music regions of Native North America before failing eyesight limited her activities. She often transcribed, notated, and analyzed the work of others, begun when Boas gave her the Haeberlin recordings, but she also worked beside other fieldworkers, such as the secretive JP Harrington of the Bureau of American Ethnology.

Roaming Scout (1845? - 1916) a Skiri Pawnee priest began in 1906 to dictate texts to George Dorsey and James Murie, another Skiri; their on-going analysis involved Boas, then at AMNH, pioneer ethnomusicologist Erich von Hornbostel, and others until it was all put aside in 1907. If HKH had taken a job at the Field, he would resume this work.

Edward **Sapir** (1884 - 1939) was a brilliant linguist who devoted himself to native languages of the Americas. He held influential positions at the National Museum of Canada in Ottawa, and the universities of Chicago and Yale. AA 41/465

James Alexander **Teit** (1864 - 1922) was born in the Shetlands, moved to Spence's Bridge among the Thompsons in BC, married a native woman, and after 1895 was encouraged by Franz Boas to undertake original research. He was particularly concerned to protect tribal rights. AA 24/490

Dorr Francis **Tozzer** (1843-1926), See Appendix K.

Thomas Talbot **Waterman** (1885 - 1936) was the first full time anthropologist, arriving after JP Harrington taught the 1910 summer term, at the University of Washington in the same year Haeberlin died; see his full biography in Appendix J. AA 38/532, 39/527

James **Wickersham** (1857 - 1939). See Appendix L.

Clark **Wissler** (1870 - 1947) devoted his career to the Plains and was long based at AMNH. AA 50/292, 51/527

Charles Gabriel **Seligman** (1873 - 1940) AA 43/437

James **Murie** (1862 - 1921), Skiri Pawnee mother, life-long student of Pawnee culture. AA 23/530

Appendix J: Thomas Talbot Waterman (1885-1936)

Waterman was one of the giants pioneering the ethnography, especially of places and abodes, of the Pacific Coast from Alaska to California. When he died in Honolulu on 6 Jan 1936, he was eulogized as a "vivid figure" and "great teacher," though his fieldwork, especially his ethno-geography, is what has stood the test of time. For both Puget Sound and northern California, he carefully plotted place names, described the major rituals localized within that terrain, and traced the regional distribution of house types and other artifacts of human manufacture.

Born the youngest of ten on 23 April 1885 in Hamilton, Missouri, TTW was the son of John Hayes Waterman, an Episcopal priest, and Catherine Shields Church, of Mississippi. His childhood was spent mostly in California, usually in Fresno. When his older brothers avoided holy orders, Thomas took up this family obligation and graduated from the U of California in 1907 with a major in Hebrew. He had taken one course in experimental phonetics with Pliny Earle Goddard, himself an Episcopal clergyman who switched from being the missionary along the Klamath River to becoming its ethnographer. In time Goddard joined the staff of the American Museum of Natural History in New York, where he became known as a comparative Athapaskanist, and closely collaborated with Gladys Reichard of Barnard College, who was from a Pennsylvania Dutch family.

Waterman went along with Goddard on at least one fieldtrip to record materials from Hupa (California Athapaskan) and, in short order, resolved to switch from the study of divinity to anthropology. He entered Columbia University to study with Franz Boas in 1909-10, finishing his PhD in 1913 on "the explanatory element" in tribal stories. His was one of three interrelated dissertations probing major themes in Americanist folklore. Another was "the test theme" by Robert H Lowie (1908).

His earliest fieldwork was in southern California among Diegeño and other Mission Indians (1908), then he shifted back to the Klamath River in the far north of that state. There he mapped Yurok places and later situated the annual rites at the Kepel Fish Dam to renew their world. In 1911 his mechanical recording of Northern Paiute speech was a first. Coming to Seattle, he visited throughout the Olympic Peninsula and Puget Sound, using $200 set aside in the summer of 1918 for an ethnographic survey of the state. When such funding ended, with a core group of enthusiastic students, his UW classes plotted the distribution of houses and canoes along the West Coast. His genuine fondness for local Lushootseed elders encouraged them to describe the Shamanic Redeeming ~ Odyssey to him, resulting in the clearest eyewitness overview of this ceremony, remaining unmatched for almost sixty years. He complemented this description of old beliefs with one of the Indien Shaker Church, which was founded shortly before he was born.

Waterman married twice. In 1910, to Grace Goodwin, and their children were Helen Maria in 1913 and TT, Jr in 1916. In 1927, he married Ruth Dulaney, a PE teacher.

A "brilliant, incisive, colorful teacher, rarely systematic and sometimes erratic, but extraordinarily stimulating" (Kroeber 1937: 527), TTW held a long series of jobs. At the University of California, he was Museum Assistant (1907-09), Instructor and Assistant Curator (1910-14), Assistant Professor (1914-18), and Associate Professor (1920-21). He set up the foundation courses in anthropology, and, with co-author Alfred Louis Kroeber providing "framework and ballast," published the first general textbook, *Source Book in Anthropology*, in 1920, revised 1931.

The most famous event in his life was being sent in 1911 to the jail cell at Oroville, California, to read long lists of native words to a forlorn man who had just materialized outside of town. He was Ishi, the last Yahi, and Waterman narrowed his choices to local languages until eventually these men were able to achieve recognition of the Yana word *siwini* for "yellow pine" by tapping the pine frame of the cot they were sitting on in the local jail. Thus begin the long process of communicating with this thoroughly native man who took up residence in the museum at Berkeley until he died of TB in 1916 (T Kroeber 1961).

At the University of Washington, TTW was Associate Professor (1918-20) when he produced the draft study of the western Washington native place names that has never been equaled, and, now, never can be. His interest in ethno-geography resulted in the published Yurok study, along with unpublished, but equally detailed, studies of Puget Sound along with the Straits of Juan de Fuca, and of southeast Alaska Tlingit. Moreover, his study of Makah whaling equipment has suddenly become extremely relevant again.

In a manuscript he finished in 1921 about the artifacts he collected around the Sound, Waterman (1973: x) acknowledged the "reputable people" who had already collected in Puget Sound, such as "Lewis and Clark, Wilkes, Boas, Culin, [George] Dorsey, Tozier, and (more recently) Haeberlin." He noted that the Tozier materials had once been on display in Seattle but were now at the Heye in New York and the National Museum in DC.

Letters in the Bancroft Library of the University of California at Berkeley reveal his life-long, bemused outlook on life. Writing from Fresno, 30 Dec 1908, he noted minor health problems limiting his career choices. On 29 Sept 1909, he wrote during graduate studies at Columbia University in New York City. Back at Berkeley, 18 June 1915, he was aware of the small academic world of jobs, noting "One of Merriam's men was ready to bite, but now he is offered an instructorship at the U of Washington."

The arrival of Ishi was not reported, but the aftermath is. Because Edward Sapir had worked on Yana, he was anxious to work with Ishi and so came from Ottawa to spend the summer at Berkeley. On 2 July 1915, "Sapir landed here with ten dollars in Canadian money and needed $150 at once." Kroeber was gone, and both Waterman and Edward Gifford were poor, so it became a "real circus" to scrounge up the money. By 7 November 1915, he was reporting details of Ishi's declining health, and, by year's end, 23 December, "I am still anxious to fly away from Berkeley."

The new year began with a most improbable proposal from John Peabody Harrington, the brilliant but unsocialized linguist of the Bureau of American Ethnology. This life of single-minded (paranoid, compulsive) research has been traced by his ex-wife of 1916-22, Carobeth Laird (1975), who soon married George Laird, a Cherokee living among the Chemehuevi. Harrington wrote to Berkeley to claim all of the southern two-thirds of California for his own research. Letters of 13/21 January 1916 explain that Harrington was willing to exchange his notes on native Californian moieties (mutually sustaining halves of these societies, often named Buzzard/Coyote) in return for J Alden Mason leaving off fieldwork among Salinans. The consensus (23 January) was that Harrington, trained only as a linguist, knew nothing of moieties and so would not have useful materials. A telegram on the 24th ordered Kroeber to write Gifford to immediately compose a 16 page paper on the Tachi so that his work would not be scooped by JP Harrington.

All this tempestuous wrangling over fieldwork and data led Waterman to muse on 1 February 1916, "I consider myself a hell of a fine teacher if that counts for anything. I will shine in the reflected light of the investigators I am training up, like [?] Outhwaite, [Thomas] McKern, and [Malcolm] Rogers."

Sadly, he reported the death and cremation of Ishi in a letter of 31 March 1916. Against the will of Kroeber and all other anthropologists involved with Ishi, an autopsy was done, and his brain removed, only to be located and repatriated eighty years later.

On 26 June 1917, TTW wrote that he was in the army and sending his wife to drafting classes so she could support their family if he is killed or "dies of boredom."

In 1918, he wrote from Seattle he was teaching Evolution of Culture 70 and American Indians 18. More ominously, 23 September 1919, reporting that UW is "busted and insolvent," he added "I can get along here cordially with the business offices, but I have a bad time with the 'scholars'." Indeed, his critical comments, in his own native place names study, on Edmund Meany's work about Washington place names indicates the level of ignorance and opposition he was up against. Still his teaching carried him through, with 400 in his Introduction to Sociology class as of 11 October 1919. Still unsettled, 3 November, he pleaded "When you go east, look around for a job for me, will you. I can't go myself, they've withdrawn the allowance for research." Unable to go into the field, he turned his classes into research outlets, reporting 14 November, "I've got a group working on Indian Houses." Among these students was Geraldine Coffin Guie, who co-authored the study of canoes with Waterman. Near year end, 10 December, he sought another source of funds and outlet for research, "I'm writing Heye to see if he wants some Puget Sound Baskets, canoe-bailers, etc," setting the stage for his manuscript on local artifacts, published in 1973, and a later job at the Heye Foundation, Museum of the American Indian in New York.

Among the manuscripts he left behind at Berkeley are Puget Sound Marriages and Geneologies (20 pp, # 100), Puget Geography (260 pp, #106), Geographical Ideas (22pp, #108), Eskimo and Puget (#110), and the mythology he coauthored with Arthur C Ballard (72pp, #107). The Bancroft also holds the manuscript by Erna Gunther (311pp, #) on Culture Element Distribution: Puget Sound (Duwamish, Skokomish, Klallam, Makah). Not a typical distribution for the Sound, by any means, though the key Duwamish entries came from Julia Siddle.

After 1921, he became "restless," shifting to the Heye Museum of the American Indian, and then the Bureau of American Ethnology. In the same BAE volume publishing the posthumous work of Haeberlin and Teit on basketry, finished by Helen

Roberts, the Administrative Report for 1922 (BAE AR 1928, 63, 73) lists Dr TT Waterman as temporary ethnologist from March 1 when he was sent to Alaska "to scrutinize certain native towns in southeastern Alaska. He collected data on totemic monuments and hundreds of place names until he returned on 15 June. On July 1, he was detached for six weeks to lecture in the Columbia University summer school.

Next he became technical director of the National Museum of Guatemala, and then, until 1927, taught at Fresno State College, where he offered geology, geography, and anthropology. He moved on to the University of Arizona for a year, then to Honolulu to teach at the Territorial Normal College ~ University of Hawaii, shifted to newspaper and public relations work, and, lastly, became Territorial Archivist.

Since his Tlingit place name study remained at the BAE in DC, and he began moving about, he sold his Puget Sound Place Names manuscript for $400 to the BAE, as mentioned in his letter of 21 March 1929.

In particular, driven by a "passion for flaming clarity ... he loved concrete facts and sharply defined findings, both presented with the same clean-cut picturesqueness which characterized him on the lecture platform and in intimate conversation" (Kroeber 1937: 528).

Gerry Guie, the former Geraldine Coffin, graduated, married newspaperman Dean Guie, and lived her life in Yakima. There, in the 1930s, she was host to Christine Quintasket, a Colville woman who had written a novel and autobiography under the pen name of Mourning Dove (1990). Gerry recalled TTW very fondly, noting that the worst criticism he could give the work of another anthropologist was "His work reads like a hardware catalog".

Writing from State Teachers and Junior College in Fresno California on 18 January 1926, he loaned Gerry Phonetic Transcription of Indian Languages.[89] Herewith a treatise on the Phonetic Transcription of Indian Languges by Kroeber, Boas, Goddard + Sapir. It was performed by these intellectual heavyweights, but is quite idiotic. I hope it helps you. Write me about your difficulties. The vowels ought to be arranged like this:

---

[89] Franz Boas, Pliny Earle Goddard, Edward Sapir, and Alfred L Kroeber, Phonetic Transcription of Indian Languages: Report of Committee of the American Anthropological Association; Washington, DC: Smithsonian Miscellaneous Collections 66 (5), 1916. It was later replaced by the more authoritative George Herzog, Stanley S Newman, Edward Sapir, Mary Haas Swadesh, Morris Swadesh, and Charles F Voegelin, Some Orthographic Recommendations: Arising Out of Discussions by a Group of Six Americanist Linguists *American Anthropologist* 36 (4): 629-631, 1934.

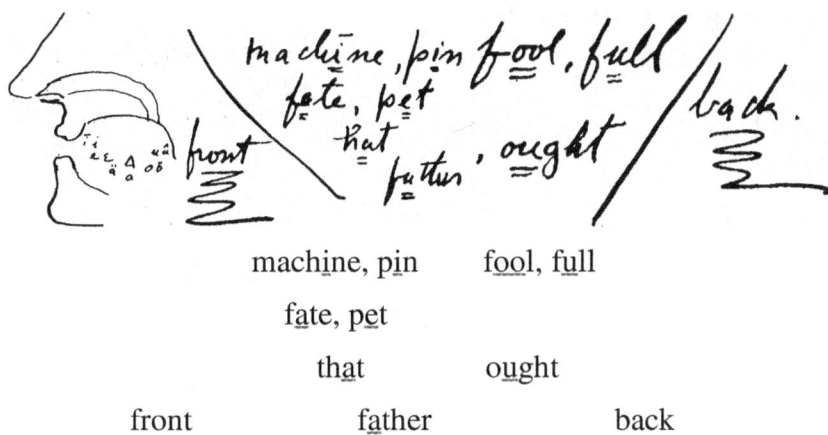

machine, pin   fool, full

fate, pet

that   ought

front   father   back

     Back vowel occurs in two forms, open + closed (the jaw dropped for the "open" sounds. The letters are put in the position in the diagram where they are produced.

Yours, hastily but with fond remembrance

+ warm regards TTW

Send pamphlet back when you are through, will you ??

On 21 March 1929, he wrote her from Hawaii.

I wish to God I could go out go out digging roots with you and the other Yakimas. A fellow wrote me a letter from Denver about basket designs. Such things make me positively hurt. Why the devil didn't I do some of this work when there was a chance. There were four hundred million place names around Puget Sound, also, that you and I and Ruth Greiner should have gotten. The Government paid me four hundred dollars for the manuscript, but it wasn't {wanst} complete.

I had some fun in the Southwest. A paper by your little friend will be in an early issue of the Anthropologist, on the sequence of cultures here. Clever, if I do say it. Your dear friend Leslie Spier (may the devil fly off with him) is full professor at the University of Oklahoma.

A former student of mine is Chief of the Bureau of Ethnology, Matt Sterling. I was in northern California last summer, and got some more material on Yurok, to complete some notes I got in 1909. I am writing the paper up now, except that I am writing to you instead. …

I'll have to send you some snaps of myself and this house. It's a Japanese house on the hill side. Gosh, what a view. This [page 2] island is all the books say it is, and then some. Honest, it's the cat's. …

Also I wrote up a good little collection of Puget Sound tales (a la Dean's [Guie and Mourning Dove's] labors), with a map, lost the map, found the map, and lost the text. It's still lost.[90] Damn. God bless you and regards. TTW

---

[90] A draft survives in TTW's papers at Berkeley, and many of these tales were recycled in the collections ACB published through UW anthropological papers.

Appendix K: Dorr Francis Tozier (1843-1926)

Captain Tozier was in command of the US Revenue Service cutter *Grant*, based at Port Townsend. Collecting all along the coast of the Pacific and Puget Sound for 14 years, he amassed about 10,000 Indien and Eskimo artifacts, of which 3,000 were baskets. He insisted that each one have been in actual use by native peoples when he bought it.[91]

He was born in Georgia, and attended West Point. In 1900, the collection was moved from Pt Townsend to Tacoma (WSHS) on loan. He began to look for a buyer when he retired and moved to LA in 1907. Most of it eventually went to Museum of the American Indian (Heye Foundation) and US National Museum, after bitter struggles. Many professionals were reluctant to get involved with the Tozier collection because of persistent rumors that he used his gunboat to force the sale or theft of artifacts from reluctant native owners.[92]

Another aspect of the long-term Tacoma/Seattle rivalry has been called "The Great Tozier Heist".[93] The Art Association of Seattle bought the collection and chartered the steamer *TW Lake* to bring it north from Tacoma. GL Berg led the assault, as it was perceived. They arrived at the Ferry Museum early on Sunday 9 Oct 1909, sidestepping the threat of a weekday injunction.

Curator William Gilstrap was locked in his own office with baskets worth $300 to compensate for remaining storage fees. The rest of the collection was boxed and placed in eleven horse-drawn vans. During the afternoon, workman began packing up the baskets set aside in lieu of storage fees. When Gilstrap protested, he was locked away until the entire shipment left town. The next day, he provided the headline for the *Daily Ledger*.

Tozier visited the collection in 1912, but the Art Association held a dubious status by 1913 and had yet to pay for the collection. By 1916, Fred E Sander was trustee of their holdings. In 1917, lead by Edmond Meany and others, an attempt was made to secure it for the state museum. Instead, George Heye purchased most of the basket collection. In 1952-53, the Burke Museum at UW purchased 227 of these Tozier baskets as part of 415 artifacts from the Alaska Fur Company.

---

[91] Nancy Jackson, Northwest Coast Basketry Collections and Collectors: Collections in the Thomas Burke Memorial Washington State Museum, University of Washington, Anthropology MA Thesis 1984.

[92] Douglas Cole, *Captured Heritage*: *The Scramble for Northwest Coast Artifacts* 1985: 219.

[93] John McClelland, *Window to the Past*, The Washington State Historical Society's First Century 1992: 57.

Appendix L: James Wickersham (1857 - 1939)[94]

Born in Illinois, raised on a farm, and schooled to the eighth grade, Wickersham taught in rural Illinois schools (1874-77) before he moved to Springfield and studied law in the offices of John Palmer, governor and senator. He entered the bar 14 Jan 1880, and married Deborah Susan Bell in October. Of their three sons, only the oldest son Darrel lived to marry but had no children. Suffering from TB, his wife died in Seattle in 1926. He married Grace Vrooman Bishop (1872 - 1963) in 1928. She was a teacher who graduated from the University of Washington in 1902, was a vital member of Juneau society, and left their Juneau hilltop home and family records to a niece, who runs it as a historical attraction.

After James and family moved to Tacoma in 1883, he supported them as a carpenter shingling roofs and building fences before he briefly formed a law partnership with Ezra Meeker. Then he set up on his own, sharing it for a time with John Palmer, Jr, son of his mentor in Illinois. His house was built at 230 South C St in Tacoma. The rest of his family moved west in 1884, then founded the town of Buckley in 1888 on the upper White River. When it was incorporated in 1890, James became town council.

A few years before, he lived much out of character. He helped organize the Union Labor Party and began an ill-judged affair with Sadie Brantner, leading into a notorious court case on a charge of seduction that was eventually dismissed. During this same two years, his second son was born and died, suggesting his uncharacteristic behavior was motivated by some sense of paternal anguish. He was a ring leader of the mob that drove the Chinese out of Tacoma in 1885 and burned all their property. He was indicted twice, but the charges never came to court. He never apologized for his actions but instead always insisted that he had helped to counter the superior threat of the Chinese, who worked so efficiently and cheaply that they would have soon taken over the West. He was afraid of their superior abilities, not any inferiority.

During the first term of Mayor Edward S Orr, Wickersham was city attorney. For his second term, however, Orr selected John A "Jack" Shackleford, whose brother Lewis was later Alaska Republican committeeman and a bitter Wickersham foe. Three Shackleford daughters had long careers in law and medicine.

Wickersham constantly engaged in land speculation for the Palmers, other Easterners, and himself, using several corporations such as the Allyn Land Company.[95] He moved to a farm near Gig Harbor in 1889, took 85½ acres on Henderson Bay to found Springfield as a summer resort, though its name soon changed to Wauna. His family avidly hiked outdoors, once walking the coast of Washington and visiting native villages along the way.

---

[94] Evangeline Atwood, *Frontier Politics*: Alaska's James Wickersham, 1979.

[95] George Pierre Castille, The Indian Connection: Judge James Wickersham and the Indian Shakers, Pacific Northwest Quarterly 81 (Oct): 122-129, 1990.

His clients included squatters on reservations at Muckleshoot and Puyallup. During a court case when he argued that Indien landowners must be regarded as citizens, and Judge Hanford agreed, some local Shakers approached him about legal protection for their church, which he provided by legally incorporating this native religion. It was founded in 1882 by the death and return of John Slocum, along with the healing power of the shake given to his grieving wife Mary Thompson Slocum. After 1890 he developed antiquarian collections of folklore and artifacts, using Mud Bay Louis Yowaluch, the head of the Shaker church, as a broker. Jack Simmons, a Shaker leader at Puyallup was a close ally; "working through Simmons, Wickersham persuaded Steilacoom John to abandon a piece of land in which [Fred G] Plummer had an interest".[96]

When the Senator Henry Dawes version of the Puyallup Bill was passed, protecting existing allotments while selling off "surplus" lands, a commission was set up. Its was ultimately composed only of Clinton Snowden, who was, at the same time, secretary of the Tacoma Chamber of Commerce.

In his famous diatribe that was anonymously signed A Boston Tillicum, Wickersham continued his bitter opposition to the efforts of Edwin Eells, son the famous missionary Cushing Eells and brother of Myron, to save as much land for Puyallups as possible. Eells avidly enrolled for an allotment any potential native who might be expected to be sympathetic to native rights. Wickersham charged in return that only a small number of the natives on these rolls were actually "real" Puyallups, as though this was some kind of indelible branding.

In 1900 he was appointed Alaska third district judge, based in Eagle City, then Fairbanks after 1904, and began his fifty years in Alaska as politician, bibliophile, and critic. As he left Tacoma and had put his artifacts in the care of the Ferry County (later Washington State Historical Society) Museum, two famous anthropologists came through on a collection trip funded by the Wanamakers of Philadelphia. Stewart Culin of the Brooklyn Museum and George Dorsey of the Field Museum in Chicago divided their efforts. While Dorsey was at Lake Sammamish purchasing the set of shamanic odyssey equipment now at the University Museum in Philadelphia, Culin spent the evening with Wickersham, "on the eve of starting his new post at Eagle City, Alaska".[97] The next day both collectors went to the museum on Sunday, where they met the unpaid curator and Wickersham. Noting that the museum was a hopeless jumble, Culin wrote that the Wickersham loan was "the only thing of real interest in all this curious medley."

Since Tacoma acquired in 1901 the only set of odyssey boards to remain in the Northwest, it seems likely that Wickersham learned from the encounter and undertook to collect the very last outfit to be used in this ceremony, knowing these artifacts were prized in the East. By contributing articles about local mythology and other native

---

[96] George Pierre Castille, The Indian Connection: Judge James Wickersham and the Indian Shakers, *Pacific Northwest Quarterly* 81 (Oct): 122-129, 1990: 128, Simmons photo 129.

[97] Stewart Culin, A Summer Trip among the Western Indians (The Wanamaker Expedition), Chapter IV, Bulletin of the Free Museum of Science and Art of the University of Pennsylvania III (1): 143-164, 1901.

subjects, his reputation as an authority increased. When James Mooney wanted an account of the Shaker Church for his Smithsonian study of prophetic movements, Wickersham complied with first hand reports as both church lawyer and supporter. He also used the occasion to again lambaste the efforts, as unnamed Indian agent, of Edwin Eells on behalf of saving some bit of the Puyallup land base.

In 1901, Wickersham was sent to Nome to clean up the corruption of the local federal bench. In 1903, he attempted a climb of Denali (Mt McKinley). He served as federal judge until 1907, then was elected territorial delegate six times from 1908 to 1920, then for a last term in 1930-32. He amassed a huge library, published a consolidation of Alaska law, and an Alaska bibliography. He always intended to write a history in retirement. Instead, failing health and eyesight, lack of funds, and lack of support frustrated his efforts. The University of Alaska received a grant for such a history, then arrogantly assumed it could station an academic in Wickersham's home library to write it. Of course he balked and the academic had to relocate to the Library of Congress in DC, where the archives of Russian America went after the sale of Alaska.

At considerable expense, he organized his library in locked cases in his Tacoma study, shipped them to DC in 1912, and then sent them to the Tacoma historical society in 1918. A decade later, they were installed in his Juneau home.

Though often characterized as a hypocrite for his duplicity in defending the rights of natives as citizens, only to use that right to buy and take their land away, Wickersham was much more complex. Full of curiosity and energy, he engaged in passions -- variously family, an affair, artifacts, or Indiens. As a Quaker, he seems to have been motivated by his "own light" to do as much as possible. After days in the office, he often spent evenings as a member of various clubs and societies. He must have been a Mason. Every night, he added to his diary, in the Quaker tradition. Much of his life was motivated by a desire for fortune, earned by billing all comers, but knowing that large funds would provide him with the leisure to undertake his research and writing projects. But he was never that successful, and old age took its toll before anything could be completed. Still, his legal incorporation of the Indian Shaker Church in 1910 has provided it with needed protection for a century. In Alaska, his ups and down with the famous Paul family of Tlingits provide a similar story of good intentions but fierce emotional conflicts. Mending fences became one of the primary duties undertaken by his wives.

Today, the large Wickersham family shares a crowded plot in the Old Tacoma Cemetery, along with the cremated remains of the judge, brought south "in state" from Alaska to Seattle and then Tacoma.

Appendix M: Stories

Raven and the Tides
{HKH 35: 24-29; 1924: 397-8}

Where the Skagit lived at Niccolum [not EG Nicolina] point there were not tides and the people could not get clams to eat because tide would not go out far enough and wind was flowing from the south all the time. People were almost starving and Kauqs = Raven was getting angry that they could get no food. The chiefs said to Kauqs who was a slave that he better go & see what he could do. Kauqs started out towards south. He traveled 10 days, night & day.

He came to a man who had 12 children, 6 boys & 6 girls. The youngest daughter was making *spegpegud*. That [is] why it was blowing all the time. "Where do you come from?" Kauqs said, "I am your nephew, I am great chief." Old man believes him, but Kauqs is just fooling him. Raven says to Southwind, "You are a great chief, who do you keep your house so dark?" Then chief had the roof boards opened. Before it was dark in the house. Raven makes youngest girl stand in front of Southwind. Then she begins to sing her sklalitut & Kauqs takes hold of girl & dances with here. Everybody was dancing violently. Then Kauqs escaped with girl through roof.

Wife of Southwind is first to recognize that Kauqs stole daughter. Southwind begins to blow & blow, but Kauqs keeps on his flight. He ties cedar bark over mouth of girl, so that she could not blow.

Kauqs takes girl to the place where Skagit lived. Old Southwind travelled north after his daughter. Kauqs kept girl tired & concealed. She was tied into a water tight basket, tied in. Southwind takes shells, blankets, etc to buy girl out. Southwind came, in canoe with his people. When he comes to Skagit, he sends one of his men to Skagit to offer them money for his daughter. But Kauqs said, "No, I don't want any money, but I want you to quit blowing. You must make tides rise & fall." Southwind agrees to this. But the tides are too high & too low, as Southwind makes them now. When tide is so low, then stench arises. Kauqs does not like this, so he makes Southwind change again. He takes two sticks & puts them into beach & show Southwind just as afar as tides must go. Southwind does this.

Southwind asks, "What other kind of food do you want?" Kauqs mentions horse clams & butter clams & cockles, mussels. "Is that all you want?" Kauqs says he wants flounders & other kinds of fish that Indians live on. Kauqs gets all he calls for. Kauqs said, "You must not blow all the time. You must only blow once in a while. And all this grub you must give so that the Indians who will live here after world is changed will have sttg [something] to live on." Kauqs then returned the daughter of Southwind.

Southwind says to Kauqs: "Northwind will be blowing too hard if I don't blow & it will be too cold." That is why Southwind blew, because if he did not, the Northwind would blow too hard. Southwind begs Kauqs to go to Northwind & see what he can do with the people there. Southwind gives Kauqs warm clothes for the trip. Kauqs promises to do what he can. Southwind goes home while Kauqs starts north. Southwind says if Northwind blows too hard, it will kill people. Kauqs goes to Northwind. He goes into house & there are 3 brothers living together: Northwind, West (N.W.) wind, and NE wind. NE wind says to N wind (his brother), "Why do you blow so hard, you make Kauqs & Eagle freeze?" < Kauqs and Eagle are relatives of Northwind. > Kauqs makes N wind agree that he will only blow during winter months, that it will let Southwind blow in summer. Kauqs tells Northwind that he has already made Southwind come to agreement.

N wind gives Kauqs a slip with writing on it & tells him to give Eagle this "note." <Little Sam said this was a "note" with writing.> Kauqs gives it to Eagle. Eagle gets angry at Kauqs. On this note it said that Eagle & Kauqs would be changed into animals, because Dik^{u}beł would soon come to change them. Eagle puts Raven out of his house. Then Dok^{u}bił came & had Raven explain what had happened. Thereupon, Dok^{u}bił changed Raven into a bird & his sister he chanted into a thieving Crow. Then Dok^{u}bił went to Eagle and changed him too into a bird too.

End

stō'bla' = N wind (oldest brother)

stūltcauq^u = NW wind (second)

stulk!ēx^u = NE wind (youngest brother)

? = S wind (oldest brother)

stō'tsī^d = SE wind (youngest)

stuldzāhab = SW wind (second)

      SW is stronger than SE and similarly

      NW "   NE

Southwind also lives together with his two younger brothers, just like N wind lives together with his two brothers.

Northwind and Southwind

{ HKH 15: 21-28; 1924: 398-99 }

Snoqualmi story told by Snoqualmi Jim.

He heard it from his grandfather who was a Snoqualmi.

Northwind was people long ago. Southwind was people too. Northwind & Southwind were different tribes. These two tribes fight together. Northwind people kill all the Southwind people. All Southwind people are killed except one woman (caul). (mountain wife??, caul name of this animal) [name for mountain beaver, not EG's Hedgehog]). She goes under ground to her father and mother. Jus as animals busies its way through the ground. This woman was married into the Southwind people. Father 7 mother 7 daughter were all of the cau'l tribe. Girl is pregnant and gives birth to a little boy who is half cau'l and half Southwind tribe. Grandfather gave the boy bow and arrow. Boy hunts wild grouse. He finds the house where his father (of the Southwind tribe) lived. There he found his father's sister living. Her name was Sqo'lats. He goes up to house and looks into house. This old woman says, "You must be the boy of the woman who married my brother." The boy says, "Yes, that is I." The woman tells boy that the Northwind people who had killed Southwind live not very far off. Then the boy got lots of wood & makes a fire for Sqo'lats. She was very cold.

Then he went home to the house of his grandfather and grandmother. There he gets made at grandfather be because he never told him who killed his father. Next morning he moved his grandparents to the house of Sqo'lats. Then the yng [young] man went to see the Northwind people who were living nearby on the river. These people have a trap (fence over river) for catching stealhead salmon. The boy pulls some fir trees <Not EG's boughs> down and lets them float down the river to the trap. He wants to make trouble for the Stomb★la <Northwind> people. Some sto'mela man sees the fir trees & tells his people that he is afraid that these trees will break the trap. The people go out & try to save the trap. The trees are too heavy for people. The boy sits on end of trap on side of river opposite the people. There he watched what the people were doing. An old Stom★la knows that the boy was the son of a Southwind man and cau'l woman. This old man tells his brother to go & ask the boy to help them remove the trees. The man goes over the trap to the boy. Man says to boy, "Won't you help us remove these trees." Boy says: "All right, I'll try." Boy takes the trees & throws them over the trap to other side, so that trap is saved of the trees. People are afraid of boy, tell him to get some salmon & then go home. Boy does this. Next day boy went to the same place. Then he took little bit bigger trees & throws them into river. Boy sits down on bank & watches trees come down against the trap. The sto'mela came & watch the trees. They try to save trap, but they could not get tree out. Then old man says: "That boy did that. He tried to hurt us. So [someone] tell him to throw trees over trap." A man goes boy & asks him to throw trees over trap. The boy goes into water and again throws trees over the other side of trap with great ease. All the Stom★la are afraid of the boy now. The boy again takes some salmon & goes away. The sto'mɛla have a meeting & talk the matter over. They are very afraid of boy. They decide that it will be best to give the boy two girls as wives and in this way make a friend of him. Two men carry this message to the boy. They say: "The Stom★la sent me. They will give you to young girls as wives." The boy says: "All right. Tell the Stom★la people to wait until tomorrow. I have to get my house ready for them today." Then the next morning the Stom★la people came in several canoes and with the two girls. The Stom★la people came into house of boy – everyone of them. They are freezing [it]. When they are all in, the boy closes the door and kindles many large fires in house. The fire makes great heat. All the Stom★la are killed by the heat including the two women. They youngest Stom★la is smart. He said to boy that he wants to urinate & that he will be right back. Boy is fooled this way & lets him out of the door. Then this youngest Stom★la runs away towards the north. He alone is saved. The other Stom★la are all killed.

Cau'l claims the trap of the Stom★la people. He would get lots of salmon from this trap & his grandparents always have plenty of fish. The youngest Stom★la never came back. He is scared of the cau'l boy.

End

People say if the youngest Stom★la had been killed too, there would be no winter. But he escaped & therefore the summer alternates with the winter.

Southwind people = stɛqaq!ᵘ

Northwind " = stōm★la

Stōqwāuq!u South Wind {HKH 35-24-28}

1

Little Sam (a Snohomish) has a tiqayui (wolf sklaletut). John Wheeler said that the stiqau sklaletut did not belong to the Snohomish but rather to the stq!ta?edjebc who lived up on the Snohomish river.

Usually a boy got a spirit that his father, gf or other ancestor had. It was possible he got a spirit from an ancestor on the mother's side as well as from one on the father's side. If a spirit is "inherited" in this way, the boy who receives the spr must got out to fast and bathe nevertheless. But it was not necessary that any ancestor of the boy had had the same spr.

2

John Williams has the q!woxq! sklaletut. Snohomish & Snuqualmi have this spirit. Carved pole with cedar bark belongs to this spirit.

John also has sgdeletz spirit. (board with two holes for hands belongs to this spirit.) This type of sgudeletz belongs on the Sdodamc.

The designs on basket #96 mad by a Snuqualmie woman are also a squdeletz skaletut, but a different kind. It does not belong to the Sdodohabc but rather to the Suqualmi.

Heyida is the same as the tiolbaxu spriit.   The following tribes had this: Snohomish, Skagit, Sdodohobc, StEq!taledjEbc. The

3

Snuqualmi, Skykobc did <u>not</u> have it

All the tribes in the vicinity had the tobcadad. They all had the following spirit, too, of which there were e different kinds:

1) sqaqkagwax a man

2) sqa'k!gwaL a man

3) sqagwaL a woman

4

Sheton

Sq!aip = war spirit

q!uax = low spirit

ts!aiq = woman's spirit

sgwigwi = potlatch (never for dead)

spaq!eksEm = potlatch for dead

What is a spegun dance?

Charlie Jules　　　　　(spirits)

yilbix^u almost as powerful as heyida

x^{u}altcab

cubadad

q! ^{u}oxqEd

5

Prof Boas would like me to see whether the different animals that appear in the tales are systematized in a different scheme of relationships, as in some of the inland Salish tribes.

Appendix N:
Catherine McLeod Mounts (1845-1933)

Born in 1845 on Clover Creek, the only daughter of John McLeod, a McCloud from the Isle of Lewis, and Cloquadote Mary, youngest child of Skanewah, Cowlitz high chief, Catherine entered her teens during the Treaty War, when her family's Muck Creek homestead was looted by US volunteer militia men while she hid and watched her pets (turkey, pig, dog) killed. Sent to Victoria (BC) for safety, she lived four years with the Rev Cridges, low church Anglicans who eventually joined the American Episcopal Church after conflict with his British hierarchy. Kitty, as she became known, valued her education there, and passed on its importance to her own ten children, several of her daughters becoming teachers and one son marrying one with photographic skills.

On1 May 1860, Kitty joined with Daniel Mounts, who had homesteaded at Dickenson Point at the mouth of Henderson Inlet until hired as Indian agent, when he moved to Nisqually. When Chief Leschi was railroaded in a second trial and hanged, Dan saw to a decent burial the first time. Unfortunately, US claims on that land led to Leschi being reburied twice more. Equally confused, Catherine was briefly and officially married to an Irish soldier from Ft Steilacoom, which soon dissolved. On August 1862, the Mounts had the first of their ten children, a girl. In 1866, they homestead above the Nisqually delta, setting up a home famously welcoming the many travelers bound for Olympia or Tacoma. In 1867, Mounts were legally and officially married, after living by "Indian custom" for years. After an 1869 flood damaged their property, they purchased adjoining land from Philander Washburn and relocated to an upland spring at Red Salmon Creek. In the 1890s, money for a railroad right of way allowed the Mounts to build a big house (eight bedrooms), bigger barn (dairy, hay), and many outbuildings. Mounts also built a school house for the area. In addition to Victorian trappings and musical instruments, the house also boasted superb native carvings and a notably well cared for basket collection that is now a pristine gem of the Washington State Museum.

Daniel died in 1904, and John in 1905, expanding the family plot at the Steilacoom Masonic Cemetery, where Mary was also relocated from the Muck homestead. Strengthening their native ties, Catherine arranged for 1909 allotments for herself and children on the Quinault Reservation, where many descendants are still enrolled. She died 20 August 1933 at 87. The huge home suspiciously burned down in 1968, but a portion of the land has been placed in a nature conservancy Nisqually Trust, and the former root cellar has sprouted a dense variety of fruit trees. Her great grandson Del McBride continued her legacy while working life long as an artist and anthropologist.

Herman Haeberlin, a young man soon to die of diabetes, just before insulin was discovered in Canada, worked with Kitty at her home in 1916 when, as she says in the notes, she was 71, concentrating on sensitive female concerns with domestic life, kinship, and medicine. Since there were German speakers among her neighbors, Herman must have felt at home. He was born, and is buried, at Akron, Ohio, where his father, a German engineer, was working, and his mother had kin. Concerned with the quality education of their son and daughter, the family returned to Germany prior to the outbreak of WW I. As a US Citizen, Herman was free to pursue his graduate and field work during that conflict, sent by Franz Boas to document the native cultures and languages of Puget Sound. As a special protégé, his death was a blow to the possibilities of anthropology in the Northwest, where a widow of 71 taught an engaged 26 year old.

Book #40 From here to end of book all from Kate Mounts (Nisqually Res) [p15]

bād = father (said by boy or girl)

skōi = mother

bada'' = son, daughter

sōqwa'' = brother, sister (younger)

sqa = older brother or sister

tsāpa'' = grandfather (mother's father & father's father) intermediate relative alive or dead

kaya'' = grandmother (both sides)

ēbats = grandson, granddaughter (on both sides)

quse'' = father's brother, mother's brother,

yilā^b = ditto (if intermediate relative dead)

pōs = mother's sister, father's sister

yilā^b = aunt (if intermediate rel. dead)

stālał = nephew & niece (said by uncle & aunt) interm rel living

qlādjūtał = nephew & niece (both sides) when intermediate relative dead (said both by aunt & uncle) [16]

sqwa'' = younger cousin (boy or girl) } on both sides

sqa = older cousin }

These 2 terms also used when interm relative dead. The terms only change for nephew & uncle when intermediate relative dead.

stālał = son & daughter of cousin on both sides

qlādjūtał = ditto (if parents of cousin are dead; but stālał is used if my own parents are dead, but parents of cousin alive)

quse'' = what I am called by son or daughter of cousin if his father is living

yilā^b = ditto (if his father is dead)

ēbats = grandchildren of cousin (interm relative dead or alive) tsāpa'' = grandchildren or cousin call me < [116b] Kwēlx^u used if intermediate relative is dead or alive.> [117]

xałtɛd = wife's brother

tc!abac = brother's wife (whether man or woman)

tc!abac = wife's sister

tc!abac = husband's brother

tc!ahabac = plural of tc!abac

xałxałtɛd = plural of xałtɛd

tc!abac = husband's sister

kwēl$\underline{x}^u$ = brother's wife's people (reciprocal) sister's brother & parents of wife of my brother

tc!abac = husband's sister

xałtɛd = sister's husband (man)

tc!abac = sister's husband (woman)

sāxāx'' = son-in-law, daughter-in-law (reciprocal) (interm rel dead or alive) (both sides)

ēbats =children of son-in-law

tsāpa'' = children of my son-in-law call me [17b]

tcābäq^u = great grand parent and great grandchild (reciprocal)

obālōtsid = for uncle's wife if uncle dead

kwēl$\underline{x}^u$ = my sister's husband sister (whether interm rel dead or alive)

sbālōtsid = if my wife is dead [18]

stciłbɛdä^{b}a^b = step son, step daughter

stciłbādɛb = step father

stciłtādɛb = step mother, uncle's wife (if uncle is dead)

stciłbɛdā'a^b = uncle's wife calls me

sbālōtsid = term that stciłtādɛb uses for parents & brothers & sisters of myself, if uncle is dead

stciłtādɛb = aunt's husband (if aunt alive)

sbālōtsid = aunt's husband calls me, if I am boy or girl) (if aunt living)

sbālōtsid = ditto (if aunt is dead)

kwēl$\underline{x}^u$ = people of sister's husband

> levirate rule: upon death of mate widow or widower marries sbālōtsid {intended} [19]

t!agɛt = noon

ts!iatqu {tsi'atko} were big people who came down from Nooksack country. The Squalli (& all other tribes around here) warned children in mid-winter not to go out after dark lest these ts!iatqu steal them. They whistled like small owls. Old people believed in them too. ts!iatqu took children (esp. girls) home, did not kill them.

<u>Pregnant</u> woman lived in a shack away from large house. Was not allowed to eat fresh meat or fish while out there. Husband did not go with her. He was not allowed to go near her while in out-house. Old women would bring her food. [20b] Shack [20] was built of mats or bark. When out camping she had to leave too & in this case shack was built of brush. Moss & ferns on which pregnant woman sat was wrapped up – put up a tree.

Menstruating women went out to the same shack. They stayed out about 5 days. During this period they bathed regularly every day & scrubbed themselves with boughs. She was not allowed to bathe in a river where there was fish. She went to pond or a spring to bathe. Sometimes several women if related stayed in the same hut. Nobody went near menstruating woman. Hunter can go out hunting if his wife has periods, provided he has not been near her. If he has been near her [21] he can not go hunting. An older menstruating woman could scratch her head with fingers. But if she was a young girl was menstruating, she was not allowed to touch hair, she scratched hair with scratcher.

Girl at first period was put out in shack made of firework & mats. No one was allowed to go near her, excepting that same old woman went with her. This was a person older than the mother. In case of a rich person, an old woman slave was usually sent out with girl to watch her. During several days (5-9). The girl was not allowed to eat or drink anything. After that she could eat vegetables & dried meat & fish (no fresh meat). The girl was kept busy making baskets & mats. Face was painted red all the time. Head face were covered [22] in such a way that girl could only see right in front of her. When girl first went out her hair was braided in 2 braids & rolled up closely to hair & tied up. Each month the braids were left down a little lower. The girl also had several strips of buckskin around one wrist & one ankle. Each month while she was out, one of these strips was untied. Besides the girl had a buckskin string (sometimes tied to a basket). In this a knot was put each month to keep count. Girls stayed out in the shack 6-8 months. After period was over framework & mats were not taken home, but were used at a following period, but were ordinarily set up at a different place. The dress that girl had worn during this period was either taken away at some [23] distance & thrown away or it was given to some old woman who might want to wear it (but it was never given to a young person). The work that girl had made (baskets, mats, etc) was given to some old person (never to a young one). Girls used rotten wood a good deal to scrub themselves, also cedar & hemlock boughs. She used different bunch of these for each different limb & only used once. After that it was tied up & put away on tree. Mrs M thinks it is 5 months that girl has to stay away from fresh mean & fish. If girl infringed upon this rule, the hunter & fisher would lost his luck.

While girl was staying in out-house, she went out at night-time (never day time) to look for sklalitut. Certain ceremonies were performed when girl [24] was first allowed to eat, but Mrs M does not know them.

At following periods, girl went out again every time, but only for 5 days. During this time fresh meat & fish were again taboo. Nobody was allowed to eat anything that she had cooked. Dress worn was _not_ thrown away, as at first period.

Hunter who had daughter who had fist monthly was allowed to hunt as long as he did not go near girl.

Each woman had her own menstruating lodge which she always used for the purpose. It was necessary to move the shack from place to place for the different periods, but the framework & mats were the same.

A shack for pregnant woman was made lie one for menstruating woman [25] but pregnant woman never used same shack that she had used for her periods. It would be a "terrible thing" to let a child be born into shacking that had been used for menstruation.

Woman who had given birth to child stayed out about 15 days after birth. In later times it was only 5. She was taken out just shortly before birth. If father of child was hunter or fisher, he must stay away from women & would not go to see child until woman came back. Person with sklalitut must also stay away. If father was not hunter or fisher, he might go to see child, but usually he kept away.

Father was allowed to eat fresh meat & fish as long as he stayed away from his pregnant wife. [26]

Slave-girl had to go to shack too while menstruating.

While woman was menstruating, she would continue her work. The baskets she made at this time could be used by young & old (not like basket made during first period while could only be used by old persons).

Rolls of cedar-bark was put in armpits of child when it was strapped to cradle. A toll was also put underneath the knees.

When woman had given birth to child, she had to bathe, but she was careful not to get her breasts wet, she tied sthg {something} over them to keep them dry.

When girl was menstruating, she did not have to keep this taboo. She might get her breasts wet then. < [26b] Roots of nettles used for colds.> [27]

Different kind of teas were given to women who were in labor. There were many different kinds of herbs which Mrs M does not know. She knows, however, of the following used as teas for helping woman in labor:

(1) Johnny-jump-ups (like violets) whole plant boiled & steeped in water

(2) Sprouts of a small wild rose used to make tea

(3) nettle tips (= buds)

(4) Lastly, a tea was also made by boiling willow and June plum bark together.

Such herbs were admonished by the midwives who were attending upon the woman. There was no obligation to having the midwives go to & fro from the woman to the other people. [28]

A dux̱ᵘda'b would tamanawus over a pregnant woman if he were called in to do so.

A hunter was careful to make a big detour around a menstruating woman's lodge, so that he would not cross a trail that she had used. If he did do that, he would have to bathe & scrub & even go to a dux̱ᵘda'b to make himself clean.

Several girls with first periods were never put together in same hut. Always separate. But at following periods woman were sometimes together in same hut if they were relatives.

Stories were never hold in day-time always on winter-nights (not in summer) [29]

Mrs never heard of any animal that the Squalli were not allowed to kill. Different tribes have different dzix̱ᵘ (not zix̱ᵘ as written in other books).

Morning star = laxel'alos } N.B. one begins with l, the other with ł

Evening star = łaxel'alos }

Thunder is a sklalitut that lives in a rock. When a person who has this sklalitut gets hurt, it is sure to thunder & rain. [29b] steelhead salmon is only salmon that goes up river & comes back. The others all die. Salmon run in following succession: tyee, humpbacked, silver, dog, & steelhead.

[30] Dog salmon are the only ones that the Indians dried. The others become strong when dried.

The first tyee-salmon caught in season was cut up & divided. The man who caught it was not supposed to eat of it. No body was allowed to step over this first fish. A general feast took place at this occasion.

Only eggs of silver & dog-salmon were dried. The eggs of tyee salmon were eaten fresh, but not dried.

Eggs of lark were given to little children to eat in order to make them become "good talkers". These eggs were cooked. [31]

Only Squalli on saltwater ate clams. But those who lived in the mountains would also get them sometimes thru' trade. Squalli from mountains came down to trade with those who live on slate water. The mountain Squalli would bring clams, camas, roots, & dried meat & trade them for clams & dried fish. The mountain Squalli never came down to beach to gather clams themselves.

Bulbs of tiger lily were eaten. They were steamed; first hot rocks put into hole, then fern leaves, then bulbs, water poured over this to generate steam, when covered with mats. Sometimes these bulbs were also cooked by simply putting them into hot ashes.

Dandelion roots cooked like camas. [32]

Roots of grandma's nightcap (bell-shaped flower, dark brown with yellow specks) cooked in ashes.

Nicknames:

logu[b] = means "young man," son of M's half-uncle.

e'e'xud = name of many boys

tse'elxud = girl's nick-name

o'olax = nickname of boy & girl, esp of an orphan

ts'xwalos = means "she's got small eyes," name of certain girl, but a boy might be called the same

tɛkwadi' = means "deaf," boy or girl

ts!ax[u] = means "little," girl's name

ɬadaila' "girlie" [33]

Twins were looked upon with great disfavor. When twins were born, the people began to howl & to make all the grub, clothes, & other property away from the parents. After some time, the people gave the parents some other property in return. The property taken from parents was divided up.

Names of adults (inherited)

yēduwa = M's oldest daughter, = name of M's grandmother

wayänät M's oldest son, = name of M's great grandfather (a Cowlitz) (woman could never have this name)

k!wanasāpab = M's second son, from a Cowlitz ancestor = man who had house at DuPont with carved house posts.

kwecāɬ = M's second daughter, means "it's fog," sklalitut name, name of M's mother's aunt.

wahau = M's 3rd son, a Cowlitz name

LeL!kwadot = M's mother's name, Cowlitz name

azōsbax = M's female cousin, Cowlitz name

batstakub = grandfather of Henry Sicade

püzoix^u = Squalli man's name

k!wayēbał = Squalli name, brother of Lecxaix

waxwilōt = man's name Squalli

ts!ōtsētēts!a' = woman, Squalli

sotqdxad = woman, Squalli

qaiq!ɛblōt = woman, Squalli

yɛt!āk!^u = man, Squalli

xaitɛd = man, Squalli

< insert Cf >

Mounts family names as printed in Haeberlin and Gunther

The Indians of Puget Sound, 1930 UWPA IV (1): 1-88.

Note switch of N for Y

[47] The names of one man of the Nisqually were the following: smūtäs, nickname; chief Stīlequem, after marrying a chief's daughter from another Sound tribe; s.oswē, a surname referring to his prowess; īnɛmał, Thunder, a name he got from his guardian spirit.

Some Nisqually nicknames are

logu^b = son of Mrs Mounts' half-uncle {means "young man"}.

'e'e'xud = name of many boys [48]

tsē'exud = girl's nick-name

ō'olax = name, especially for an orphan

ts!xwālos = "she has small eyes," nickname for a girl, but a boy might be called the same

tɛkwādi' = "deaf," boy's or girl's nickname

ts!ax^u = means "little," girl's name

łādaila' "girlie"

Names of adults (inherited)

xēduwa = Mrs Mounts' eldest daughter {Christina Mounts McAllister 1862-1946 = 83}, inherited from Mrs Mounts' grandmother

wanänät Mrs Mounts' oldest son {John Morgan 1868-1922 = 53}, inherited from Mrs Mounts' great grandfather (a Cowlitz)

k!wanasāpab = Mrs Mounts' second son {Frank 1870-1949 = 79}, meaning "man who has house with carved posts (Cowlitz name)

kwēcāł = Mrs Mounts' second daughter {Mary Ann ~ Polly 1972-1955 = 83}, means "it's fog;" guardian spirit name of Mrs Mounts' mother's aunt.

wahan = Mrs Mounts' 3rd son {James Tighe 1874-1924 = 50}, a Cowlitz name[98]

LēL!kwadōt = Mrs Mounts' mother {Mary McLeod} (Cowlitz) {azōsbax = M's female cousin, Cowlitz name ~ missing}

bātstakub = grandfather of Henry Sicade

punōix̱^{u} = Nisqualli man's name

k!wanēbat = Nisqualli name, brother of Lecx̱aix

wax̱wilōt = Nisqually man's name

ts!ōtstēlēts!a = Nisqualli woman's name

sotqadx̱ad = Nisqualli woman's name

qaiq!ɛblot = Nisqualli woman's name

nɛt!āk!^{u} = Nisqualli man's name {xaitɛd = man, Squalli ~ missing}

< Return to Handwritten notebook >

    Each tribe had its own set of names. This one name is know as belonging to Squalli, another one as belonging to Cowlitz, etc. and each family had its own set of names. It was an offence to take the name of the ancestor of some other family but my own. If I did take a name belonging to another family, the other family made a row & I would be forced to give a potlatch to this family. If this be done, I could keep the name. The same thing was done if I took a name belonging to another tribe. Then I had to give a potlatch to the Cowlitz family to whom the name belonged (not to the whole Cowlitz tribe). [36]

---

[98] The others of these ten children are Belle Zoura 1876-1948 = 72, Tristen Burgess 1879-1913 = 35, Hilda Pearl 1882-1952 = 69, Florence Ella 1884-1968 = 84, Catherine Kity 1887-193 = 76.

I could not give my daughter the name of my father's brother's wife, unless the woman had consented to giving my daughter this name while she was living. But of my father's brother's wife were dead & I gave my daughter her name, the people of the deceased made a row. This was done because the woman was not an ancestor of my daughter. I could get the name of brother of father. Two persons never took the name from the same person. For instance, my cousin would not take the name from a common ancestor. Bitter quarrels sometimes arose between two people who wanted the same name. these quarrels might be divided by one part making a payment to the other. < [36b] Different families had same nick names for children.>

If a person mentioned the name of a deceased person, he had to make a payment [37] to the people of the deceased. It was against the rule to mention the name of a dead person, he was always referred to the father, brother, son etc of some living person. A person was not allowed to speak of his <u>own</u> dead father, son, etc by name. This taboo, however, only held good for a certain length of time. After a year or two some other member of the family of deceased might take name of deceased, he never did this however right after death, he had to wait a year or two.

Nicknames of a deceased child was also avoided for a certain time. But after a while another family might give its child the name nickname. In such a case this family was however careful not to let the bereaved family hear this name.

(continued in book 42)

Pheasant Composition Book ~ School Series No 160

#42 pp 1-3 Kate Mounts (Nisqually Res) [15]

It was against etiquette to refer at all to a person who had recently died even in the indirect terms of brother of father, etc of so and so. It such a reference was made, all the people would at once begin to cry & wail.

2 cousins might have the same nickname, but not 2 brothers.

Slaves were ordinarily simply called by name of tribe from which they had been captured. For example, a slave captured from the Skykomish was simply called sk!ēxobc. But sometimes slave held his own name, they this would be used.

Adult person never went by his or her nickname, not even a low calls person. It the latter was too poor to give a naming-feast, then he took the name of his father or grandfather nevertheless [2] without giving a feast. If one person got angry at another one he might call him by his nickname, this was a slur.

At time of taking a name from ancestor a feast & potlatch was given. A high class person would call in other friendly tribes at such an occasion.

When woman became married, she <u>never</u> took the name of an ancestor of her husband. Very often when girl got married, her own folks gave her another name from her own ancestors (this was done too when the girl already had had a "real" name.)

Children of parents from 2 tribes could be named from either side.

All Indians agree that among the Cowlitz the women had a more important public role than among the Squalli , although among the latter the women too shared in same fasting with men. The Cowlitz women were known to be "great speakers" in public.

Fire is set up with bark. When traveling, Indian had a pɛdāq. This was made of shredded cedar bark inside wrapped with non-shredded cedar bark outside & tied up. About 4 ft long. One end of kept burning. This would burn for a day or two.

Martha Washington

Composition Book No 154

All notes in this book {#41} are from Mrs Kate Mounts. Mrs Mounts (raised among Squalli).

Squalli had basketry hats. No rim. Evidently twined technique. Soft, Flat on top. Rim fitted head. No extra rim inside. Squally made them themselves. Designs on hats. Squally had water baskets of cedar. Only used for water. No lids. Handle made of cedar limbs (stidgwad)

Dishes always oblong, Mrs Mounts never saw a round dish. Spoons made of wood + of horn. Squalli had no weaving at all. Spoons had animals carved on handle. These animals refer to sklalitut of owner. Squally used no buffalo blankets, excepting [1b]

Mrs Mounts father was a Scotchman, her mother's father was a Cowlitz, her mother's mother was Clallam & Puyallup. She was raise among Squalli. [2]

The squally who were related to Klikitat. The ones that were related to Klikitat sometimes went east of the mountains. These alone wove buffalo skins, no other Squalli did so. House posts were carved & painted with sklalitut designs of owner. Mrs M only saw one house with these carvings inside, this one stood at Dupont. It was used for living in (not just for tamanuwus). The other houses Mrs M knows had no carvings of this kind. Bunks all around the house, shelves above them for storing. The later slanted, thus |↗

Bunks were double. The bunks for sleeping were next to wall & about 2½ ft high. In front of these beds were bunks bout 1 ft high for sitting on. Fires were in center of house. No mat partitions between the families. Mats hung along the walls of house [3]

Slaves usually slept on lower bunks. But if there was enough room on top bunks, then they were permitted to sleep there.

In war raids the men were killed & the women & children were taken as slaves.

People who lived on opposite sides of house usually belonged to one family & had a common fire. Each family ate alone, not all people in house ate together.

Doors either on long or short sides. No swinging doors. Slave of cedar was set in front of door opening. House was made of cedar boards. The boards of the walls stood vertical & stood in a trench. Roof was gabled. Framework of house was tied together with stēdgwad. For letting smoke out boards of roof were pushed aside.

If owner of house died in the house [4] then the house was either burnt up altogether or given away to some other people. But in later case all the people who lived in house previously had to move out. But if owner did not die in the house, he people would not have to move out. If a person to whom house did not belong died in it, then the house was not burnt down, but it was deserted for a while. People could move back after 1 or 2 month. A person who was about to die was not taken out of house to die.

Mrs M does not know if corpse being taken out thru hole in wall. Corpse was carried out thru door. Belongings of deceased were burned u outside (not inside of house). Some of his property might also be given away to some old people (never to young ones). Dead were either buried or put up in tree in canoe. [5]

If people had no canoe, body was wrapped up & put on board in tree. After burial a feast & a cultus {faux?} potlatch was given to friends who had taken part. Men & women were fed. There does not seem to have been special group of women who were engaged as "waiters". Dead person went to land of skayu {ghosts}.

Squalli & Puyallup had not sgwēgwē' (autumn cultus potlatch) in olden ties, but later they have acquired custom. In older days only Chehalis, Cowlitz, Skokomish, Clallam, Snohomish & other Sound Indians had sgwēgwē'.

Squalli did spigpigud from November until Feb or March. One person only would spegpigud at a time.

Sklalitut was looked for only in winter time & only when it was stormy. However children were sent out in summer too when [6] it thundered. Spirit could be gotten any time in winter, not in special months.

When a man lost a wife, or a woman a husband, the he or she had to go out to bathe every night (never in daytime) for several weeks & rub himself with boughs. Father or mother did same when child died. This was not down for sister or brother.

When a child is born, woman is not allowed to touch her hair. She uses head-scratcher for 4-6 weeks. <[6b] Father may touch his hair.> If a boy was born, then women's hair is washed by other women (not by herself) after 4 days & then again on 8th day. If it is a girl, then hair is washed after 5 days & again on 10th.

When man or woman loses relative (either father, mother, wife, husband, child brother, or sister), hair of both men & women [7] is cut twice, first a part is cut off after 4 or 5 days, then a 2nd part is cut off after 4 or 5 days more.

When husband dies, wife must marry his brother or his cousin. Same thing is down by wife's people when wide dies. Brother, cousin or 2nd cousin was thus married off to widow.

Cousin of Mrs M mother had about 20 wives. This man never went out to get a wife, different tribes brought girls to him. He would then pay for them as he thought fit. Whenever his wives' people came to bring him food wood etc, he would give them something. One wife was always the favorite. This was generally the first wife he had married.

Wife usually stayed with man's people. Father & mother (or uncle & aunt, if parents dead) of man went over to girl's [8] people to negotiate for girl. Man himself would not go. If marriage was agreed upon the man's people brought the girl back, the man himself did not go over to get girl. A payment for girl was made. Wife's people would sooner or later make a small payment back to the girl. This latter was supposed to hand this over to the man's people.

Squalli do not have custom of man who wove build of pile of bark. Mrs M knows of this custom, but says Squalli did not do it. If women left man, then her people have to refund marriage payment to man (not only half, but usually most of it). But if man left woman, the he could not make demand.

Squalli never in time before white man came, married within his tribe, but always [9] married girl of some other tribe. He would not even marry a girl from another village of thee same tribe. This applied alike to high & lower class people. Squalli looked down on person who infringed upon the rule. He would have to pay a fine. If he did that, the wife's people consented, then he could live on with his wife, provided he had paid enough. If he did not pay, he ran in danger of being killed. The disgrace of marrying a girl of the same tribe was greater for a high class man than for a low class one & he had to pay a larger fine. It was regarded a disgrace even when the girl loved the man, in such a case a man had to pay the fine to wife's people nevertheless.

Person of 25 was sometimes dux^{u}dā'b & would cure. x^{u}dā'b was acquired in [10] youth, just like skaletut. < [9a] xudab could also be inherited.>

Cousin (woman) of Mrs M's mother had two sklaletut. As a young girl this woman had gone out to look for a spirits, but had never been able to get one. But she inherited her two sklatetut when the relative who had the respective sklalitut died. The gwoxq she got from her mother's people & sL!alqab she got from her father's people.

Indians told their children to stay away from persons who had a big sklalitut. This did not apply to their own children.

Man or woman might get sklalitut from a deceased relative (father, grandfather, uncle, aunt, etc). When a person died, he might designate the heir of his sklalitut, but this wa not necessarily the case. When person died, the sklalitut went away. When it came [11] back, it might come to an heir of this sklalitut. Then this person would begin to spigud & to give a cultus potlatch. This person did not change his name & did not acquire the man of the person from whom he got the spirit. The skalitut might not come to him until years afterwards. x^{u}dā'b was inherited in same way as sklalitut. Sklalitut when inherited was no good unless person made spigud & potlatch. The same applied to x^{u}dā'b. A person who had inherited x^{u}dā'b must also spigud. In order to get a x^{u}dā'b it is necessary to have a sklalitut.

Never heard of dāhadad. Squalli did have sacred formulas used with herbs for curing. < [11b] This knowledge was not the same as x^{u}dā'b. > But this was kept secret & could only bought or handed down to son or child.

Women also had x̣ᵘdā'b. Sally Jackson [12] found some of her spirits, others she inherited. Sklalitut & x̣ᵘdā'b always go to <u>nearest</u> relative of deceased. If deceased leaves a wife & son, it goes to son. If he leaves a brother, & son, it goes to brother, if son is not of age, but if son is old enough it goes to him in preference to brother.

Person does not linger around grave to get spirit of deceased. < [12b] tcādzats = to inherit anything, not only spirits. >

Children were told to stay away from graves. Older people would sometimes go to graves to wail. Relatives were buried together. Burials were at considerable distance from village. Several years after death bones were gathered up & buried. The handling was done by man who had special power for this. The bones of different people were wrapped up separately, but they were all [13] buried in one & the same hole. Man who handled bones was paid for his services. A person with special power was also hired to carry dead person out of house. Corpse was not kept in house longer than a day & a night. Sometimes it was buried right away after death. Dead body was wrapped up in mats.

Other kinds of sklalitut: sqēip, sqāgwał, hēyida.

Sally Jackson is supposed to have tiōłbax̣. This is the highest sklalitut there is.

Mrs M never heard of tsaiq. She does not know much about sklalitut.

M's mother had qwoxq (from father), sqēip (from mother's people) & tiołbax from mother's father. [14]

February wāqwāqos = frog month

March x̣ᵘpopohēgwad ("it blows, the buds open")

12 months in year.

String (called gwasō^b) was made of cat-tail rushes. It was split & twisted & braided gwasō^b refers only to string made of these rushes.

sxaltɛed = cradle board baby was wrapped up in shredded cedar bark & tied to board by means of buckskin thongs or by gwasō^b. Cradle was carried on the back. Roll of cedar bark was put under neck of baby. Padd {Pad} of same material was put on forehead & lashed to board to flatten head. Cowlitz flattened head of baby in somewhat different way from Squalli. The Cowlitz made head "thinner" in direction from front to back. [15]

Babies were kept in cradles about a year 7 a half. Mrs M says that in older times children were one washed in cold water (not in warm.)

High class Squalli wore sōlax in their septum. Men & women wore this. One shell was stuck thru septum. Squalli did not wear abalone shell in nose. Nose of child was pierced when child was about 5. Rim of ears was pierced all around. Sōlax was also worn in ears hanging down from string. Squalli never wore abalone shells in ears.

Tattooing was done with gooseberry thong & charcoal. It was almost exclusively confined to women (very few men had it). Girls of 10-12 were tattooed. Sometimes young women got some more. The tattooing was restricted to the underarm & to leg [16] below knee. At either end of tattooed area (at wrist & elbow, and at ankle & below knee) there was a zigzag line around limb. The designs within these areas were just for ornamentations, had no reference for sklalitut. M has a mark thus >--< on wrist. She says this is a design taken from beadwork on top of moccasin. Klickitat did no bead-work in old days. Mrs M thinks Squalli learned bead-work from half-breed French.

Women wore hair parted & braided in two braids & hanging down on either side in front. Women wove no band around head. Men wore hair parted in middle & hanging down loose or braided in two braids. Men let hair grow long.

< [16b] Carrying straps of baskets were made of maple bark. Sometimes they used buckskin carrying straps, but they were not frequent & were only acquired thru' trade.>

Men sometimes (but not often) wore [17] a band of mink or weasel fur (with hair on) around head with feathers stuck in here & there.

Men often tied hair together on back of head in order to keep it from getting into the face.

Squalli did not keep wool-dogs.

M is 71 years {1916}, Squalli had coiled baskets as long as she can remember.

Spoons were made both of horn & of wood.

Loose twined baskets with twilled bottoms were made by old Squalli used for packing and storing of grub. Dried food was put into these baskets, the latter was lined with maple leaves & tied together & then the baskets were put away fro winter use.

The close twinned baskets (see my [18] Chehalis basket) was not made by Squalli in olden days. < [17b] Only a few persons left to-day who can talk Cowlitz. Ann Highton is a Cowlitz. She lives sometimes on Squalli, sometimes on Chehalis reservation. Is a friend of Langfred's on Squalli reservation & lives with them sometimes.>

Mountain grass was often used to overlay the strip of which the loose twined baskets (with twilled bottoms) were made. The carry straps were braided of maple bark & also often interwoven with white mountain grass.

Wickerweave baskets their (potato baskets) were used in olden times for roots.

Squalli made their own basket hats. Men never wove these.

Mats of cat-tail rushed were made by Squalli in old times, always made by women. The rushes are held together by string made of split & twisted rush string (= gwasō[b] cf p14)

Summer houses were either square or round = tipi formed. The Squalli tipis [19] were made of poles tied together at top & covered with mats (which run horizontally around tipis). The square house was also made of a framework (gambled poles with horizontal one lying cross-wise) and covered with mats. The roof was not gabled but simple slanting. A loose mat on high side of square house served as door. Fire was outside never inside.

Squalli often built summer-house of branches when camping up in mountains. These were square like mat-houses with framework cut of gabled poles with horizontal ones lying on them. This framework was covered with branches of maple alder or fir.

Squalli ate lots of acorns. These acorns were cooked in the ground like camas (hot [20] rocks underneath covered with dirt, fire on top). After the acorns were cooked, they were put into open work baskets & these baskets were then cached in the mud of a lake & kept there for winter use. The acorns must be completely covered with water & mud. This mode of caching was never done without first cooking the acorns. When acorns were gathered out of water, they were ready to eat, were not cooked again.

While Squalli were traveling, they cached camas in tree (never in ground). The camas were cooked & dried put into baskets lined with maple leaves & put on tree.

Hazelnuts with shells on were cached in the ground. Dried hazelnuts were cached in trees. Hazelnuts were not cooked.

Acorns, fern roots, & sprouts of salmon-berries were eaten with salmon eggs. Hazelnuts were not eaten with salmon eggs. [21]

Roots of sunflowers were cooked like camas. This flower is about 2 ft high & has blossoms & seeds like out sunflower.

Cowlitz & Klickitat also ate acorns. Squalli did not mash up acorns. Meat was cached on tree (never in ground), it was covered with cedar-bark to keep rain out.

Man or woman who had lost a relation thru death was not allowed to eat any fresh meat or fish. He had to eat dried meat & fish for about 6 months. But this taboo did not apply to vegetable foods. Person could eat fresh roots & berries.

When a man lost his wife or a woman lost her husband, he or she was not allowed to touch their hair with fingers. They wove a head-scratcher of wood – tied to string around neck. But if a man or woman [22] lost a child, he or she was <u>not forbidden</u> to touch hair with fingers. When hair was cut for mourning, this was not done by person but by some other person, i.e. old person (never by young one). The cut of hair was either buried secretly or kept in some secret place.

Slaves were sometimes killed at death of a big chief. Never heard of wife of chief being killed at such an occasion.

Tc!auwai' & sōlax were used by old Squalli tc!auwai' was made of white clam shells, these beads were strung on strings & were round& flat. Tc!au'wai & sōlax were put on body of dead person. No grub was put with corpse. But a certain number of days after the death a morsel of each kind of food eaten by the survivors was thrown into the fire [23] for the deceased. This was thrown into the ordinary fire, no special fire made for purpose. At death property of deceased was burnt in a special fire <u>outside</u> of home.

Squalli were not strong on cultus potlatch, like other tribes. At of time of spegigud was only time Squalli had cultus potlatch. When a young man or woman took the name of some dead ancestor (this person must never be alive), the friends were called in & a feast given & some of the old quests might get some presents. The man would never himself call out the name he was taking, but another person was always hired for this purpose. The feast for this naming might last several days. This acquisition of a name had nothing to do with the inheritance of a sklalitut. At such a [24] naming-feast, the Squalli did not invite other tribes. But the Chehalis & Cowlitz would invite people from each neighboring tribe & a man from another tribe hired to call out the new name.

Girl got name from female ancestor & boy from male. Girl never took a name from a male ancestor. Boy or girl were about 10-12 when they acquired such a name. before that they just had a nickname. A person might change his name 2 or 3 times, each time taking a new name from an ancestor & abolishing the old one.

Puget Sound Lushootseed
dxʷləšutsid ~ xʷəlšutsid Researchers
Alphabetical, with clues ~ hints to affiliations and archives

1   Thelma Adamson (1901 - 1983) - Melville Jacobs Collection, UW

2   Pamela Amoss – UW

3   Clarence Bagley – UW Archives

4   Arthur Ballard (1876 - 1962) – Auburn

5   Ann Bates – Seattle

6   Dawn Bates - Arizona State University

7   Dave Beck - Toronto, U of Alberta

8   Astrida Blukis Onat – Seattle

9   Franz Boas - American Philosophical Society (APS), Philadelphia

10   Nels Bruseth - UW Archives, Darrington

11   Charles Buchanan, MD – UW

12   Francy Calhoun – UW

13   Eugene Casimer Chirouse (1821 – 1892, ordained OMI 1848)

14   June Collins - Buffalo, NY

15   Myron Eells - Whitman College, WA

16   Roger Ernesti – UW

17   Paul Fetzer – UW

18   Brent Galloway – Berkeley, Saskatchewan

19   George Gibbs (1815 - 1873) – DC, National Anthropological Archives

20   Erna Gunther (1896 - 1982) – UW MSCUA, Burke Archives

21 Herman Haeberlin (1890 - 1918) – National Anthropological Archives, DC; APS Philadelphia; American Museum of Natural History, NYC

22 John P Harrington - National Anthropological Archives, DC

23 Thom Hess – UW, Victoria, BC

24 Vi Hilbert - Lushootseed Research

25 Frederick Hulse – UW, U Arizona, Ca

26 Hyong Joong Kim -

27 Sandra Patricia Kirkham -

28 Toby Langen – Tulalip

29 Ezra Meeker – UW, Puyallup

30 Leon Metcalf - Burke Museum, UW

31 Bruce Miller - Vancouver, UBC

32 Jay Miller – NWC

33 Jay Ellis Ransom – UW

34 Marilyn Richen – Portland, Shakers

35 Natalie Roberts – DC

36 Martin Sampson - Tacoma, WA

37 Aileen Satushek - UC-Davis

38 Claude Schaeffer – Glenbow, Calgary, Portland, Or

39 Seaburg, William (1947 -) – UW Bothell

40 Sercombe, Laurel – UW

41 Roderick Sprague - Northwest Archives, U Idaho

42   Marian Smith (1907 - 1961) - Royal Anthropological Archives, London

43   Harry Smith – NYC

44   Sally Snyder (1930 - 1986) - Melville Jacobs Collection, UW

45   Warren Snyder – CA

46   Wayne Suttles - Friday Harbor

47   Robert Theodoratus - Ft Collins, CO

48   Kenneth Tollefson – Seattle

49   Harriet Turner (1920-2015) – UW

50   Colin Tweddell - Bellingham

51   Thomas Talbot Waterman (-) - Hawaii, Berkeley, DC

52   James Wickersham - Juneau, AK; Tacoma

53   Joyce Wike – Cusik, Nebraska

54   Johnson Williams – Klallam

55   Zalmai Zeke Zahir – UO,

US Archives with Lushootseed Materials

The Seattle Public Library
> Pioneers File
>
> Seattle Room
>
> Northwest Regional Shelves

Museum of History and Industry MOHAI, Seattle
 (archives now at Georgetown away from new Lake Union museum)
> Photo Archives
>
> Denny Family Papers (Seattle founders), particularly David (1832-1903)
>
> Newspaper Files (P-I photos)
>
> Lucile Saunders McDonald (1898-1992) features and articles

Special Collections, University of Washington (until 2004 MSCUA = Manuscripts, Special Collections, and University Archives) Seattle
> Biography Files
>
> Isaac Stevens Papers (below, territorial governor, senator, Indian agent)
>
> Edmond Meany Papers (1862-1935, early Historian)
>
> Jerry Meeker 3 Notebooks (Puyallup Elder, Land Developer)
>
> Erna Gunther Papers (1896–1982, early anthropologist, museum director)
>
> Lushootseed Research Archives (Vi Hilbert's notes, texts by elders)
>
> Melville Jacobs Papers (1902-1972, early linguist, folklore, Oregon coast)
>
> Seattle Directories, Local Histories, Biography Files, Newspapers
>
> John Peabody Harrington microfilms (1884–1961, early linguist)
>
> Hill Family (Nathan was local BIA agent at Holmes Harbor, 1850s)
>
> Anthropology Department Records
>
> Local Histories
>
> Microfilms & Newspapers
>
> John Peabody Harrington Files (early anthropologist)
>
> Willoughby Family (Sarah, artist, Charles, Quinault Indian Agent)

Burke Museum, Seattle

> Erna Gunther Papers (see above)
>
> Leon Metcalf (first tape recordings in early 1950s of native languages)
>
> Director's Files ~ car & boat use, correspondence
>
> Ronald Olson, typed Quinault stories

Lushootseed Research Archives {now @ UW SC above}

> Native language texts ~ transcriptions
>
> Elder biographies
>
> Vi Hilbert Biography
>
> Fieldnotes

Ethnomusicology Archives, UW, Seattle

> Lushootseed Research Video and Sound Tape Archives
>
> Thom Hess field recordings

Harriet Turner Archives

> Fieldnotes
>
> Photos, Tapes
>
> Hand drawn maps

Suquamish Archives

> Court Records
>
> Elder Interviews Tapes & Files

Duwamish Archives

> Recognition Petition

Filipino American National Historical Society, Seattle

> Biography Files
>
> Indapino [Indian – Filipino Offspring] Records

National Archives and Records Administration, NARA, Seattle

    Homestead Records & Plats & Tract Books

    Reservation Agency Records

      Tulalip, Suquamish, Swinomish, Puyallup

    Census Records

    Microfilms ~ M5 > Washington Superintendency Records

Tacoma Public Library

    Pioneer Files

    Open Shelves by Locale (look the books)

    Local Histories

    Newspaper index

Washington State Historical Society in Tacoma

    Edwin Eells Papers (Pioneer, Indian Agent)

    Photo Archives

    Ezra Meeker Papers (1830-1928, Pioneer, Hops King)

State Library in Olympia

    Pioneer Files

    Newspaper Clipping Files

    George Gibbs Letters and Tribal Censuses, esp. Nez Perce

    Isaac Stevens Library (First Governor, Senator, Bureau of Indian Affairs Official, federal grant to purchase books for first state library)

Washington State Regional Archives in Bellevue

    King County Tax records (marked "I" for Indian)

White River Valley Museum

    Arthur Ballard (1876-1962) biography (lost copy of "Listen My Nephew")

    Muckleshoot Records

    Hops Farming Records, Photo Archives

Port Townsend, Jefferson County Historical Society

      Nathan Hill family records, Snoqualmie 1856 Census

      James Swan materials (his watercolors at Yale)

Bancroft Library, University of California, Berkeley

      T T Waterman fieldnotes & drafts

      Arthur Ballard stories

      Erna Gunther Element Distribution (CED) manuscript (300pp)

American Philosophical Society

      Franz Boas (1858 - 1942) archive

      Herman Haeberlin (1891 - 1918) letters

      James Teit 1910 letters

      Ethel Aginsky (1910 - 1990) Puyallup linguistics (notebooks at Willits, Ca)

      Edward Sapir (1884 - 1939)

National Anthropological Archives, Smithsonian, DC

      George Gibbs (1815 - 1873), in the Northwest 1854–1859, native word lists

      Herman Karl Haeberlin (1891 - 1918), in NW 1916-17 (Leslie Spier donation)

      Thomas Talbot Waterman (1885 - 1936), in Seattle 1918-1920

      John Peabody Harrington (1884 - 1961), at UW in 1910, in NW in 1942.

American Museum of Natural History, New York

      Franz Boas (1858-1942), in Washington State many times, especially in 1910, 1927

      Herman Haeberlin, (1890-1918), Tulalip 1916–1917, artifacts accession records

Royal Anthropological Society Archives, London

      Marian Smith, Puget Sound, Sto:lo (microfilm at RBCM Victoria, Ottawa)

UPDATED HAEBERLIN TERMS
by Zalmai Zahir

Haeberlin	Lushootseed	English
1. spEtcu'	spəču? ~ syalt	hard basket
2. ƛ̓amqEs	ɫamqs ~ ɫabqs	spoon
3. xʷᵘtci'ɫqs	xʷčiɫqs	abalone
4. tc!au'wai	čəway?	shell
5. xatske'lus	x̌ackilus ??	step-wise design
6. sL!iɫtc	sx̌̓ič	tattoo
7. uyomatc	yu?yubəč	butterfly
8. slaha'lb	sləhalb ~ sləhaləb	disk game
9. sxalo'ltc	sx̌aləlč ~ sx̌ax̌əlč	sword fern
10. xai'o'xua	x̌ayux̌ʷə?	flies, fly
11. xelai'utsid	x̌alayucid ~ x̌əlayucid	type of basket
12. ts!ayu	c̓ayu ??	dark brown cedar bark for basketry
13. cau'ɫ	šaw̓kʷɫ	mountain beaver
14. Leq!ted	ɫəq̓təd	mountain beaver trap, "side lure"
15. gwakakᵘ	gʷada?kʷ	wedge, antler
16. skatcid	š(ə)qačid	stone hammer
17. kᵘlayuɫtc	qʷəɫay?ulč (NL), st̓ək̓ʷabulč (SL)	dish, "wooden container"
18. xpai'	x̌pay	cedar
19. qatsaqwats	qacagʷac, qcagʷac	iron wood
20. stsa'dzax	c̓a?suč (NL) c̓ac̓us (SL)	bow

21. sqalax	sq̓alax̌	digging stick
22. saxwaqed	səx^wuk^wəd, səx^wəsk^wəd	handle of digging stick, "by means of holding"
23. sqwe'L!Es	sq^wiƛ̓əs	war spear
24.	skəki^ʔi^ʔł (NL) sx̌altəd (SL)	cradle board, -i^ʔł *infant, child*
25. dzakidił	d^zak^wtədi^ʔł	stick for rocking baby
26. x̌uoted	x̌^wutəd ??	type of trap
27. tc!ax^wwadid	č̓ax^wadid, č̓ax^w=adi^ʔ=d	beater, "hit on the side of something"
28. sq!osid	ck̓^wusəd, c(ə)k̓^w=us=əd	cane, "straighten up the face"
29. dukwiL!babc	dx^wk^wiƛ̓əbabš dx^w-k^wiƛ̓=əb=abš	The red people
30. ləkwa't	ləq^wa	type of "soft" basket
31. stidgwad	stidg^wəd	cedar limbs, cedar limb rope
32. cabEdultc	šəbədulč	šəbəd design, šəbəd (for) container i.e., basket
33. cabEd	šəbəd	troll net, pocket net
34. ts!aut	sc̓ay^ʔt	gills of salmon
35. ts!aitolitz	sc̓ay^ʔtulč	salmon gill design
36. kwaix^u	kwayx^w/kwayx̌^w ??	dip-net
37. sduxwiL	sdəx^wił	hunting canoe
38. L!ots!Lots!itoib	ƛ̓uč̓ƛ̓učičtəb	webbing net
39. cEpcEpa's	šəpšəpac	comb
40. qwuxq	q̓^wux̌^wq^w(əd)	type of sqəlalitut
41. golatc	q^wulač	dip net
42.		

Possible morphological analyses

x̌ack=il=us

x̌əcq=il=us

sx̌ʼiⱡč

c̓ayuʔ

ⱡəq̓=təd

Principles of Esthetic Form in the Art of
The North Pacific Coast
A Preliminary Sketch

Herman Karl Haeberlin

IN so far as esthetics is not merely a fanciful structure of metaphysical postulates, but deals with demonstrable relations, it is a study of the artistic principles characteristic of a certain cultural group or epoch, or of a certain school of artists. The very fact that such principles can be found demonstrates the cultural significance of the phenomena in question and gives to the science of esthetics a place in the series of cultural sciences. If artistic expressions were individualistic in the sense that they were *disjecta membra*, we could indeed not speak of principles. But everywhere . in cultural growth do we become conscious of broad underlying laws which we abstract from the individual phenomena by conceptualization and which make a scientific study of cultural phenomena possible beyond the stage of pure description. This seems to be the essential trait of culture history in contradistinction to individualistic history in which we deal with the succession of dynasties, the fates of armies, and the intrigues of statesmen. Thus from a culture-historical point of view we study the principles which under- lie the art of a certain cultural group, how in the progress of cultural development the principles become gradually metamorphosed into new ones, and how the whole presents the continuity of organic growth. All of our culture-historical concepts, such as culture areas, cultural specialization, assimilation of cultural borrowings and the like, are based on the existence of principles by which a cultural area or a cultural epoch may be characterized. But more than that we gain even our norms of cultural evaluations from the conception of such principles. For surely we do evaluate when we [259] speak of cultural centers and of the fringes of cultural areas. We actually do place the stress accent on the cultural centers and not upon the marginal areas. Purely descriptively there is no reason why the marginal areas should be of less significance or popularly speaking "lower" in degree of cultural development than the nuclei of the areas with their highly specialized cultural forms. We place the culture centers there where we discern broad principles underlying the complexity of cultural life. It is illusory to believe that a purely descriptive culture history is possible.

Our study of underlying cultural principles may be either extensive or intensive. If it is extensive, we investigate the cultural life of a people as a whole, we correlate its different phases, study their associations one to another, and determine the common ideas which dominate them. But if our study is intensive rather than extensive, then we abstract a certain phase from the other phases and study the principles involved in the relation of its elements. In the following I propose to consider a sphere of culture-historical study of the intensive type to which very little attention has been paid. It consists in a study of the relations of form in the art products themselves. When these relations are such that we recognize them as typical of a certain culture area, we call them stylistic. The typical nature of these relations of form is the essential point, because only in so far as phenomena are typical do we speak of culture-historical principles. Most of those erratic markings which have been collected as the "Anfänge der Kunst im Urwald" seem to be equally void of culture-historical bearing as are the helpless scribblings of children on which so much interpretative energy has been spent.

In the case of the carving and painting of the northwest coast we are dealing with an art whose style is felt " by every one. To whatever objects this art is applied, be it to totem poles, house fronts, canoes, dishes, or spoons, we are always confronted by certain characteristic features of style. Certain characteristics of this art have been discussed. For instance, attention has been called to the fact that invariably the whole of the animals represented is given in the carving or painting, no matter how [260] disproportionate the size of the different parts of the body may be. Furthermore, it has been pointed out that in order to make such an entire representation possible the device of showing the animal "unfolded" either along the front or the back has been resorted to. These important principles refer still to the contents of the representations of this art, not really to the relations of forms, for which it would seem to me the term "artistic" is properly reserved. Such problems, for instance, as the relation of the forms of the mouth of the crest animals to the form of their eyebrows, if investigated, would reveal principles of "Formgebung" which might be as feasible of demonstration as is the principle of "unfolding." The mouth of the animals is either quite horizontal or its corners are turned down very considerably. Similarly, the eyebrows either lie about in the same plane or are considerably on the slant. Even a superficial survey I think is sufficient to impress one with the correlations which exist between these different forms of the mouth and the eyebrows. Similar problems of the artistic relations of lines arise in the case of the relation of the eyes to the superimposed ears of the animals and of the beak or nose to the rest of the face. Furthermore, such phenomena are of interest as the curvature of surfaces and the persistency with which painted lines are given artistic "character" by making them lighter and heavier at different points, as for instance in the outlines of the eyes which represent joints. By such a method of analysis we should arrive at the formulation of a number of esthetic principles which underlie the art of the northwest coast and which have thus far only been "felt. " Only after the definite formulation of such principles can we attempt a scientific comparison of the artistic qualities in the style of different cultural groups.

We should study not only the relations of lines and surfaces within the individual figures represented. An equally important task is to ascertain the principles which underlie the artistic combination of the different figures of a totem pole, of a spoon handle, or the like. A hasty survey reveals devices of composition that are in principle the same as some employed in our own art. For instance, a composition of crest animals is sometimes effected by [261] having a line in one figure continue in a succeeding one. In such a case the function of the line may be different in the two figures as far as the content is concerned, but from the point of view of form the continuity of the line results in a pleasing harmony in the outline of the figures represented. Another device of composition is the relation into which the projecting ear of a figure is brought with the figure above it. This relation is often worked out with great skill and presents an example in which the primitive artist solved an esthetic problem of composition, – a problem consisting in this case in the bold composition of the ear of the lower figure with the legs and haunches of the one above. Under this heading of the relation of different parts of a totem pole to one another occur some of a very subtle nature. For instance, in some memorial columns on the top of which a bird is placed, the curvature of the back of this animal and the outline of its wings appear to be adjusted with a wonderful feeling of form to the rigid vertical lines of the undecorated section of the column.

The most striking demonstration of the esthetic sense of the northwest coast artist lies in the adaptation of his subject matter to a given surface. There are a great diversity of surfaces to which he must adjust his composition. The totem poles offer cylindrical surfaces, the handles of spoons horn-shaped ones, dishes are round or oval, and canoes and the fronts of the houses have again different shapes. The given surface is the primary condition of composition and its utilization as an esthetic factor presents to the artist ever new problems. The solution of these problems involves truly artistic imagination. To speak here simply of technical mastery is not right. If this term should have any meaning whatever in our study of art, it must be made to refer strictly to the automatic motor habits which are bound to result from specialized activities. Certainly it must not vitiate the concept of artistic imagination, which is as indispensable in the study of primitive art as in that of our own. The adjustment of the same designs to different given surfaces is one of the most fruitful fields for studying the effective- ness of this imagination. The criteria are the different form-relations of the same design on different kinds of surfaces. Such [262] comparisons I think can be demonstrated in concrete terms. In the art of the northwest coast comparisons of this kind are rendered especially feasible on account of the conventions of a non-artistic character by which the artist is bound to represent all parts of an animal as well as never to omit certain characterizing features (for instance, the cross-hatched tail of the beaver, the long beak of the raven, etc.) whatever the shape of the surface may be.

To summarize briefly there are then three distinct lines of research in our study of principles of form:

1. The study of the principles which underlie the formal relations of the different parts of the animal figure to one another;
2. The study of the principles of the formal combination of successive figures;
3. The study of the methods of composition with reference to a given surface.

The pursuit of these lines of investigation is bound to lead us to a more exact determination of what constitutes the style of the northwest coast art. Our study will attain culture-historical depth by comparing the stylistic form relations of the cultural center with those of the marginal areas, or probably just with the absence of such form relations. Certainly the gradual waning away of the principles of esthetic form, which are valid among the Haida, as we proceed southward to the Kwakiutl and finally to the Nootka and Salish tribes, and northwest to the northern Tlingit and southern Eskimo, is very instructive.

The relations of forms, the analysis of which is urged here, will be of varying degree of demonstrability. Some relations like the continuity of lines in different figures will be directly and geometrically demonstrable, while others will be more or less recondite. And there are even bound to remain such relations which can only be "felt" and to which the student of art can only call attention in order that others may experience them. But certainly such a condition of affairs is in no way characteristic of the esthetics of primitive art. The study of our own art is confronted by the same situation. For example on the one hand we may study the spatial relations of a Gothic cathedral in the purely mathematical terms of [263] the relation of the intercrossing of the longitudinal and the transversal naves (= *das Quadrat der Vierung*) to the other dimensions of the edifice; on the other hand no one doubts the legitimacy of studying the purely psychic relations inherent in the different elements of a modern piece of art. It is well known, for instance, what wonderful use Rodin makes of the human hand for purposes of characterization. In his sculptures the relation of the hand to the rest of the figure may be indispensable for the unity of artistic conception and still, in spite of this innateness, a pragmatic demonstration of this relation would be inconceivable on account of the purely ideological nature of the relation. The result is that the relation can be only experienced intuitionally. It must be "nacherlebt." The more spiritual the synthetic unity in art becomes, the less are the relations pragmatically demonstrable.

The only plea I wish to make is that we study the formal principles in primitive art by methods comparable to those applied in the esthetics of our own. We are likely to look on primitive art simply as an ethnographic element and to limit our study to its relations with the other elements of a cultural unit. This I have called the extensive line of research. By an intensive study of primitive art we become conscious of the essential identity of problems in primitive art and in our own. Surely both lines of study may become mutually helpful. The study of primitive art has the great advantage of an ethnological perspective in which the cultural relations, I mean borrowings, assimilations, specialization of cultural elements, are far more plastically outlined than they are in the history of our own art. On the other hand the esthetic study of our art is privileged by being able to become individualistic and biographical, so to say, thanks to the detailed documentary evidence bearing on its historical development. It is true that this may become an evil when the student is not able to look beyond the historical details and to see the broad underlying principles of cultural relations. But in the study of primitive art it is just this biographical feature of the history of modern art that we need for stimulation. We tend too much towards conceiving the art of a primitive people as a unit instead of considering the primitive artist as an [264] individuality. . It is necessary to study how the individual artist solves specific problems of form relations, of the combination of figures, and of spatial compositions in order to understand what is typical of an art style. A purely ethnological point of view in the study of primitive art is inadequate. We need a broader culture-historical outlook. It may seem paradoxical, but it is nevertheless true that ethnology becomes the more scientific, the more it forgets that it is a science. It is the culture-historical point of view that counts. Ethnology is a fortuitous unit. It is the culture-historical point of view that counts.

Columbia University,
New York City

American Anthropologist N.S 20: 258-264 1918

Bibliography

Amoss, Pamela

1975   Catalogue of the Marian Smith Collection ~ Fieldnotes, Manuscripts, and Photographs in the Library of the Royal Anthropological Institute of Great Britain and Ireland.

1979 *Frontier Politics*: Alaska's James Wickersham. Portland:

1978   *Coast Salish Spirit Dancing*, The Survival of an Ancestral Religion. Seattle: University of Washington Press.

1981 Coast Salish Elders. pp. 227-261 in *Other Ways of Growing Old*. Pamela Amoss and Steven Harrell, eds. Stanford University Press.

1982 Resurrection, Healing, and 'the Shake': The Story of John and Mary Slocum. pp. 87-109 in *Charisma and Sacred Biography*. Michael Williams, ed. Journal of the American Academy of Religion, Thematic Studies XLVIII (3/4): 87-109.

1987   The Fish God Gave Us: The First Salmon Ceremony Revived. *Arctic Anthropology* 24 (1): 56-66.

1988 Erna Gunther (1896-1982). *Women Anthropologists, A Biographical Dictionary*. Ute Gacs, Aisha Khan, Jerrie McIntyre, and Ruth Weinberg, eds, pp. 133–139. New York: Greenwood Press.

1990 The Indian Shaker Church. Wayne Suttles, ed. Northwest Coast. Handbook of North American Indians, Volume 7: 633-39. DC: Smithsonian Institution Press.

Atwood, Evangeline

1990 The Indian Shaker Church. *Northwest Coast.*

Ballard, Arthur

1927   Some Tales of the Southern Puget Sound Salish. University of Washington Publications in Anthropology 2 (3): 57-81.

1929 Mythology of Southern Puget Sound. University of Washington Publications in Anthropology 3 (2): 31-150.

1935 Southern Puget Sound Salish Kinship Terms. *American Anthropologist* 37 (1): 111-116.

1950 Calendric Terms of the Southern Puget Sound Salish. *Southwestern Journal of Anthropology* 6 (1): 79-99.

1951 Deposition on Oral Examination of Arthur Condict Ballard. November 26, 27, 28. Testimony before the Indian Claims Commission of the United States, Docket 98. Carolyn Taylor, court reporter. 2 volumes.

1957 The Salmon-Weir on Green River in Western Washington. *Davidson Journal of Anthropology* 3: 37-53.

Barnes, RH

1984 *Two Crows Denies It: A History of Controversy in Omaha Sociology.* Lincoln: University of Nebraska Press.

Bates, Dawn, Thom Hess, and Vi Hilbert

1994 *Lushootseed Dictionary.* Seattle: University of Washington Press.

Bierwert, Crisca

1986 Tracery in the Mistlines: Semeiotic Readings of Sto:lo Culture. Seattle: UW Ph.D. Dissertation.

1999 *Brushed by Cedar, Living by the River.* Tucson: University of Arizona Press.

Bierwert, Crisca, ed.

1996 *Lushootseed Texts ~ An Introduction to Puget Salish Aesthetics.* Translated by Crisca Bierwert, Vi Hilbert, Thomas M. Hess; Annotations by Toby C.S. Langen. Lincoln: University of Nebraska Press.

Bliss, Michael

1982 *The Discovery of Insulin.* University of Chicago Press.

Blukis Onat, Astrida

1984 The Interaction of Kin, Class, Marriage, Property Ownership and Residences with Respect to Resource Locations among Coast Salish of the Puget Sound Lowland, *Northwest Anthropological Research Notes* 18: 86-96.

Castille, George Pierre

1982 The 'Half-Catholic' Movement: Edwin and Myron Eells and the Rise of the Indian Shaker Church. *Pacific Northwest Quarterly* 73: 165-174.

1990 The Indian Connection: Judge James Wickersham and the Indian Shakers. *Pacific Northwest Quarterly* 81 (Oct), 122-129.

Castile, George, ed.

1985   *The Indians of Puget Sound.* The Notebooks of Myron Eells. Walla Walla: University of Washington Press for Whitman College.

Cole, Douglas

1985   *Captured Heritage.* The Scramble for Northwest Coast Artifacts. Seattle: University of Washington Press.

Collins, June

1949   John Fornsby: The Personal Document of a Coast Salish Indian. pp. 287-341 in Smith 1949.

1950a   Growth of Class Distinctions and Political Authority Among the Skagit Indians During the Contact Period. *American Anthropologist* 52 (3): 331-342.

1950b   The Indian Shaker Church. *Southwestern Journal of Anthropology* 6, 399-411.

1952a   An Interpretation of Skagit Intragroup Conflict during Acculturation. *American Anthropologist* 54: 347-355.

1952b   The Mythological Basis For Attitudes Toward Animals Among Salish-Speaking Indians. *Journal of American Folklore* 65 (258): 353-359.

1966   Naming, Continuity, and Social Inheritance among the Coast Salish of Western Washington. Papers of the Michigan Academy of Science, Arts, and Letters 51: 425-36.

1974   *Valley Of The Spirits*, The Upper Skagit Indians of Western Washington. Seattle: University of Washington Press.

1979   Multilineal Descent: A Coast Salish Strategy. *Currents in Anthropology*, Essays in Honor of Sol Tax: 243-254. Robert Hinshaw, ed. The Hague: Mouton.

1994   Kinship, Social Class, and Religion of Northwest Peoples. *North American Indian Anthropology*, Essays on Society and Culture: 82-107. Raymond DeMallie and Alfonso Ortiz, eds. Norman: University of Oklahoma Press.

Compton, Brian

2003   December 7 Letter containing comments on Appendix E.

2003   December 17 Letter containing comments on Notebooks.

Cowan, Ian, and Charles J Guiguet

1978 The Mammals of British Columbia. Victoria: BC Provincial Museum, Handbook 11.

Culin, Stewart

1901   A Summer Trip among the Western Indians (The Wanamaker Expedition). Chapter IV. Bulletin of the Free Museum of Science and Art of the University of Pennsylvania. III (1): 143-164.

Dalquist, Walter

1948 Mammals of Washington. Lawrence: University of Kansas, Museum of Natural History, Publication, Volume 2.

Darnell, Regna

1990 *Edward Sapir ~ Linguist, Anthropologist, Humanist*. Lincoln: University of Nebraska Press.

DeSola, Ralph

1946 American Wild Life Illustrated. Compiled by WPA-NYC. New York: William H Wise & Co.

Dos Passos, John

1930 *U.S.A.: The 42nd Parallel, Nineteen Nineteen, The Big Money*. New York: Harcourt, Brace and Co.

Donald, Leland

1997 *Aboriginal Slavery on the Northwest Coast of North America*. Berkeley: University of California Press.

Eells, Myron

1887 The Indians Of Puget Sound (nine parts). *American Antiquarian* 9.

1889   The Twana, Chemakum, and Klallam Indians of Washington Territory. Smithsonian Annual Report For 1887: 605-681.

1985 *The Indians of Puget Sound. The Notebooks of Myron Eells*. George Pierre Castille, ed. Seattle: University of Washington Press.

Elmendorf, William

1935   The Soul Recovery Ceremony Among The Indians of the Northwest Coast. Master of Arts Thesis. University of Washington.

1946 Twana Kinship Terminology. *Southwestern Journal of Anthropology* 2: 420-432.

1948 The Cultural Setting of the Twana Secret Society. *American Anthropologist* 50: 625-633.

1960 The Structure of Twana Culture. Pullman: Washington State Research Studies, Monographic Supplement 2. (with Comparative Notes on the Structure of Yurok by Alfred Kroeber).

1961a   Skokomish and Other Coast Salish Tales. Washington State University Research Studies 29 (1): 1-37; (2): 84-117; (3): 119-150.

1961b   System Change in Salish Kinship Terminologies. *Southwestern Journal of Anthropology* 17 (4): 365-382.

1970 Skokomish Sorcery, Ethics, and Society. Chapter VI: 147-182, *Systems of North American Witchcraft And Sorcery*. Deward Walker, ed. Anthropological Monographs of the University of Idaho 1.

1971   Coast Salish Status Ranking and Intergroup Ties. *Southwestern Journal of Anthropology* 27: 353-381.

1993 *Twana Narratives*. Native Historical Accounts of a Coast Salish People. Seattle: University of Washington Press.

Fitzpatrick, Darlene

1968 The 'Shake': The Indian Shaker Curing Ritual among the Yakima. University of Washington: MA Thesis.

Fox, Ruth

1950 Milestones of Medicine: The Discovery of Insulin. 7: 185-221. New York: Random House.

Frisbie, Charlotte J

1991 Women and the Society of Ethnomusicology: Roles and Contributions from Formation through Incorporation (1952/53-1961). *Comparative Musicology and Anthropology of Music. Essays on the History of Ethnomusicology*: 244-265. Bruno Nettl and Philip Bohlman, eds. University of Chicago Press.

Frykman, George A.

1998   *Seattle's Historian and Promoter* ~ The Life of Edmond Stephen Meany. Pullman: Washington State University Press.

Gilstrap, William H, ed.

1905?   Art and Crafts of the Totem Indians – Collected by DF Tozier, US Revenue Cutter Service. Tacoma: Central News Co. {sales catalogue}

Glenn, James

1983   De Lancey Walker Gill: Photographer for the Bureau of American Ethnology. History of Photography ~ An International Quarterly 7 (1): 7-22. January ~ March.

Golla, Victor, ed.

1984   The Sapir-Kroeber Correspondence. Letters Between Edward Sapir and A L Kroeber, 1905-1925. Berkeley: Survey of California and Other Indian Languages, Report 6.

Gunther, Erna

1925   Klallam Folk Tales. University of Washington Publications in Anthropology 1 (4): 113-170.

1927   Klallam Ethnography. University of Washington Publications in Anthropology 1 (5): 171-310.

1928   A Further Analysis of the First Salmon Ceremony. University of Washington Publications in Anthropology 2 (5): 129-173.

ms.   Culture Element Distributions: Puget Sound (Duwamish, Skokomish, Klallam, Makah). Berkeley: Bancroft Library.

1949   The Shaker Religion of the Northwest, *Indians of the Urban Northwest*: 37-76. Marian Smith, ed. [below]

1973   *Ethnobotany of Western Washington*. The Knowledge and Use of Indigenous Plants by Native Americans. Seattle: University of Washington Press. [1945]

Haeberlin, Herman, and Erna Gunther

1930 *Indians of Puget Sound.* Seattle: University of Washington Press.

Haeberlin, Herman

1974 Distribution of the Salish Substantival [Lexical] Suffixes. M Terry Thompson, ed. *Anthropological Linguistics* 16 (6): 219-350.

Hess, Thom

1971   Prefix Constituent With /x^w/. pp. 43-69 in *Studies in Northwest Indian Languages*. James Hoard and Thom Hess, eds. Sacramento Anthropological Society, Paper 11.

1976 *Dictionary of Puget Salish.* Seattle: University of Washington Press.

1977 Lushootseed Dialects. *Anthropological Linguistics* 19 (9): 403-419.

Hilbert, Vi (taq^wšəblu)

1976 Recording in the Native Language. *Sound Heritage* IV (3-4): 39-42.

1979 Yehaw. Privately Printed.

1980a Huboo. Privately Printed.

1980b Ways of the Lushootseed People: Ceremonies and Traditions of the Northern Puget Sound Indians. Seattle: United Indians of All Tribes Foundation, Daybreak Star Press.

1985 *Haboo*. Native American Stories From Puget Sound. Seattle: University of Washington Press.

Hilbert, Vi, Jay Miller, and Zalmai Zahir

2001 *Puget Sound Geography*. sdaʔdaʔ g^wəɫ dibəɫ ləšucid ʔacaciɫtalbix^w. Original Manuscript from TT Waterman, Edited with Additional Material. Seattle: Lushootseed Press.

Hodge, Frederick, ed.

1910 Handbook of American Indians North of Mexico. Smithsonian: BAE-B 30.

Jacknis, Ira

1992 "The Artist Himself" : The Salish Basketry Monography and the Beginnings of the Boasian Paradigm. *The Early Years of Native American Art History ~ The Politics of scholarship and Collecting*. Janet Catherine Berlo, ed. Seattle: University of Washington Press.

Johnson, Nancy

1984 Northwest Coast Basketry Collections and Collectors: Collections in the Thomas Burke Memorial Washington State Museum. University of Washington, Anthropology MA Thesis.

Jonaitis, Aldona

1988 *From the Land of the Totem Poles*. The Northwest Coast Indian Art Collection at the American Museum of Natural History. Seattle: University of Washington Press.

Kroeber, Alfred L

1937 Thomas Talbot Waterman. *American Anthropologist* 39: 527-29.

Kroeber, Theodora

1961 *Ishi in Two Worlds*. Berkeley: University of California Press.

Kruckeberg, Arthur

1991 *The Natural History of Puget Sound*. Seattle: University of Washington Press.

Laird, Carobeth

1975 *Encounter with An Angry God. Recollections of my Life with John Peabody Harrington*. Banning: Malki Museum Press.

McClelland, jr, John

1992 *Window to the Past*. The Washington State Historical Society's First Century. Tacoma: Washington State Historical Society.

Miller, Jay

1976 The Northwest Coast Of What? Final Address at Conference on Northwest Coast Studies. Simon Fraser University and Canadian National Museum of Man. 12-16 May.

1979a A Strucon Model of Delaware Culture and the Positioning of Mediators. *American Ethnologist* 6 (4): 791-802.

1980 High-Minded High Gods in North America. *Anthropos* 75: 916-919.

1981 The Matter of the (Thoughtful) Heart: Centrality, Focality, or Overlap. *Journal of Anthropological Research* 36 (3): 338-342.

1982 People, Berdaches, and Left-Handed Bears: Human Variation in Native North America. *Journal of Anthropological Research* 38 (3): 274-287.

1985a Salish Kinship: Why Decedence? pp. 213-222. 20th International Conference on Salish and Neighboring Languages. August 15-17. University of British Columbia, Vancouver.

1985b Art and Souls: The Puget Sound Salish Journey to the Land of the Dead. 5th Conference of the National Native American Art Studies Association. Ann Arbor and Detroit.

1988a *Shamanic Odyssey.* The Lushootseed Salish Journey to the Land of the Dead, in terms of Death, Potency, and Cooperating Shamans in North America. Menlo Park, CA: Ballena Press Anthropological Papers 32.

1988b Viola Edmundson Garfield (1899-1983). *Women Anthropologists, A Biographical Dictionary*: 109-114. Ute Gacs, Aisha Khan, Jerrie McIntyre, and Ruth Weinberg, eds. New York: Greenwood Press.

1992a Native Healing in Puget Sound: 1-15. Portrayal of Native American Health and Healing. *Caduceus - A Museum Journal for the Health Sciences.*

1992b A Kinship of Spirit. Society in the Americas in 1492: 305-337 in *America in 1492.* New York: Alfred Knopf.

1992c North Pacific Ethno-Astronomy: Tsimshian and Others: 193-206 in *Earth and Sky*: Visions of the Cosmos in Native American Folklore. Claire Farrer and Ray Williamson, eds. University of New Mexico Press.

1992d Society in America in 1492: 151-169 in AMERICA IN 1492: Selected Lectures from the Quincentenary Program, The Newberry Library. D'Arcy McNickle Center for the History of the American Indian. Harvey Markowitz, ed. Occasional Papers in Curriculum Series 15.

1997 *Tsimshian Culture.* A Light Through the Ages. Lincoln: University of Nebraska Press.

1997a Back to Basics: Chiefdoms in Puget Sound. *Ethnohistory* 44 (2): 375-387.

1999 *Lushootseed Culture and the Shamanic Odyssey*: An Anchored Radiance. Lincoln: University of Nebraska Press.

1999a Suquamish Traditions. *Northwest Anthropological Research Notes* (NARN) 33 (1): 105-175.

2000 Inflamed History: Violence Against Homesteading Indiens in Washington Territory. *North Dakota Quarterly* 67 (3/4): 162-173.

2000a Religious Background of Salish Aesthetics by Helmi Juvonen. Jay Miller, ed. *Northwest Anthropological Research Notes* (NARN) 34 (1): 17-48.

2001 Ashes Ethereal: Cremation in the Americas. *American Indian Culture and Research Journal* 25 (1): 121-137.

2002 Dr Simon: A Snohomish Slave at Fort Nisqually and Puyallup. *Journal of Northwest Anthropology* (JONA) 36 (2): 145-154.

Miller, Jay, and Vi Hilbert

1993   Caring for Control: A Pivot of Salishan Language and Culture: 237-239 in *American Indian Linguistics and Ethnography in Honor of Laurence C. Thompson.* University of Montana, Occasional Papers in Linguistics 10.

1996   Lushootseed Animal People: Mediation and Transformation from Myth to History: 138-156 in *Monsters, Tricksters, and Sacred Cows*: Animal Tales and American Identities. A. James Arnold, ed. New World Studies. Charlottesville: University of Virginia Press.

Norton, Helen H

1980   Evidence for Bracken Fern as a food for Aboriginal Peoples of Western Washington. *Economic Botany* 33 (4): 384-396.

1985 Women and Resources of the Northwest Coast: Documentation from the 18th and Early 19th Century. University of Washington, PhD Dissertation, Anthropology.

1990 Fort Nisqually: A Little Known Historical Treasure, Index for 1833-1849, Seattle Genealogical Society Bulletin 39 (3, Spring): 103-118.

1990a   Fort Nisqually: A Little Known Historical Treasure: Part Two, Seattle Genealogical Society Bulletin 39 (4, Summer): 161-177.

1990b   Fort Nisqually Index, Part Two, Index for 1849-1859, Seattle Genealogical Society Bulletin 39 (5, Autumn): 7-14.

1990/1   Fort Nisqually Index, Part Three – Settlers' Accounts of 1841-1879, Seattle Genealogical Society Bulletin 39 (3, Winter), 59-67.

1991   Index IV: Fort Nisqually Servants' Accounts 1836-1867, Seattle Genealogical Society Bulletin 39 (3, Spring): 111-115.

1991   Fort Nisqually Index 5:   Women and the Frontier – 1840-1872, Seattle Genealogical Society Bulletin 39 (5, Autumn): 5-10.

ms Huntington Microfilm, misfilm inventory. (See Norton 1990-91).

Pierpont, Claudia Roth

2004 The Measure of America. How a rebel anthropologist waged war on racism. Annals of Culture. *The New Yorker*. March 8, 48-63.

Sampson, Chief Martin

1972   Indians of Skagit County. La Conner: Skagit County Historical Society Historical Series 2.

Schmidt, Erich

1927a The Mrs William Bryce Thompson Expedition. Natural History 26 (6): 635-644.

1927b A Stratigraphic Study of the Salt-Gila Region, Arizona. Proceedings of the National Academy of Sciences 13 (5): 291-298.

1928 Time-Relations of Prehistoric Pottery Types in Southern Arizona. American Museum of Natural History, *Anthropological Papers* 30 (5): 247-302.

Seaburg, William

1999 Whatever Happened to Thelma Adamson? A Footnote in the History of Northwest Anthropological Research. *Northwest Anthropological Reseach Notes.* 33 (1): 73-83.

Seaburg, William, and Pamela Amoss

2000 *Badger and Coyote Were Neighbors. Melville Jacobs on Northwest Indian Myths and Tales.* Corvallis: Oregon State University Press.

Smith, Marian

1940 *The Puyallup-Nisqually.* Columbia University Contributions to Anthropology 32.

1941 The Coast Salish Of Puget Sound. *American Anthropologist* 43: 197-211.

Smith, Marian, ed.

1949 *Indians of the Urban Northwest.* Columbia University Contributions to Anthropology 36.

Snyder, Warren

1956 "Old Man House" on Puget Sound. Washington State University Studies 24: 17-37.

1968 Southern Puget Sound Salish: Texts, Place Names, and Dictionary. Sacramento Anthropological Society, Paper 9.

Suttles, Wayne, ed.

1990 *Northwest Coast.* Handbook of North American Indians ~ Volume 7. Smithsonian Institution Press.

Suttles, Wayne, and Barbara Lane

1990 Southern Coast Salish, *Northwest Coast*. Suttles, Wayne, ed. Handbook of North American Indians. Volume 7: 485 - 502. Smithsonian Institution Press.

Taylor, Holly

2003 December E-mail comments on Regaining Haeberlin.

Thompson, M Terry, ed.

1974 Herman Haeberlin's Distribution of the Salish Substantival [Lexical] Suffixes. *Anthropological Linguistics* 16 (6): 219-350.

Valentine, Lisa Philips, and Regna Darnell, eds.

1999 *Theorizing the Americanist Tradition*. Toronto: University of Toronto Press.

Waterman, Thomas

1908 Diegeño Identification of Color with the Cardinal Points. *Journal of American Folklore* 21.

1909 Analysis of the Mission Indian Creation Story. *American Anthropologist* 11.

1910 Religious Practices of the Diegeno Indians. *University of California Publications in American Archaeology and Ethnology* 8.

1910 Collections from the Hudson Bay Eskimo. American Museum of Natural History, *Anthropological Papers* 4.

1911 The Phonetic Elements of the Northern Paiute Language. *University of California Publications in American Archaeology and Ethnology* 10.

1914 Explanatory Element in the Folk-tales of the North American Indian. *Journal of American Folklore* 27.

1916 The Delineation of the Day-Signs in the Aztec Manuscripts. *University of California Publications in American Archaeology and Ethnology* 11.

1917 Evolution of the Chin. *American Naturalist* 50.

1917 Bandelier's Contribution to the Study of Ancient Mexican Social Organization. *University of California Publications in American Archaeology and Ethnology* 12.

1917a The Yana Indians. *University of California Publications in American Archaeology and Ethnology* 13.

1920 The Whaling Equipment of the Makah Indians. University of Washington Publications in Anthropology 1 (2).

1920a   Yurok Geography. *University of California Publications in American Archaeology and Ethnology* 16 (5): 177-314. [Transmitted 21 June 1918].

1922   The Geographical Names Used by the Indians of the Pacific Coast. *The Geographical Review* 12 (2): 175-194.

1924   The Shake Religion of Puget Sound. Smithsonian Report for 1922: 499-507.

1925   North American Indian Dwellings. Smithsonian Institution, Annual Report for 1924: 461-85.

1927   The Architecture of the American Indian. *American Anthropologist* 29.

1930   The Paraphernalia of the Duwamish 'Spirit-Canoe' Ceremony. New York: Museum of the American Indian, Heye Foundation, Indian Notes 7 (2): 129-148, 295-312, 535-561.

ms   1935 The Sons of Ham.

ms   1935a Side-lights on the American Indian.

1973   Notes on the Ethnology of the Indians of Puget Sound. New York: Museum of the American Indian, Heye Foundation, Indian Notes and Monographs, Miscellaneous Series 59.

2001   See Hilbert, Miller, and Zahir.

Waterman, TT, and Alfred Kroeber

1919   Selected Readings in Anthropology. University of California Syllabus Series, No. 101. Prepared for Department of Anthropology, University of California, Berkeley and Department of Sociology, University of Washington, Seattle.

1920   *Source Book in Anthropology.* University of California Syllabus Series 118.

1931   *Source Book in Anthropology.* Trade Book.

1934   Yurok Marriages. *University of California Publications in American Archaeology and Ethnology* 35.

1938   The Kepel Fish Dam. *University of California Publications in American Archaeology and Ethnology* 35 (6): 49-80.

Waterman, Thomas Talbot, and Geraldine Coffin

1920   Types of Canoes on Puget Sound. Indian Notes and Monographs, Museum of the American Indian, Heye Foundation, New York.

Waterman, Thomas, and Ruth Greiner

1921   Indian Houses of Puget Sound. New York: Museum of the American Indian, Heye Foundation, Indian Notes and Monographs, Miscellaneous Series 5.

Waterman, Thomas, and Collaborators

1921 Native Houses of Western North America. New York: Museum of the American Indian, Heye Foundation, Indian Notes and Monographs, Miscellaneous Series 11.

Whitaker, jr, John

1980 *The Audubon Society Field Guild to North American Mammals.* New York: Alfred A Knopf.

Wickersham, James

1892 A. Boston Tillicum ~ A Plea for the Puyallups. Tacoma: Daily News Print.

1896 Pueblos on the Northwest Coast. *American Antiquarian* 18: 21-24.

1898 Nisqually Mythology, Studies of the Washington Indians. *Overland Monthly* 32: 345-51.

1899 Notes on the Indians of Washington. *American Antiquarian* 21: 269-375.

Wickwire, Wendy

2019 At The Bridge ~ James Teit and an Anthropology of Belonging. Vancouver: UBC Press.

Wike, Joyce

1941 Modern Spirit Dancing of Northern Puget Sound. University of Washington: M.A. Thesis Draft.

1952 The Role of the Dead in Northwest Coast Culture. *Indian Tribes of Aboriginal America*, Proceedings of the 29th International Congress of Americanists: 97-103. Sol Tax, ed.

Wirsing, Dale R

1977 Builders, Brewers, and Burghers. Germans of Washington State. The Washington State American Revolution Bicentennial Commission.

Wright, Robin, ed.

1991 *A Time of Gathering, Native Heritage of Washington State.* Seattle: University of Washington Press.

Zahir, Zeke Zalmai

2004 Translations, Meals, and Advice, 17 May. And many times before and since.

Ziontz, Lenore

1986a Erna Gunther and Social Activism: Profit and Loss for a State Museum. *Curator* 19 (4): 307-316.

1986b The State Museum Comes of Age. Washington Trust for Historic Preservation *Landmarks* 4 (1): 4-10.

Zumwalt, Rosemary Lévy

1992 *Wealth and Rebellion: Elsie Clews Parsons, Anthropologist and Folklorist.* Urbana: University of Illinois Press.

2019 *Franz Boas ~ The Emergence of the Anthropologis*t. Lincoln: University of Nebraska Press.

Mythology of Puget Sound.

Hermann ⋔ Haeberlin
Franz Boas, Erna Gunther Spier

The following collection of tales from Puget Sound was made by Dr. Herman Haeberlin on an expedition which was made possible by the generosity of Mr. Homer E. Sargent of Pasadena, California. Unfortunately Dr. Haeberlin died before he had time to work out his material, and the tales have been written out from his notebooks by Erna Gunther Spier.

The first group (pp. 372-391) are transformer tales which belong to the group characteristic of Vancouver Island and Puget Sound. The name Hālākᵘ by which the transformer is called by the Skagit may be related to the name Xals or Xäls by which he is known on southern Vancouver Island. In a number of cases tales belonging to different cycles, or isolated tales, have been incorporated into this cycle. Thus the first tale of our series describing the origin of the transformer is not known in this form from the Gulf of Georgia (see F. Boas: Mythology of the Tsimshian, RBAE 31, pp. 586 et seq.). The Star-Husband story has also been made part of this cycle.

Mink and Raven who are important figures in the origin myths of the northern coast tribes, appear here also in a number of tales. The modern version of the origin of daylight (which is identified with the clock) is rather peculiar.

The tribes of the east coast of Puget Sound represented here have been deeply influenced by those of the interior, as is manifested by the series of Fox tales in which Fox takes the place of Coyote of the interior. The story of how Coyote deceived the wives of his son and ascended to heaven belongs to all the interior Salish tribes. This is followed by the story of the introduction of the salmon which is also characteristic of the interior of British Columbia and Washington.

Another group of tales relating to the five wolf brothers is analogous to similar tales of the Chinook (F. Boas, Chinook Texts, BBAE 20, Washington 1894; Kathlamet Texts, BBAE 26, Washington 19o0; E. Sapir, Wishram Texts, PAES 2, New York, 1909).

Our knowledge of the folk-lore of Puget Sound is still very imperfect. While from the west coast of Washington we have collections from the Chinook, Quinault (L. Farrand, Traditions of the Quinault Indians, Publ. Jesup Exped, 2: 77-132) and Quileyute (L. Farrand and T. Mayer, Quileute Tales, JAFL 32: 251-279, 1919). Puget Sound is represented only in the collections of Phillips: "Totem Tales" (Chicago 1896), which, however, is useless from a scientific point of view and in which a great [372] many tales from other parts of America are included. Some Puyallup and Chehalis tales have been recorded by F. Boas (Globus, 1893, 63: 154-157; 172-175; 190-193). One tale represented in the present collection (No. 35) is contained in Paul Kane's "Wanderings of an Artist" (London 1859, pp. 250 et seq.).

A collection of Klallam Tales has been published by Erna Gunther Spier (University of Washington Publications in Anthropology, Vol. I, No 4). Comparative notes are reserved for a comprehensive treatment by her.

Franz Boas.

1. SYMPLEGADES.
(*Snuqualmi: told by Little Sam.*)

Five women traveled from the west. They were dog salmon (*L!wai*), tyee salmon (*yō'batc*), silver salmon (*sk'wets*), steelhead salmon (*qeuxu*) and rainbow salmon (*xobade'*, *xuba'de'*). These women came to the Snuqualmi River near the Falls before the world had changed and they found an old woman who had fallen asleep holding a baby in a cradle in her arm. The five women stole this child and puts {ok} some rotten wood in the cradle instead. They took the child away to their home in the west.

When the people found out that the child had been stolen they hunted everywhere for it. Finally the Bluejay, the child's grandmother flew to the west where the end of the world was. There were two big rocks there which were always opening and closing. On the other side of the rocks it was dark. Bluejay tried to get through and succeeded, but the rock hit her in closing and flattened the back of her head.

When Bluejay got through the rock she met a man who made all kinds of fish nets. This was the stolen boy whom the salmon women had reared, and when he was grown to manhood they had married him. Bluejay flew past him and as she did so the man took up some dust and threw it into her face. Bluejay began to cry and said: "I have been looking for you for years, and now you throw dust into my face." Then the man who was *Dō'kᵘibɛɫ* showed Bluejay all the salmon who were his children and he taught her how to make all kinds of nets. Bluejay brought all this information to her people, the Snuqualmi.

As Bluejay was returning through the opening and closing rock she put the net gauge which Dō'kᵘibɛɫ had given her for the fish nets in between the rocks and in this way kept them open, until she had passed through.

Dō'kᵘibɛɫ returned to this world and he brought all his salmon children with him so that they could spawn in the rivers. Before *Dō'kᵘibɛɫ* came, there were no salmon in this world, and when he brought all the species of salmon the humpbacked salmon were forgotten and so this kind of salmon comes only every second year.

2. STAR HUSBAND (FIRST VERSION).
(*Snuqualmi: told by Skookum George.*)

About two miles beyond Snuqualmi Fall near the mountain called *Q'albits* several women were camping and digging fern roots. Among them were two sisters, *Yeselbc*, the younger, and *Tapaltxᵘ* the elder. When the women were asleep the sisters looked up to the sky at night. The younger one said, "Where can we find men?" - "We want fishermen so that we can eat fish with our fern roots," replied *Tapaltxᵘ*. "We don't want fishermen, we want hunters; then we can eat meat." - "How would you like it if we got those stars up there as husbands? There is a red one and a white one." - "Don't say that," *Yeselbc* answered. "I will take the red star and you can have the white star," said *Tapaltxᵘ*.

They had been awake for a long time so both sisters slept very soundly that night. While they slept both stars came down and took the two sisters up to the sky.

When the girls awoke they did not know where they were; it was a different place from where they had been. The red star took the older girl and the white star took the younger girl as wife. Both were fine men and fine hunters, but the red star had sore eyes.

As soon as the men had had breakfast they would go out hunting, while the girls stayed at home. They worried because they did not know where they were. They found some ferns just below their home and they dug for the fern roots which they took home and cooked. Every evening the stars came back with a deer. The four then ate deer and fern roots together. The men said, "Don't follow those roots very deeply." Every time they went hunting they gave the girls this advice.

The younger one who was the smarter of the two, said, "Why don't they want us to follow these roots deeply?" The next day she told her sister, "Let us follow the roots deep into the ground." They followed the roots and the wind came up from below. They made the hole larger and as they looked through it, they saw the place where they had come from. The younger sister called to *Tapaltx*[u] and said, "Look down here; see that is where we belong." Then they covered up the hole with dirt and went home to decide what was best for them to do. The girls twisted cedar twigs and made a rope ladder. It took them a long time to make it. When it was finished they went back and opened the hole. They put the ladder through but is was too short and would not reach the earth. They gathered more cedar twigs and made the ladder longer. Meanwhile they had stayed in the sky about one year and the younger girl was pregnant. They brought home only a few fern roots now, because they had not much time to dig while they worked on the ladder. The men asked them why they brought home so few roots. "Fernroots are so hard to get now," they replied. Again they opened the hole and tried the ladder. This time it was long enough; it reached to the Snuqualmi country [374] could not start on that day any more, so they left the ladder in the hole, but covered the hole up.

The next morning the men went out hunting and the girls decided to leave. The men knew nothing about what the girls were doing. The girls went to the ladder and the elder one went down first. She went down until she came to the mountains. The younger one followed and she covered the hole with dirt before leaving the sky. They told the people that they had been in the sky. Many people heard about this and they wanted to see the ladder. The people had thought that the girls were lost. The ladder was swinging into the *Q'albits* mountains (near North Bend). Lots of people swung on the ladder and they swung through a valley that runs from North to South. The many gulches there are caused by this swinging. Many different kinds of people came there to have a good time.

The younger girl gave birth to a boy. She had no time to take care of the child so she hired Toad to care for the baby. Toad was a blind woman. She made a cradle for the baby. Somebody stole the baby because he was such a fine boy. The people searched for the lost child but they could not find him. While they looked for the baby they had no time to take care of the swing. The Rat had been swinging and he gnawed at the swing and it dropped down into a pile and formed a large round rock in Snuqualmi valley. (*Midoad* { } is the name of this rock to-day, the Indian word for rock.)

The people looked everywhere for the stolen baby. Finally Hawk found out that the baby was at the end of the world where the salmon lived. The mother hired some birds to get the baby. Salmon had stolen the baby and taken him to the end of the world beyond the rocks that open and close. It was very hard to get there and even the birds were not able to pass the rocks. The people looked for the smartest bird who would be able to pass through the rocks. Finally they found that Bluejay was the smartest one. He was sent to get the child. This bird was slow but smart. He came to the place where the rocks open and close. He saw the baby as he watched through the rocks. As soon as the rocks opened he flew through. He came to the baby, took him and watched the rocks. When the door opened Bluejay flew through. With the baby he could not fly as quickly, and as the door closed it struck the back of his head. This is the cause for the peculiar form of the bluejay's head in the back.

The child had grown and could talk now. Bluejay left him on the safe side of the rocks and flew to tell the boy's mother that the boy was big now and would soon be coming home to show the people what he could do. The boy came back and he made rivers and creeks and changed everything. He made animals, ducks and birds. He made big rocks. The boy's name was Xweq!^{u}. [375]

2a. STAR HUSBAND (SECOND VERSION).[99]
(*Told by Henry Sicade*.)

In those days when the earth was young, trees were scarce; the land at large was open and easy to go over; there was no moon, no sun and the people lived in a kind of perpetual twilight. They mingled with the animals; birds, beasts and men having a common tongue.

There dwelt on the earth at that time three sisters, the oldest called *Tapalt*, the next *Yeslamish* and the youngest, *Callocoblow*. At seasons when the fern roots were good for food these sisters would dig them to store for other times. When evening came they built a fire in camp, dried their roots and made their bed as comfortable as they could with the scanty means at their command. At early dawn they would return to work and repeat this for several days.

One evening when they retired *Yeslamish* exclaimed, "I wish that red star would be my husband." *Tapalt* seconded her and said, "I wish the white star would be mine."

------

[99] I. Copied from the *Tacoma Evening News* (no date). Five versions of this story have been recorded. Two of these are very short, stopping after the sisters return to earth where the elder girl gives birth to a son who becomes the ancestor of the Snuqualmi. The most complete versions are the two given above. In a fifth one the baby is stolen by its star father.

The two short versions were told by Snuqualmi Jim. Skookum George told the first version given above. These ~~informants~~, both Snuqualmi, claim that this is a Snuqualmi story and although the Snohomish know it, they never tell it.

Venus in the west in the evening (*ła'xēlalōs*), is identified as the white star who married the elder girl and Venus in the east in the morning, is the red star who married the younger girl. These women were Snuqualmi.

The next morning, much to their surprise, they found themselves in an unknown land, each with her wish satisfied. *Tapalt* found that her husband had sore eyes. The youngest sister, who had expressed no wish was left alone in the camp to carry back to her people the wonderful story of her sisters.

Hitching their matrimonial wagons to stars had its drawbacks, as the women soon found out. The world where they lived was a pleasant place, much like the earth, but without wind or storms or rain. Their husbands guarded them jealously and strictly forbade their following fern roots downward. *Wecook*, the grandmother of the women, who seemed in some mysterious way to have gotten to the land of the star-husbands, always went with the sisters when they dug for fern roots.

A son had been born to *Tapalt* and the White Star. She called him *Arh-hade* (the Moon), because he was born in a strange land and some day would be a famous and wonderful man.

Curiosity and homesickness soon became the supreme considerations of the women. One day they dug down until suddenly a gust of wind blew through and they saw far below their native land. Their husbands felt the air moving and came to see what the women were doing, but they had stopped up the hole and pretended to be otherwise occupied.

The women whispered among themselves when the backs of their husbands were turned and planned to make a long ladder of cedar roots to reach downward. After days and days of hard work they had made a ladder long enough to span the distance. To deceive their husbands they would take home large quantities of roots each night, so that they might have no notion of other activities. Deer meat was pressed into a tiny cake by each of the sisters and when the appointed time came *Tapalt* and her baby boy and *Yeslamish* went down the ladder. *Wecook*, the grandmother, volunteered to remain and cover the opening behind them and then, being afraid the angered husbands would kill her, quickly covered herself up in the hole and turned into a fern.

There was great rejoicing and a big gathering when the sisters returned. The center of attraction was the swing ladder, used by the women as a clinching proof of their wonderful adventures. The years passed and the ladder finally fell down from the sky and was turned into Snuqualmi Falls.

During the excitement of their return the sisters had given the baby, Arh-hade, to a blind old woman to care for while they told of their adventures and distributed bits of food which had miraculously increased to great abundance. *Skulley*, a monster disguised as a strange woman, and her two daughters appeared and in the excitement stole the baby boy from his blind care-taker and fled with him to a distant and unknown land.

Clamorous rejoicing gave way to wails of grief and the best prophets and guessers were summoned to find where the baby had been taken.

Bow-klish, the bumble bee was the best guesser, and after several attempts, lying flat on his back and working his toes first one way and then another, finally announced the direction of the kidnapper's flight and told the people by a great noise of pounding on boards. *Sky-ky*, the bluebird, grandfather of the boy, being bold and daring and swift in travel, was decided to be the proper man to follow.

After overcoming many dangers and suffering untold hardships, *Sky-ky* reached his destination only to be confronted by a new difficulty. There was a dividing line constructed so that it opened and shut at very short intervals. Beyond this was a strange land unknown to his people and there the baby had been taken. The great barrier was like a wall cut in two, the lower part moving up and down, while the upper moved down and up. It looked impossible for any living creature to go through without being crushed to death. There was only one opening at a great distance from the ground. Above the opening the wall stretched to untold heights. [377]

Sky-ky, knowing that he had come from afar and that to return with no news would be to carry bad news, determined to go farther if he must die in the attempt so that his people might know he had done his very best. Finally, after he had been long baffled, he assumed the form of a bluejay and hopped back and forth, studying the wall and the best and quickest way to go through. After several efforts with many narrow escapes he finally made a desperate attempt to go between the two walls as the walls came together. Quick and agile as he was, yet the great walls nearly crushed his head as he quickly jumped through feet first. The peculiar shape of the bluejay's head and the tuft of black feathers at the top bear witness to his narrow escape in this great adventure.

Sky-ky beheld a strange and unknown land, a land full of streams abounding in all kinds of fishes. The country was open, a vast expanse where game of all kinds was plentiful. There was perpetual day there and the climate was temperate and fine. People dwelt there and for years he kept up his search for his grandson, *Arh-hade*, until one day he found a lonely man in a lonely place. The hermit was melancholy and troubled. *Sky-ky*'s curiosity was aroused and he asked the stranger why he should be so unhappy when all about him the people were so well and happy and contented in this great, fine land.

"I do not belong to this happy land. I was stolen from my people. Those who come here to live are the dead from our land," the stranger replied. The *Sky-ky* greeted him as his long lost grandson. The oldman exclaimed, "You shall return the way you came. Take this stick to, open the wall so as not to harm yourself. For me there are many years of hard labor. Tell my people, I, too, shall return sometime."

Arh-hade then became the great changer of things. He subdued monsters, made the fire useful to man and many other things. Finally that he might be always helpful he changed himself into the moon in order to give light by night. So it was that from the "man in the moon" came the only tidings of the happy hunting grounds to people who have feared death.

3. DŌ'K^UIBEŁ AND THE ANIMALS.

Grizzly Bear was originally a person and lived with his brothers and cousins, Blackbear, Wildcat, Cougar and Raccoon. Grizzly Bear was very powerful and killed many Indians. For this reason Fox killed Grizzly Bear and cut off his nose. This he changed into a grizzly bear and he told the bear that now he would not be so powerful anymore and could no longer kill so many Indians. Fox was tricky and not as powerful as Grizzly Bear had been, but he had killed Grizzly Bear by making him fall asleep first.

The excrements of Fox were his five brothers[100]' and they helped him. [378] His wife was Mole. When Fox had killed Grizzly Bear the brothers of the latter, Black Bear, Wildcat, Cougar and Raccoon made war on him. But *Dō'k^uibeł* came along and changed them all into spirits. Dō'k^uibeł changed Fox into an animal and let him be tricky but he would not let him be a spirit.

4. DŌ'K^UIBEŁ AND THE SQĀ'HAQATCET.[101]

Six people of the Sqā'hāqatcEt tribe lived at Holmes' Harbor on Whidby Island. They were catching pofferts {sculpin, flounder?}. As they were cutting up the pofferts, Dō'k^uibeł came along and changed the six people into rocks. The poffert was also changed into a rock which was large at one end and cut into four pieces at the other. These rocks are on the east side of the island.

Dō'k^uibeł went south from there and hit a bluff with a stick and made gulches into rocks. These rocks now look like tents. Dō'k^uibeł went on and met a man whom he changed into a rock. But this man was powerful and changed himself back into a human being. He did this three times. Then Dō'k^uibeł promised him that he would give people all kinds of game in the future for food. Thereupon the man allowed himself to be changed into a rock. The man told Dō'k^uibeł that children must not come near him when he became a rock because he was going to be dangerous. There would be lots of sharks around this rock. Then Dō'k^uibeł made a little island called *Q!oq!sɛdō'* on the east side of Holmes' Harbor.

Another man that Dō'k^uibeł changed was also powerful and bargained with the Transformer. He asked Dō'k^uibeł, "Do you know how people will be protected against sharks when they dive for powers?" Dō'k^uibeł said, "No." Thereupon the man told Dō'k^uibeł that in the future Indian's should have an instrument for killing sharks. From this the Snohomish got the instrument they use when diving for spirits.

Dō'k^uibeł made a man whom he called *Luxwē'us* in place of the man he had changed into a rock. Dō'k^uibeł gave *Luxwē'us* the power of making fire by striking two rocks together and thus igniting cedar bark. Before this the people had no fire. This was the method of fire-making which Dō'k^uibeł taught the SqāhāqatcEt. ** He gave each tribe another way of doing it. He gave the Snohomish a fire drill. Other tribes he gave other ways of making fire.

---

[100] i. See note p. 38.

[101] I. The SādādqatcEt were partly Snohomish and seem to have been a historical people who died out before Little Sam's time. They died out because they were harassed by other tribes and they themselves had no warriors.

5. DŌ'KᵁIBEŁ CHANGES THE SNAKES AND THE FROGS.
(*Snohomish.*)

Long ago the snake and lizard were human beings, but the servant of [379] Dō'kᵁibeł changed them into animals and made them great shaman's spirits for the future people of the world. The frogs were sisters of the snakes. In the early spring when the frogs began to sing they were calling for their brothers, the snakes. The Frogs said that the snakes had crooked eyes. The snakes were offended at this and to get even they ate up the frogs.

6. DŌ'KᵁIBEŁ AND THE DEER.
(*Snuqualmi : told by Little Sam.*)

Dō'kᵁibeł went to the deer people. One of them was filing at a spear-head of bone and was singing that he would kill Dō'kᵁibeł." What are you singing about?" asked Dō'kᵁibeł. "No, I was not singing at all," said the man. "Oh yes," said Dō'kᵁibeł, "you were singing." - "I was singing that I am filing this bone in order to kill Dō'kᵁibeł with it." Thereupon Dō'kᵁibeł took the bone, pushed it into the man's armpit and made a deer of him.

7. PHEASANT (*SGLOB*) AND RAVEN (*KAUQS*.)
(*Skagit : told by Josephine Leclair.*)

Raven was the brother-in-law of Pheasant. They lived in separate houses. Both of them were human beings at the time. Raven was a very greedy fellow. He made a fish-trap of the type called *pɛda's* (a funnel-shaped trap of basketry). At first Raven put this trap into the river with the opening facing downstream. But he caught no fish at all that way. Then Raven turned the trap so that the opening lay in the direction of the current. He was successful in catching a few fish with the trap in this position, but not very many. Finally he placed the trap with its opening facing upstream. Now he caught lots of fish.

Both Pheasant and Raven had lots of little children. Raven's wife would only give her brother, the Pheasant, all of the small fish Raven caught. This made Pheasant angry. He decided to go away. So he made himself bow and arrows, took feathers from his own wings and put them on his arrows. Then he went off hunting. He was not a bird then, but a person. As he was looking for game, he came across a pheasant. He killed the bird and hung it up on a tree. Then he went farther and found another pheasant. He killed this one too and hung it up on a tree, as he had done with the first one. Going on he killed a third pheasant and hung it up likewise. Finally he killed a fourth pheasant and hung it up on a tree. While he was busy with this fourth pheasant, he heard the barking of dogs in the distance. He knew that these dogs were those of *Hālākᵁ* (Skagit name of *Dō'kᵁibeł*). He became very much alarmed. Then he saw a great elk running towards him. The animal ran past him and then [280] fell down and died. Pheasant went up to the elk and saw two big arrows sticking in its sides. He knew that these arrows

157

belonged to Hālākᵘ. Very much frightened he went to hide in some bushes. Now the dogs came running up to the elk. Then Hālākᵘ came himself. He was carrying a big cane. Hālākᵘ caught sight of Pheasant, and said to him, "Why do you hide?" Pheasant came out from his hiding-place trembling all over. "Did you kill this elk?" asked Hālākᵘ. "No," answered Pheasant, "I did not kill it, you did it." - "Are these your arrows?" continued Hālākᵘ. "No, they are yours." - "Are these your dogs?" - "No, I have no dogs, they are yours." "Can you dress an elk?" - "No, I cannot do that." - "Can you make a fire?" - "No, I do not think so, but I will try." - "Very well then," said Hālākᵘ, "if you make a fire, I will dress this elk."

Pheasant succeeded in making a large fire. In the meanwhile Hālākᵘ dressed the elk. Every bit of fat he cut off from the animal he gave to Pheasant, who put it all into his crop. Pheasant did this because he wanted to save the fat for his children. His crop became quite full. Hālākᵘ was just like God, and therefore knew that Pheasant was really not swallowing the fat but was keeping it in his pouch.

When Hālākᵘ had finished dressing the elk, he asked Pheasant, "Can you pack?" - "No," answered Pheasant, "I cannot pack." - "I will see to it that you will be able to pack."

So Hālākᵘ went up to Pheasant and put sinews on his arms and neck. This made Pheasant strong. He had been without sinews on his arms and neck before. Now Pheasant was able to pack. Hālākᵘ made a very small package of the elk-meat and packed it on the back of Pheasant. Then he said to him, "Now you must go home. On the way you will hear all kinds of strange sounds behind you, but you must not look around. You must always look straight ahead. As you pass the pheasants you killed and hung up on the trees, you must take each one down with your left hand."

Pheasant went back home and did exactly as Hālākᵘ had told him. He did not look back in spite of the strange noises he heard. He took the pheasants down from the trees with his left hand. He was a poor man. When he arrived at his home, he found that his children were starving. So he took the fat which Hālākᵘ had given him out of his crop and let his children eat it. Then he told his wife all about his experiences with Hālākᵘ. He told how good Hālākᵘ had been to him, how he had pitied him and given him all of the elk-meat. While the little pheasants were eating, they made the same kind of noise which pheasants usually make when they eat. The old Raven heard this noise over in his own house. He became suspicious and said to his wife, "There must be something going on in the other house. I hear the little pheasants smacking. They must have something good to eat. Probably you gave them some good fish." He sent his wife over to his neighbor. [281]

Pheasant knew that the stingy old woman who always kept the best fish for herself was coming over to see them. So he said to his wife, "Now she is going to bring us something good to eat, because she knows we are eating well and now expects to get something in return. But we will not bother about her, nor will we give her any of our own food." The wife of Raven paid them a visit and saw them all eating. She gave them a basket of fish. When she returned to her husband, she told him that Pheasant had met Hālākᵘ and that he had received lots of meat from him. Raven decided to go himself and hear about the experiences of Pheasant. He said to Pheasant, "Tell me all about Hālākᵘ, I want to go to see him too." Pheasant said, "I frightened Hālākᵘ by telling

him that I owned everything that really belonged to him. In this way I frightened Hālāk^u
to such an extent that he gave me the elk which he had killed." - "Very well," said Raven,
"I will go and scare him too." So he went away to meet Hālāk^u. He travelled over the
same trail that Pheasant had taken. He also killed pheasants just as he had done. When
he had killed the last one, he heard the barking of dogs. The sound was coming closer
very quickly. But he did not hide as Pheasant had done. An elk approached him, passed
by, then fell down and died. Raven went up to the animal, pulled out from the dead
body the arrows of Hālāk^u, and put some of his own arrows in their place. Soon after,
the dogs came up to the elk and then Hālāk^u himself arrived. Raven sat down and
uttered a loud sigh, as if he were very tired.

"Is that your elk?" asked Hālāk^u. "Yes, surely," answered Raven, "I am the man
who killed it." - "And are those your arrows in the animal?" - "Yes, they are mine." - "Are
those your dogs too?" - "Yes, of course," said Raven, "they belong to me." - "What are
the names of your dogs?" - "Their name is Ta'blic." - "Well then call your dogs." Raven
did so and called "Sta'blic, sta'blic!" but the dogs only began to growl at him, as if they
were about to bite him. Then Hālāk^u asked again, "Can you dress elk?" - "Certainly, I am
a man, I can dress an elk." Raven went up to the elk and tried to dress it, but he did not
succeed. Thereupon Hālāk^u started to dress the elk himself. While he was doing so he
thought to himself, "Certainly, this man is quite different from my friend Pheasant." As
he was dressing the elk, Hālāk^u gave the fat to Raven, who was so greedy that he ate it
all himself and did not store it away in his crop the way Pheasant had done. Hālāk^u now
asked him, "Can you make a fire?" - "Certainly I can make a fire," answered Raven, and
at once tried to make one, but he did not succeed. Then Hālāk^u asked, "Can you pack?"
- "Certainly, I can do that."

Hālāk^u made a pack of elk-meat, but Raven was not able to carry it. So Hālāk^u
made a very small pack of meat and put it on Raven's back. Now Raven was able to
carry it. Hālāk^u told him the same thing he had told Pheasant when he went away, "On
your way home you will [382] hear all sorts of strange noises behind you, but you must be
sure not to look around. The pheasants which you have killed and hung up you must
take down from the trees with your left hand." Raven assured Hālāk^u that he would
obey the instructions, and then started on his way. He travelled a long distance. Then
he heard many strange noises back of him. He tried very hard not to look around. He
took the pheasants from the trees. The strange noises followed him. Finally he could
restrain himself no longer, he looked around. At once his pack broke down and fell to
the ground. He picked it up and managed to knot the rope. Then he got the meat back
in the proper position and continued his journey. But after a while he again heard the
strange noises and was forced to look around a second time. Again the pack fell down.
As before Raven knotted the rope and adjusted the pack. He travelled on only to have
the same experience. Thus Raven was tormented repeatedly, and every time the pack
broke down it got heavier. Finally it was getting too heavy for him to carry. Although he
was still a considerable distance from his house, he laid the pack down and went home
without it. When he got home, he said to his wife, "You go and get my pack. It is not
very far from here." The woman went out to fetch the pack. She looked for it very
carefully, but could not find it anywhere. So she went back home, and said to her

husband, "Where is your pack? I cannot find it." Raven said, "It is there where I told you. Go and look for it again. It has a rope of cedar-twigs tied around it." The woman went out again, but was unable to find it. She had to come back without it a second time. Raven was very angry at his wife, he scolded her, "You are always able to eat, but you can never do anything I tell you." This time he went out himself to look for his pack. He came to the place where he had left it, but now he found nothing there but a piece of rotten wood around which was tied a rope of cedar-twigs. Raven thought to himself, "Hālāk^u is a person who cannot be fooled." Then he went back home.

***

Josephine Leclair said that, at the end of this story, the narrator would give the following moral injunction: "Even if you are poor, you must always be honest. Never be like Raven!"

8. DŌ'K^UIBEɬ TRANSFORMS MINK.
(*Snuqualmi.*)

Mink caught a dog-salmon and roasted it. When Dō'k^uibEɬ found this out he put Mink to sleep. He ate the salmon and smeared the fat on Mink's hands and mouth. As Dō'k^uibEɬ went away Mink woke up and saw him. He reprimanded Dō'k^uibEɬ. The latter turned back and converted Mink into different forms. The first time, at Mink's own request, he changed him into a doll. Mink wanted to be a doll because the girls would play with him. As soon as Dō'k^uibEɬ turned away, Mink attained his real form again and scolded Dō'k^uibEɬ. The latter then changed Mink into a flat rock. Mink wanted to have this form because then the girls would sit down on him. As soon as Dō'k^uibEɬ turned away he changed back to his real form and scolded Dō'k^uibEɬ. The latter then changed Mink into a tree. Mink liked this because the girls would sit astride on him when they went bathing. Again Mink assumed his real form and scolded Dō'k^uibEɬ. Then he was changed into a sandy beach. This also pleased Mink for the girls would slide down on him. Once more as soon as Dō'k^uibEɬ started to go Mink attained his real form. Now Dō'k^uibEɬ lost his patience so he turned around, split Mink right in two, tore off his nose and threw it into a snag and called it "Mink ". This is the end of Mink.

9. HOW SALMON WON THE GIRL.
(*Snohomish.*)

A man invited all the people and promised his daughter to the one who could split elk antlers. Nobody could do it. Later on eight fish[102] went up the Skykomish River and came to the place where this man lived. He gave a feast for them. Spring Salmon

---

[102] 1. The fish were: Tyee Salmon (*yo'batc*); Spring Salmon (*yoibatc*), Steelbead Salmon (*qewax^u*); Rainbow Salmon (*xuba'de'*); Speckled Salmon (*p!satc*); Trout (*k!ua'pɬ*); a fish like a trout (*xoitsid*); small salmon (*tuwatsk^u*).

had received from his grandfather the power of splitting elk antlers easily. Spring Salmon won the girl but he gave her to his elder brother, Tyee Salmon. The girl resented this.

Wolf was one of the guests who could not split the elk antlers and now he was jealous. When the salmon were all in a canoe he killed from the shore the elder brother of Spring Salmon. Wolf made the others come ashore and stole the girl. Spring Salmon began at once to make himself strong by rubbing himself with stones so that he could take revenge.[103]2

There were five wolves living together. They never drank from a basket, but always from running water. Spring Salmon hid underneath the platform from which the wolves used to drink. Wolf smelt Salmon but the stolen woman reassured him that there was no one near. Wolf drank and Spring Salmon jumped up and killed him. In this way Spring Salmon killed the four eldest wolves; the youngest, he only wounded.

The youngest wolf went to the shamans, Grizzly Bear, Black Bear, Wild cat and Cougar and asked for help. The shamans performed a dance to make the fish fight among themselves for the girl. Trout was the survivor and won the girl. Then Dō'kʷibɛɬ came to the girl and told her that the fish were fighting for her. Dō'kʷibɛɬ struck the girl four [384] times and made her a large black bird with red under the wings. She flew away. Dō'kʷibɛɬ then changed Trout into a fish and revived his dead companions and made salmon of them. But Trout never travels down to the Sound as the salmon do.

Dō'kʷibɛɬ asked Trout whether there were any people living around. Trout said, "Yes, there are Snake and Lizard, his wife, living over there. "Dō'kʷibɛɬ changed Snake and Lizard into Snohomish. This is the reason why almost all Snohomish today have shaman's spirits and hardly any ever become warriors.

10. RACE FOR THE GIRL.
(Skykomish.)

Xʷbɛtca'al and Qē'qē (birds) were brothers and lived in the mountains. Qē'qē had a daughter. He invited a great many people to a feast and promised his daughter to the one who could win in a race against her. All kinds of animals tried to win her - the animals were all human beings then, but none could beat the girl. Qē'qē was a cousin of Mountain-goat who was the first Indian. He was a Skykomish and had four grizzly bears as dogs. Qē'qē invited Mountain-goat and his ten children to the feast. They arrived in the evening and Mountain-goat said, "I won't let my children run until tomorrow morning." Qē'qē agreed to this. So the next morning after breakfast when the oldest boy refused to run, the youngest of Mountain-goat's children declared that he was ready to try the race. The people laughed at him for he was a very little fellow and had a big belly. So far Mink had been the only one who could run as fast as the girl and even he could not beat her. Qē'qē said, "Don't be ashamed of my daughter." He knew the mountain-goats were great runners.

---

[103] 2. Boys rubbed themselves with rough rocks and sticks to become strong and tough.

The smallest Mountain-goat and the girl got ready to run around the track. The race was run between two poles set up at a distance from each other. The boy gave the girl a head start. As she moved ahead of the place where he was standing, she spit on the ground where she stood. This happened repeatedly. Qē'qē beat the drum and urged his daughter on. The boy caught up to the girl and gave her a shove as he passed, then he got ahead of her. The girl began to cry because she was ashamed to marry this ugly little mountain-goat. She only ran around the track once but the Mountain-goat ran around three times. The little Mountain-goat did not marry the girl but gave her to his eldest brother.

In ten days a child was born to the girl. She wanted to show her boy to her people so she made a pack of some meat and told her husband where she was going. He told her not to take the right hand road but after she had gone along a while she forgot the warning and went down the right hand road. She came to the *Sxwayō'k!ᵘ*, the Five Sisters. They were glad to see the woman and the child. In two days they ate the meat in her pack and then they were going to eat the woman and the child. They hung the woman and her baby high up in a basket. On the morning before they were to be eaten the woman and the little boy cut a hole into the bottom of the basket with a child's knife. They escaped and put the bottom back into the basket, and set in a piece of rotten wood to make the basket appear heavy.

The Five Sisters made a fire and heated rocks. They took down the basket. When they found that the woman and the child were gone, the older sisters whipped the youngest one who was supposed to keep guard over the basket. Then all five chased the woman and the boy. The child knew that the Five Sisters were pursuing them and told his mother to climb up a tree. There were fifteen trees growing close together. The Five Sisters finally found the woman in the tree and they sent the youngest sister home to get a chisel. With this they felled the tree, but the woman jumped over to the next tree and she repeated this as they felled each tree. When there were only four trees left the woman told the boy to run to his grandfather and tell him that his mother was in danger. The child obeyed. When only three trees were left, the four grizzly bear dogs came running up. Only one tree was left when they reached the scene. The woman began to cry. The dogs killed the four oldest sisters; the youngest ran home to close the door and save their children from the dogs. But she could not reach home before the dogs killed her also and then they rushed into the house and killed all the children.

The woman started to go home, but on the way she met Dō'kᵘibeł who changed her into *xubɛtca'al* (Hawk in mountains). The boy was changed into the same kind of bird. Father Mountain-goat asked Dō'kᵘibeł, "What is going to be the spirit of the Skykomish?"[104] He gave them a kind of *tsaiq* spirit which helped the Skykomish be great hunters of the mountain-goat. He also made them great mountain climbers. He told

---

[104] I. All the tribes about here have a tsaiq spirit, but each one is of a different variety. The tsaiq of the Skykomish was good for hunting mountain-goat while that of the Snohomish was effective in helping them hunt on the sound.

them to make staffs of fir-wood but not of hemlock. On account of this the Skykomish are the only tribe that kill the mountain-goat.[105]2.

11. THE CANNIBAL WOMAN.
(*Skagit: told by Josephine Leclair.*)

There were two orphans, a boy and a girl. They lived with their grand-father whose name was Carrot (*ca'gaq*). This old man had four dogs who were wolves. The boy was older than his sister and getting sensible. One day he told his grandfather that he wanted to go home and visit his uncle and aunt who lived in another part of the country. The two children got ready to go. Their grandfather told them that they were going to a strange and unknown land. There were two roads. He said, "First you will follow a single road, then you will reach a place where this road forks. The road to the left is wide and good, but do not take that one. Take the one to the right, it is very narrow and can hardly be seen; that is the road you must take, it leads to your uncle." Before they left, their grandfather told them to take some of his water along.

Then the children started out and travelled a long way until they finally came to the place where the roads forked. There they sat down and rested. The boy had forgotten what his grandfather had told him and he said, "We will take the wide road." The little girl said, "No, grandfather told us to take the narrow road." They talked about the matter, but finally the girl yielded to her brother because he was older. They travelled along the wide road for a long distance and came to a river. There was a big house on the other side of the stream and a great big woman came out. The boy called to her and asked for a canoe to take them across. The little girl began to cry and said, "Now we don't know what will become of us. Grandfather told us to take the narrow road." The woman came over and put the children in a canoe. It was towards evening. She took them across the river and put them in her house.

There were five women of enormous size in the house. They were called *swayo'k!*[u]. These women used to eat persons alive. That evening the oldest woman said, "We will keep the children until tomorrow." Then they were going to have a big feast. The little girl began to cry. The children were put in a basket and hung up. The women danced all night. The boy knew that they would sleep very heavily towards morning after such vigorous dancing. He had a small knife with him. When the women were sleeping he told his sister not to cry. "We will try to get out in some way." He cut the bottom out of the basket and said, "Now be careful." He put the girl down through the bottom of the basket and then he followed. They walked over the women without waking them. The youngest woman was the smartest. Her name was Young-Woman

---

[105] 2. Before the old mountain-goat was changed into a mountain-goat he gave Dō'k[u]ibEł a trap for catching mountain-goats and told him to give it to the future Skykomish so that they might catch mountain-goats. The Skykomish are the only tribe that use this trap. It consists of a loop of cedar rope, one end of which is attached to a rock and this contracts as the goat runs into it. The loop strangles the goat.

(*txo'mx*). She always slept by the door. The children passed over her and got into the canoe and crossed the river. They went back along the same road by which they had come.

When the women woke up it was very late. They made a fire and then one of them said, "Take the children down for our breakfast." The basket was very light. They looked into it and saw that it was empty. The women said, "The children cannot be very far away; let us follow them." They were great runners, especially the youngest one. They chased the children and finally caught sight of them. The little girl looked around and saw the women. She began to cry. The boy remembered the water his grandfather had given them. He poured a few drops of this water in four different places and the drops became four big trees. The children climbed up one of these trees. When the women came they saw the children up the tree. How would they get them? They decided to gnaw around the foot of the tree and fell it. They started to gnaw and after a while the tree began to fall. Just before it fell the boy took his sister over to another tree. The women went to look at the fallen tree and saw that they were fooled. Then they began to gnaw at the second tree and when it fell the children were sitting on the third one. The women gnawed on the third tree and when it fell the children were on the fourth tree. The little girl began to cry and said, "What shall we do when the fourth tree falls?" The women started gnawing at the fourth tree. The boy had one drop of water left. As the tree began to fall he poured the water on it and it became whole again. The women promptly started again gnawing around the butt end. At this moment the boy remembered that his grandfather always told him that when he was in danger he should call for him. The children's grandfather was a great man and could hear over a great distance. The boy thought, "I will call and my grandfather will send his dogs." The boy called for his grandfather three times. Then the women heard a noise like thunder. They asked one another, "What kind of noise is that?" One of them said, "That was my long hair." But it really was the noise made by the dogs, as they were coming toward the place where the children were. When the dogs shook themselves there was a noise like thunder. The youngest woman said, "I hear the noise coming nearer." She was the wisest one among them; but the older women told her to go on working and not pay any attention to the noise. "No," she said, "I will go away." She had just left when the dogs came. The other women were still gnawing. The dogs bit and killed them all except the youngest one; she got away safely. The children came down from the tree and went back to their grandfather with the dogs. The grandfather was glad to see that they were safe.

Fox (*smyau*) who lived near by heard of the witches and knew that the youngest one was still alive. He came to the place where the children had been. He went into the house of the witches. There were many little children in the house and they came and picked at Fox and bit [388] him. The woman was not there. The children bothered Fox so that he left the house. But his spirit[106] told him to go back into the house even if the children did bother him. "You will see many hearts hanging on the wall. They are the hearts of the children and of the youngest woman. Take a stick and hit every heart.

---

[106]   I. Shelton always speaks of the two little girls in Fox. Mrs. Leclair calls it his "superstition" or sklaletut; she never mentions little girls.

Then all these people will die." The woman was out gathering fern roots. Fox went into the house and struck all the hearts with a stick and every time he struck a heart, one of the children died. Every time a child died the woman would know that something had happened at home because her digging stick broke." Something must be wrong," she said, "because my stick is breaking all the time." She started to go home. While she was on her way Fox struck her heart and she fell dead. Fox came out of the house and began to sing, "Their uncle killed them all, *hai'ya*." He walked on towards a mountain singing this.

He had heard of some wonderful birds a long way off. He thought that this might be the place where those birds lived. He came near a house, so he stopped singing. He went into the house and saw many birds sitting around the fire. He said, "I shall kill all of you." He made a hole where the ashes were, took all the little birds and put them into the hole and covered them up with the hot ashes. He came out of the house and began to sing the same song. He walked higher and higher up the mountain, singing the same song. Finally he came to the very summit. Then the mother birds heard him and knew it was Fox. They flew over him and this killed Fox and he rolled down the mountain.

Fox had a brother who was a very much better man than he. His name was Dō'kᵘibɛɫ. He discovered that Fox was dead and travelled to the place where his body lay. Only the fur was left. Dō'kᵘibɛɫ said, "Fox does not know what is good for him." Then he placed the bones in the position in which they had been when Fox was alive. He walked over the body three times and then Fox woke up and became alive. Fox fixed his fur and shook himself and said, "I must have been asleep a long time." Dō'kᵘibɛɫ said, "No, you were dead. Don't bother those birds any more, they are wonderful birds and they can kill you." Dō'kᵘibɛɫ left Fox.

Fox went out on new adventures. He met a tiny boy who was dragging a large bow and large arrows behind him. Fox said, "Why have you that bow and those arrows? Don't you know that they belong to your father?" Fox scolded in this way as if he had sense himself. The boy said, "I have no father, the bow and arrows are mine." Fox answered, "If they are yours, then shoot me." Fox did not believe that they belonged to the boy. The boy said, "You are too near." Then Fox went off at some distance and called, "Shoot me now." The boy said, "No, [389] you are too close." Then Fox went on a great distance and called again, "Shoot me now." Again the boy replied, "No, you are too close." Fox was angry then and said, "I'm not going to call for you again." He walked on for many days and never thought any more of the boy. Then one day he was struck by an arrow in the back of his head. This was the boy's arrow. The boy was Woodpecker (*tsɛsa'q!ᵘ*).

Fox was dead three days when Dō'kᵘibɛɫ came along. He found the arrow and recognized it as Woodpecker's. Then Dō'kᵘibɛɫ placed Fox's bones in order as he had done before and passed over the body. Fox woke up and said, "I have been asleep a long time." Dō'kᵘibɛɫ said, "No, you have been dead. You must not meddle with Woodpecker again. He is a great shooter." Then Dō'kᵘibɛɫ left Fox.

Fox walked on and finally heard a great noise and much shouting. He came near and found all kinds of birds and animals. He saw them shoot arrows right up to the sky. The arrows would come right back to where the people were. Fox asked them, "What are you doing?" The people said, "Our land has no fire. There are people in the sky who have fire and we want to make war on them. We want to get the best shooter so that we can make a road of arrows up to get fire." Fox tried to shoot but he could not do anything. The best shooter was the youngest brother of Wolf (so'pxɛn•ŋ). He was the only one who could come near to the sky with his arrows but even he could not reach it. Fox said, "There is a boy whose name is Woodpecker. He is a great shooter. I guess he will shoot for you. "The people said," We will pay him the finest plumes for his arrows." They made this offer to Woodpecker. He agreed, but he said he was not at all sure that he could reach the sky. He had a grandmother, Snail. "What do you think, Grandmother, do you think I can shoot that far?," he asked her. His grandmother said, "I will go with you." She tied a tumpline around her waist. They travelled a long distance to the place where the people were. The people made room for the boy and his grandmother. The boy shot up to the sky and the old woman looked up and started to sing and dance. She sang, "I see the arrow of my grandson, I see it yet, I see it yet." Finally she said, "Now I see it stop." She saw it stop in the sky. Every time the boy shot she would sing and dance. She sang, "Now I see the arrow of my grandson, I see it yet, now I see it stick to another arrow." As the boy shot, the arrows stuck end on end and formed a chain. He shot four times and the people themselves could see the last arrow. The boy said to the people, "Now you can shoot for yourselves." Then the best shooter shot arrows until the last one touched the ground. When this was done, the old woman, Snail, went up the chain of arrows and fastened them together. When she had reached the top she came down again. She told the people when she got to the ground that they must be careful in going up, otherwise the chain would break. Then all the people climbed up to the sky. Towards the end two sisters began to climb up. They were [390] Black Bear (tcɑ'tkᵘɛn) and Grizzly Bear (sta'mtamɬ). Black Bear went ahead. This looked so funny to Grizzly Bear that she said, "Oh, sister, how funny you look," and they started to laugh. Then Black Bear said, "Then you go first." They went down and this time Grizzly Bear started up the chain. Black Bear had to laugh and she said, "You look just as funny as I do." They laughed and Grizzly Bear wanted to have her sister start again. By trying to change the chain broke and the sisters were left down below.

When the people reached the sky they talked with one another, "Who will go to these people and steal the fire without fighting? Who can lie just like a dead person and not laugh when he is tickled? That is the person who will have to get the fire for us." So they started to tickle everybody but they all laughed and could not lie still like a dead person. Finally they came to an old man named Beaver (statxᵘ). They put him down and tickled him but he would not move and did not even smile. The people said, "Here is the man who will get fire for us." They put him in the water and he floated to a fence which was a fish trap. One of the sky people who owned the fire came to the trap and found Beaver. He said to himself, "That is a wonderful animal. There are no beavers around this part of the country." He told his people that there was a beaver in their fish trap. A chief said, "This may be just a trick. Haul him out and see if he is dead." They pulled him out and began to tickle him all over. "Surely he must be dead," they said. They took him to the house and laid him near the fire.

Now one of the people who had come from the earth said, "Now the sky people will cut up Beaver. Which one of the birds will fly to the house where Beaver is and distract the attention of the sky people?" Thunder Bird (slεhe'm) said he would go. He flew there and just as the sky people were about to cut up Beaver he alighted on the house opposite the one where Beaver was. The sky people saw the bird and said, "Oh, there is a wonderful bird over there, come and see!" They all ran out to see it. Immediately Beaver snatched up the fire and ran away. The people who had come from earth had chosen the fastest runner to meet Beaver and take the fire from him and run back to earth with it. This person was the youngest brother of Wolf. Young Wolf took the fire and ran to his people. The people did not know how to get back to earth. They said, "Our grandfather lives near by. We will see if he can take us back to earth. We will pay him grass for netting (q!a'g^{u}aɫ)." They went to him. He was called Spider (sopsa'pεn). They asked whether he could help them get back to earth. He took their pay and let them down on his rope. And the people got back to earth with the fire.

When they reached the earth they heard of a man whose name was Dō'k^{u}ibεɫ. They heard that he was going about making all things different. Dō'k^{u}ibεɫ had a long rod which he carried with him and every time he touched the earth with this rod he would make a hill. When Dō'k^{u}ibεɫ came to the people who had been in the sky he turned them into animals and birds.

But the fire was there. When the people got back to earth the fire began to burn and the world was all ablaze. Dō'k^{u}ibεɫ was frightened by the fire. He started to run and came to a trail. The fire burned along behind him and he knew he could not save himself. So he lay right down in the trail. The fire swept over him and burned his back. When he got up he went down to the river. He saw a little fire across the river. He stepped right over the stream and there he found his brother Fox again. Fox was cooking some fish and Dō'k^{u}ibεɫ thought he would play a trick on him. He put Fox to sleep and took all of Fox's fish away and then he turned Fox into the animal that he is today. He was no longer a human being.

When Fox woke up he said, "I am still hungry. I must have been eating fish, for my hands and face are all greasy, but still I am hungry." He went to the river to drink. There he saw his reflection in the water. He said, "Somebody must be in the water." Then he became frightened. He looked in the water three times and each time he became more frightened. He went and asked his spirit[107] who the person in the water really was. The spirit answered, "Why don't you know that that is yourself? Don't be afraid of yourself. You have been changed into an animal." Fox went over to the water again and drank; he was no longer afraid of himself.

Then Dō'k^{u}ibεɫ continued his journey.[108]2

---

[107] I. See note on p. 388.

[108] 2. According to the narrator this is the usual formal ending of the transformer tale.

12. HOW THE SONS OF MINK AND RAVEN STOLE LIGHT.
(*Skagit : told by Charlie's wife.*)

In the beginning of the world the people lived in a village. Raven had one son and Mink had one son. They said, "Let us train our children." Where Mink and Raven lived it was dark, but in the east there was light. They agreed to train their sons to be strong young men. Young Mink and young Raven practised running and became good runners. They came home and told their fathers that they were good runners so their fathers told them to steal light from the people in the East.

In the East there is a light country. When they came to a house in this country Mink went inside, but Raven stayed without. Mink disguised himself as an old man before he entered the house. The people let him come in and lie down for he acted as if he could not walk. When night came he tried to steal the light. He got up and touched the light. It flickered. The people woke up and asked where Mink was. But Mink [392] quickly got under the covers and the people did not find out anything. The next night Mink tried the same thing again. The light flickered again and the people woke up and looked to see whether Mink was in bed. Again Mink got under the covers. Mink did this the third night and the same thing happened. The fourth night he made up his mind to get the light this time.

Raven had been waiting outside at some distance. Mink now acted like a young man again and caught the light quickly and ran away with it. The people woke up and saw that Mink was gone. They followed him. Mink ran until he was almost tired out. Then he shouted to Raven to take the light. Raven took it and ran on. The people followed Mink and Raven until they reached the dark country. The people of the dark country saw the light coming and their country became light. Old Raven and old Mink were proud of their sons for having stolen the light from the country in the east. Old Raven wanted to have the light all the time, but the other people wanted it to go down from time to time. The wish of the latter prevailed.

13. HOW MINK GOT DAYLIGHT.
(*Skagit.*)

In olden times it was dark all the time and the only light was the moon. But there was daylight in the east. Mink and his younger brother Sole and his cousin Raven talked about the man who had daylight and set out eastward to get it. They took fifteen strings of dried clams with them. They went as far as possible in a canoe. Then Mink left the two others and gave them the fifteen strings of clams which were to last fifteen days. He went off alone and made himself so old that he could hardly walk. As soon as Mink had left Raven sent Sole away and in three days ate all the clams.

Mink came to the man who had the daylight and who was the chief of the tribe. Mink told the man, "I am the oldest brother of your father, in time of war the people took me away with them. Now I have come back to see you." The man with the daylight believed what Mink said. Meanwhile Mink was watching how the man controlled the sun. It was like a clock. The man called his people together and told what Mink had said.

There were three different keys used in winding the clock and Mink found out how to work them. Then while the people were still asleep Mink stole the clock. He took off the mask that made him look like an old man. One of the people saw Mink go away. They chased him. Just as Mink was tired out he met Raven who took the daylight and ran on. The little boy Sole had the canoe in readiness. All three jumped aboard and paddled away. The people could not follow because they had no canoes.

Mink had the clock which was the sun wrapped up. He went to his grandmother's where he lived. She said, "What is Mink doing? He could not get daylight." Mink made the sun work and it became daylight.

The chief's daughter saw the daylight come. She went to Mink's house and listened to the clock striking. The girl went to her father and said, "Your cousin has secured the daylight." Mink was a slave[109] before but now the girl called him chief. There were two chiefs in this tribe, one was the father of this girl. The one chief said to the other, "We will give a feast and let Mink tell how he got the daylight." They called him chief too. At first Mink said that he did not want to be chief and stayed a slave. He locked himself up in his house and the chief sent his daughter to listen all night. Mink knew that the girl was outside. He went out. The girl wanted to marry him and followed him indoors. She watched him wind up the clock with the three keys in the morning. After winding with the third key the sun rose.

Mink said to the girl, "Go to your father and make him call all the people together." The people came and Mink said to them, "If you are going to call me slave all the time then I shall take the daylight back to the east, but if you call me chief I will leave the daylight here." The chief put the matter up to the people. They voted that Mink should become chief in place of the old chief. The old chief gave his daughter to Mink and said, "Bring Mink into the house and he will now be our head man."... [110]

14. MINK.
(Skagit: told by Skookum George.)

Mink (*ts!balqed*) was a young unmarried man. He liked to go swimming. He knew of a girl whose father was *SL!a*, a great chief. Mink watched the girl very closely. One day as he was swimming in the lake he saw her bathing on the other side of the water. Mink wondered how he could get at the girl. Finally he decided to stretch his penis under the water to the place where the girl was. He did this and reached the girl. It was impossible for her to get away from him. A little bird flew close to the girl. At first she did not notice it but when it flew by for the third time, she heard it tell her to

---

[109] 1. Mink had been a slave among the Skagit. They captured him east of the Mountains.

[110] 2. This tale is unfinished. {The next tale explains the very first pregnancy and birth due to the bit of Mink still inside.}

take a piece of swamp grass and cut off Mink's penis. She did this, but a part of Mink's organ remained in her. Very soon she became pregnant and gave birth to a boy.

The girl's father *SL!a* was very much ashamed that his unmarried daughter should have given birth to a child. He was determined to find out who the child's father was. For this purpose he called together all [394] his people. He took his grandchild in his arms and said that the person at whom the child pointed his finger would be regarded as his father. *SL!a* carried the child all around the circle where his people were standing, but the child pointed to no one.

In the meantime Mink told his grandmother that he wanted to go to the meeting of the people. The old woman told him that he should not go, but Mink did not obey her. He arrived at the house where all the people were assembled and took his place near the door. At once the child pointed to Mink and cried, "That is my father there." *SL!a* now made his daughter marry Mink. He gave her a canoe and two women slaves and sent her off with Mink and the baby.

They went away in the canoe, Mink and his wife sitting side by side and the child in a cradle in front of them. One of the slave women looked down into the water and saw some sea eggs (*sqoegwetc*) {sea urchin}. The slave pulled some of these out of the water. The two slaves and Mink's wife began to eat, but Mink claimed that he did not know what they were and he would not touch them. This was not true for Mink knew what they were eating. He asked his wife, "How does it taste?" - "Fine," she answered. "Then let me taste a little," said Mink. He tasted a little and said that it was very good. His wife then ordered the slaves to fetch some more. Mink was very greedy, so he said to his wife, "I want to dive down into the water myself and fill a basket." His wife objected, "No, let the slaves do it." But Mink was so insistant {ok} that finally his wife let him go. He dove down into the water and brought up a single sea egg. Then he dove down again and this time he brought up two. A third time he brought up three. Each time he stayed down a little longer. The fourth time he dove in he stayed down a long, long time, from noon almost until nightfall. While he was in the water one of the slave women looked down and she saw Mink eating sea eggs with his mouth and with his anus as well. The slave called the attention of Mink's wife to this. When she saw him doing this she said, "Let him go, we shall leave without him." So the canoe started off, but before they had gone very far Mink came up to the surface and called to his wife to wait. She paid no attention to him and ordered the slaves to paddle on and throw the baby into the water. Mink was deserted. He told his baby to save himself by getting underneath a snag. The child did this. That is why the minks always go under snags.

15. MINK AND HIS BROTHER.
(Snohomish: told by Shelton.)

There was once a mink and his little brother. They were living alone and every day they would go out fishing or hunting. One fine day they went spearing fish. The water was beautifully calm and it was very clear. For a long time they did not see any fish to spear. Mink was always getting into mischief. The nickname of his little brother was Tɛtis'ka. Mink told him to jump into the water and swim around like a flounder.

Little Tɛtis'ka said, "Oh, no, you might hurt me." Mink said, "No, I would not be so foolish as to stick you with this sharp spear. I will just make believe that I am spearing, but I won't hurt you." He urged him, "Go ahead, we cannot travel like this, this is no fun." Then finally Tɛtis'ka said, "All right," and jumped into the water and swam around like a fish. Mink chased him in the canoe, just as if he were chasing a fish. Mink made a motion as though he were going to spear the fish, but he bore in mind what he had promised Tɛtis'ka. Then his little brother would come up and Mink would tell him that he looked so well in the water. "Do it again, we are having a nice time now." Tɛtis'ka would dive down again and Mink chased him. The little brother really looked like a fish. Mink forgot his promise for a moment and speared him. Mink put his little brother in the canoe and went home. He cried and mourned. He felt very badly about this accident so he wanted all the white fir trees to fall into the water. His grandmother was at home. She heard Mink cry and said to herself, "I should not be surprised if that foolish boy has killed his little brother Tɛtis'ka."

16. MINK GETS FOOD.
(*Skykomish.*)

Mink was staying with his grandmother, Frog. It rained and the wind blew and they had nothing to eat, so Mink said, "I might look on the beach to see if there are any mussels there." Every day he looked around but found nothing, until finally one day he found one mussel shell. He took it home and showed it to his grandmother and told her that this was all he could find. After this they moved to a large house. He went again to look on the beach and found another mussel shell. When his grandmother saw it she said, "You better look out for a boy just like you who comes out of the water every evening and walks around on the beach." This boy's father was Tiō'łbɛx and he was a very rich man who lived in the sea. Mink watched for this boy and when he saw him, he captured him. Mink took the boy to his house and made him a slave, because his father was a rich man. When his son did not return home for five days, Tiō'łbɛx realized that something must have happened. He called his friends together and they rose to the surface of the sea. Tiō'łbɛx suspected that his son must be in the large house that belonged to Mink. Mink watched from his house and saw Tiō'łbɛx coming. He became afraid because Tiō'łbɛx had so many people with him, and he feared that he and his grandmother would be made slaves. So Mink and his grandmother made large fires and filled the house with smoke. Then [396] the grandmother called in many frogs to make a great noise in the house. All this was done to frighten Tiō'łbɛx and keep him away from the house. The grandmother went out to meet Tiō'łbɛx on the beach, but Mink stayed in the house.

First Tiō'łbɛx offered Mink and his grandmother five slaves for his son, but Mink was not satisfied. Then he offered much shell money, but Mink would not accept that. The third offer that Tiō'łbɛx made, was mountain-goat wool blankets. Still Mink would not give the son in exchange. Finally Tiō'łbɛx offered grass, found in the mountains, of which rope is made. This also did not satisfy Mink. Then Tiō'łbɛx said, "What am I going to do? Mink will not accept anything I offer in exchange for my son." But Mink was clever; he let his grandmother tell Tiō'ɫbɛx that he did not want any property, he wanted food. Tiō'ɫbɛx was glad to hear this, and said, "I will give him much food." Tiō'ɫbɛx was very rich and all the sea animals, fishes, seals, and clams belonged to him. He promised Mink that the sea would be calm for five days and that he would be able to get all the fish he wanted. Then Mink released the son of Tiō'ɫbɛx and sent him back to his father. Tiō'ɫbɛx kept his promise and Mink got plenty of fish. There were so many fish that Mink and his grandmother got tired from carrying them into the house. Meanwhile other people had nothing to eat. They came in canoes and got fish from the beach. So Mink secured many friends and became a great man because he gave the people food.

17. RAVEN CHANGES THE RIVER COURSES.

The Snuqualmi, Snohomish, Swinomish and all the other tribes came together before the world was changed. Eagle was the head man of the gathering. He was a great man and lived up in a tree. When the people wanted to decide an important question they called up to him as he sat in his tree and in the conference that followed, each one of the people below was allowed to give his opinion. At this time Mink, Eagle's cousin, and Raven were slaves. Matters were talked over and the people agreed that one side of all rivers should run up and the other side down. The rivers should go up to the falls and turn around there. Eagle wanted this so that the people would have an easy time travelling both up and down stream. Raven disagreed with Eagle because the salmon would have no chance to stop, they would go up to the falls and come right back. Raven could always give good arguments. He wanted the rivers to go only one way and at turns he wanted little eddies. Mink agreed with Raven. Now Raven had fine judgment, although he was a slave and he convinced the other people that the only proper thing to do was to adopt his plan. So now the rivers run only one way and the salmon have a chance to go up the river and spawn.

18. RAVEN AND THE TIDES.

Where the Skagit lived at Nicolina Point there were no tides and the people could not get clams to eat because the water would not go out far enough and the wind was blowing from the south all the time. The people were almost starving and Raven was angry that they could get no food. The chiefs told Raven who was a slave, to go and see what he could do to help the people. Raven started out and travelled towards the south for ten days and ten nights. He came to Southwind who was an old man with twelve children, six boys and six girls. The youngest girl was making *spegpegud* and that was why it was blowing all the time.

"Where do you come from?" asked the old man. Raven said, I am your nephew, I am a great chief." The old man believed this but Raven was just fooling him. Then Raven said, "If you are a great chief, why do you keep your house so dark?" The chief had the roof boards opened to make the house lighter. Raven made the youngest girl stand in front of Southwind; she began to sing her spirit song and Raven took hold of the girl and danced with her. Everybody was dancing violently and Raven escaped with the girl through the roof. The wife of Southwind was the first to realize that Raven had stolen their daughter. Southwind began to blow, but Raven kept up his flight. He tied cedar bark over the girl's mouth so that she could not blow. Raven took the girl to where the Skagit lived and concealed her by tying her into a water tight basket. Southwind took blankets and shells with him to ransom his daughter. Southwind came with his people in a canoe and when he reached the Skagit he sent one of his men to offer money to them for his daughter. But Raven said, "No, I don't want any money, I want you to stop blowing. You must make the tides rise and fall." Southwind agreed to this, but as he made the tides they were too low and too high. When the tide was low a stench arose and Raven did not like this, so he made Southwind change it again. He took two sticks and put them on the beach to show Southwind just how far the tides must go and Southwind followed Raven's directions. Then Southwind asked, "What kind of food do you want?" Raven mentioned horse clams, butter clams, cockles, and mussels." Is that all you want?" Raven added flounders and other kinds of fish that the Indians ate. Raven got all he asked for and then he said, "You must not blow all the time, you must only blow once in a while. And you must give all this food so that the Indians who will live here, after the world has been changed, will always have enough to live on." Then Raven returned the daughter of Southwind.

Southwind told Raven that Northwind would always be blowing too hard if he did not blow, and then it would get very cold. Southwind begged Raven to go to Northwind and see what he could do with the people there. He gave Raven warm clothing for the trip. Then South wind went home and Raven started on his journey north. [398]

When Raven reached his destination he found three brothers together in the house; they were Northwind, Northwestwind, and Northeastwind. Northeastwind said to Northwind, "Why do you blow so hard? You are making Raven and Eagle freeze." Raven made Northwind agree that he would blow only during the winter months and let Southwind blow in summer. Raven told Northwind that he had already made Southwind come to an agreement. Northwind gave Raven a slip with writing on it and told him to give it to Eagle. Raven obeyed and gave it to Eagle who became very angry, for on the note it said that Raven and Eagle would be changed into animals by Dō'kᵘibɛł. Eagle had Raven put out of his house. Then Dō'kᵘibɛł came and had Raven explain all that had happened. Thereupon Dō'kᵘibɛł changed Raven into a bird and his sister into a thieving crow. Then Dō'kᵘibɛł went to Eagle and changed him into a bird too.

19. NORTHWIND AND SOUTHWIND.
(Snuqualmi: told by Snuqualmi Jim.)

Long ago Northwind and Southwind were tribes which were constantly at war with each other. Finally the Northwind people killed all the Southwind people except one woman, Hedgehog. She always went underground to visit her parents. This woman married into the Southwind tribe and gave birth to a son who belonged half to the Southwind people and half to the Hedgehog tribe. The grandfather gave the child a bow and some arrows and he hunted wild grouse. While hunting he found the house where his father of the Southwind tribe had lived. At that time Sqa'lats, his father's sister was living there. The boy went up to the house and looked in. The old woman said, "You must be the child of the woman who married my brother." The boy answered, "Yes, I am." The woman told the boy that the Northwind people who had killed all the Southwind tribe lived not very far away. Then the boy gathered lots of wood and made a fire for *Sqa'lats* for she was very cold. Afterwards he went home to his grandparents. Now he became very angry at his grandfather because he had never told him who had killed his father. The next morning he took his grandparents to the house of *Sqa'lats* and he started out to find the Northwind people who were living near the river. These people had a trap in the river for catching steel-head salmon. The boy pulled some fir boughs down and let them float along to the trap, for he wanted to make trouble for the Northwind people. A man of the tribe saw the boughs and told his people that he was afraid the branches would break their traps. The people all came down to the river and asked the boy to save their trap for the boughs were too heavy for them to move. The boy sat on the end of the trap opposite the people, and watched what the people would do. An old [399] man of the tribe knew that the boy was the son of a Southwind man and of a woman of the Hedgehog tribe. He told this to his brother and the latter went to the boy and asked him again to remove the boughs. The boy promised to try and he took the trees and threw them over the trap to the other side so that the trap was saved. The people were afraid of the boy and told him to take some salmon and go home. He obeyed them but the next day he returned and did the same thing again, this time taking heavier boughs. The Northwind people tried to take the boughs out but failed and they said, "The boy did that; he is trying to hurt us. Let someone ask him to save the trap." A man went and asked him to save the trap and the boy threw the boughs over to the side with great ease. All the Northwind people were very much afraid of the boy now. Again he took some of their salmon and went home. The Northwind people had a meeting and talked over the whole matter, for they were very much afraid. They decided that it would be best to give the boy two girls from their tribe as wives and in this way to make a friend of him. Two men from the tribe were sent to the boy with this message. The boy told them, "I will take the girls, but tell your people to wait until tomorrow for I have to get my house ready." The next morning the Northwind people came in several canoes bringing the two girls. The Northwind people came into the boy's house. They were freezing. When they were all in the house, the boy closed the door and built many large fires in the house. The fires made a great heat and all the Northwind people were killed, even the two girls. The youngest of the Northwind tribe was very clever. He told the boy that he wanted to urinate and that he would be right back. The boy let him out and the Northwind child ran away. In this way he alone was saved when all the others of his tribe were killed.

The boy then claimed the trap of the Northwind people. In this way he could get plenty of salmon and his grandparents would always have enough to eat. The youngest of the Northwind people never came back because he was afraid of the boy.

The people say that if the youngest of the Northwind people had been killed also there would be no winter. But since he escaped summer and winter alternate.

20. FOX.
(Snohomish: told by Shelton.)

At the time when the animals were human beings, Fox and Mink planned what they would do together. They decided to travel together and show one another what they could do and how clever they were. They were both tricky. They travelled for a while and wondered which one would play a trick on the other. Mink thought that it would not do [400] to travel together all the time for if they separated they would have a better chance to trick one another. So Mink said to Fox, "I am going ahead to see what kind of country lies before us." They were cooking their meal at camp and Mink went on while Fox stayed behind. Mink found a clear creek and deliberated on how he could play a trick on Fox. He fixed a small trap (*'idā'd*) of wickerwork and put it into the deepest part of the creek, but there were no fish in the stream. He urinated in the water and told his urine to become a fish. It became a fine trout. Mink went back to camp and told Fox that there were nice trout in the creek. Fox was always hungry so he went to the stream and built a fire. Mink knew that Fox was caught by this trick and he went away and left Fox alone. Fox caught the trout and ate it. It tasted very well, but soon after he felt sick. The next day Fox realized that he had been tricked. He felt as though he were pregnant and as he swelled up he found out that he really was with child. Fox had two little girls[111] inside of him. They were very clever. Fox called to them to come out and asked them what was wrong with him. The girls laughed at him and said, "What a fool you are; you always think that you are so smart, but this time Mink got ahead of you. He urinated into the water and you ate his urine in the form of a fish." Fox said, "I thought so." He always said this. He decided to settle down somewhere because he knew he would soon have a child. He got busy and made a brush shelter. A few days later he gave birth to a child. It was a boy who was very clever and grew up very fast. In a few days he was a big boy. He made bow and arrows and hunted small game. Later he made a larger outfit and hunted elk and deer. He became a good hunter and Fox began to look around for a good wife for his son. Fox went and asked Butterball to be his son's wife and a bird woman became the boy's second wife. The boy went out and hunted every day and he became very wealthy. The son liked Butter-ball but he did not care much for Bird-Woman. Old Fox wondered how he could get rid of his son so that he could marry his wives. Fox called his little partners inside of him. The girls laughed and said, "You must make two *ha'm'tcal* (birds with white feathers) of us." Fox said, "I thought so." The two acted their parts well. Fox went home and told his son that he saw two *ha'm'tcal* on a tree. The son was very anxious to kill these valuable birds. Fox led him to the tree where the birds were. The young man took off his trousers, his shirt and the tie around his neck. He had a garter of fur and moccasins. These he stripped off too. He climbed the tree. Fox winked to the girls and knowing what he wanted, they flew higher and higher up into the tree. The young man wondered why he could not catch the birds. Meanwhile the birds flew higher and higher and the boy followed them until he reached the sky. The little girls

---

[111] I. Evidently his excrements, see, p. 388.

returned to Fox. Then Old Fox put on all the clothes which his son [401] had left so that he looked like him. Fox went home and when he arrived at the camp he began to wail and cry. He wanted to make the women believe that Young Fox had just lost his father. He told them how Old Fox had been killed. Butterball knew at once that this was Old Fox, but the other woman thought that her husband had come back. Fox said that he did not want to stay where they were now living, so they left the house and travelled a long way. In the evening they made a camp. Butterball was sure that Old Fox had killed her husband. Old Fox told her that he would love his other wife better. Butterball was glad to hear this because she did not like Old Fox. The other woman was glad because now she could enjoy the favor that Butterball had always had. Butter-ball cried and cried for she knew that her husband must be dead. The next day they travelled on and Fox had a fine time with the other woman. Butterball still continued crying and touched no food and walked behind Fox and Bird-Woman.

The young man, after he was blown away, came to a strange country. He sat down and wondered where he was, for he saw nobody about him. He began to walk along and finally he came to an old man with large white whiskers. The old man was busy making twine for fish nets and did not have much to talk to the stranger. At last the old man asked the boy where he came from. The young man gave the name of the earth. The old man told him that he was a spider and made nets of all kinds. Then he told the young man that he could take him back to his own country. The young man said, "How will you take me back?" He did not know where he was. Then the young man promised Spider four buckskins already tanned which he had hidden away in his own country, provided the old man would get him back there. Spider said, "I can use my ropes here to lower you down to your own country. You live on the third country below. You have to go through two countries before you come to your own. You must do what I am going to tell you. I will tie you to this rope and lower you down. When you get to the first country, don't untie the rope, but roll and roll so that you wear out {wore through} the earth and descend through the hole to the next country. There you must roll again but don't untie yourself, otherwise you will get lost." The young man did as he was told. When he got to the other country he rolled and rolled. This rolling caused all his hair to wear off. Then he went through the country which was worn through by rolling and finally came to his own country. He knew this as his country because it was so much warmer than elsewhere. The old man had told him that his country would be warmer than the others. When the young man had untied himself the old man waited patiently wondering whether the stranger would remember his promise about the buckskins. At last the old man felt the rope jerk four times and he knew that the buckskins had been tied on and he was glad and wished the young man good luck. The young man travelled and looked for his old home where his father and his [402] wives had been. He came to the place and found it deserted. He walked about and found their tracks. His hair was all off and he was naked, for Old Fox had gotten all his clothes, but he travelled on. Finally he caught up to his father and his wives. Only his loving wife was far behind the others and walked alone crying. The other woman was ahead with Fox enjoying herself. The young man wondered whether to tell Butterball who he was. She was carrying her little bundle on her back and the packing straps were hanging down and dragging on the ground. The young man stepped on the strap. She jerked it away for she thought it had been caught. He stepped on the strap again and she became angry, "What is that bothering me?" She looked back and saw her husband smiling at her. But he did not look as he used to, because he was all naked and had no hair. She recognized him and they sat down and embraced. Butterball was so happy but she was still crying and she told him how the others had treated her. "The old man does not want me to camp with them. The other woman was fooled but I knew that he was Old Fox." The young man told his wife that he had been in a strange country and that he did not know how to get back until he found the old man who let him down on his ropes. She told him that she was going to try to do a big thing. The young man asked what this was and she said that she was going to try to make his hair grow so that he would look as he used to before he went away. She embraced him and put her hands over his head, then she made a motion and there a fine crop of hair began to grow. Then the young man looked as before. He said to his wife, "Tonight when the couple ahead camp, go right up to them and even if the old man does not want you, tell him that you are going to sleep with him." The woman said, "No, I don't want to do that. I don't want to go near Fox unless you are with me." Her husband answered, "But then he will see me." - "Why I can pack you in my basket."

They agreed upon this plan and after she had packed him into her basket Butterball went to Old Fox's camp. Old Fox told her to stay away." I told you to stay away until I asked you to come." She said, "What is the matter with you? I have just as much right to be with you as the other woman." Old Fox said, "I like you, but I don't want you until I ask you to come." The woman answered, "But I must stay with you tonight." Old Fox thought that she must have some power, otherwise she would not speak like that. He was fixing the camping place for the night. The woman untied her basket and let it down and out came the young man. Old Fox was very much ashamed of himself. He said to his son, "Here are your trousers and your shirt and here are also your garters and scarf and your hair ribbons." The young man said to the women, "What is the matter with your husband?" Old Fox returned the clothes and said, "These are yours. "But Young Fox did not put on the clothes for he was wondering in what way he could get even with the old man. [403]

At last he evolved a scheme. "Tomorrow I will go hunting and I am going to kill a deer; then I'll come home and tell the old man that I killed a deer some distance away and I'll make him and his woman get the deer to our camping place." The next morning he went out. His wife was very much ashamed of herself for having lived with her father-in-law and wanted to excuse herself, but Young Fox would not listen to her. Old Fox tried to be very good and did all the work to please his son. But Young Fox would not believe his father any more for he had found out how tricky he was. The young man killed the deer as he had intended and he went back to camp to call the whole family to help him bring it home. Old Fox was very glad to have a chance to be helpful to his son and he wanted to bring the deer back all alone. The young man had everything planned out. He talked to the meat of the deer and said, "I want you to turn into rotten wood after the old man and Bird-Woman have carried you home, break the packing strap repeatedly and bother them every way you can. I want to get ahead with my wife. I don't want to have them around me any longer." Old Fox and Bird-Woman packed up the meat and they had no more than started when the strap broke. This happened again and again. Bird-was stronger and she was not so far behind the young man and his wife. Finally at the last breakdown, the meat changed into rotten wood. Old Fox wondered what had happened. He thought he had been carrying meat. "Certainly my son must have played a trick on me." The same happened to the load which Bird-Woman carried. She let her load go and started running to catch up with Young Fox and his wife. The old man did the same. Soon Bird-Woman came to a creek and she was surprised because they did not cross it when they were coming up. She swam across and Old Fox after her. They continued to follow the tracks of the young man and his wife. Then they came to a bigger river. Bird-Woman tried to swim but she got into a drift and was lost. Old Fox started to swim and drifted a long way before he was able to reach other side. He was tired and weary. He did not know what had become of Bird-Woman. She was lost and he never saw her again. The young man and his wife were gone and Old Fox did not want to live with them any more. He sat down by the river and began to wonder how he get something to eat, for he was getting very weak and hungry. Finally he thought of his two little girls so he called them out. They came started laughing at him. Old Fox asked them, "What shall I do now I am getting thin and I don't know where to go." The girls said, "we will tell you and then you will claim that you know all about it after we told you. There are two women down below here and they have salmon trap. Their name is *Wiłwił*. You had better turn yourself a wooden dish and then drift along the river until you come to the trap. You will be caught in the trap and the women cannot help but see there." Then Old Fox said, "That is what I had thought of." He always said this. [404]

He turned himself into a wooden dish and floated down the river until he reached the salmon trap. The women came down to catch some in the trap. They saw the wooden dish and thought that somebody must have met with disaster up the river; "This is a fine dish. We have like it, so we will take it home for our salmon." Old Fox thought, "Now I see where I'll get something to eat very soon." One of the women said, "You had better handle this dish very carefully, it looks like a delicate dish." In the evening one of the women said, "Let us try this little dish and have some salmon." They got some salmon out of the trap and began to cook it. When it was done they put it on the little dish. The women started eating. They had just started when the salmon all gone. One of the women said, "I haven't had enough, let us cook another one." So they cooked another fish. When this was cooked put it on the dish and again it disappeared rapidly. "There must something the matter with us. We never ate more than two salmon and now we have hardly had enough." They washed the dish and put it away.

The next morning one of the women went out and brought back salmon. They cooked them and put them on the dish. They had hardly started to eat when all the fish was gone, so they put the second fish the dish and that went even faster than the first. One of the women became angry and she threw the dish on the ground. As she did this she said, "This must be a Fox dish." The dish broke and old Fox cried just like a baby. "Did you hear that? It is a baby." The dish cried, "I am your little brother." - "Did you hear that?" said one of the women." It will be nice to have a little companion; we will raise him, for we need a boy to stay at home when we travel." They picked him up and wrapped him in a blanket. The baby was very smart. He sucked his hand as if he were hungry. They gave him a salmon fin. "My, but that's a smart baby," they said. He grasped the fin just like a big boy.

The next day the women went back to the woods, away from the river to get Indian potatoes. They did this every day after getting their fish. They tied the baby to a post in the house. They fixed an Indian cradle for him. As they went away they looked around and saw the baby smiling at them and making motions with his arms. "My, but he's a smart baby," they said. As soon as they were out of sight Old Fox untied himself. He went down to the trap and got some salmon. He cooked and ate all the fish he wanted. He would stop for a while and then commence to eat again. In the evening he thought it would be best to go back, so he returned to the house and tied himself into the cradle just as the women had left him. When the women came back he jumped in his cradle. "My, what a fine baby." They thought that in a few days they would have a big boy to attend to their traps. This made Old Fox laugh and think, "I shall have some fun with you later on."

The next day the women went again to dig for potatoes and they left him alone. Old Fox was getting far too big for the cradle. He untied him [405] self again and cooked salmon at the trap. He got bigger and stronger after eating so many salmon. Now he wondered what he should thought that he would like to work his way up to make himself a better man than he was now. He called again on the two little sisters within him. He said to them, "I am tired of this, what can I do?" The girls said, "You always say that you know all about it after we tell you. There is a woman and her daughter living far up this river. They are almost starving on account of this trap. The trap keeps the fish going up the river. If you could tear down this trap, then the salmon would go up the river and you might travel along with them. Then people will think you are a great man because you will be taking salmon along with you." - "Yes," said Fox, "but when I tear the trap the women will kill me. It will take some time for me to tear down." The girls said, "There are only two vulnerable spots on body, your head and your anus. We will tell you what you can do. There are two baskets in the house of the women. You must put one over head and one over your anus. Then you can go ahead and break the trap and the salmon will go right through."

He went and put the baskets over himself and he was just finishing his work of tearing up the trap when the women came home. As they entered the house they saw the cradle empty. Their first thought that someone had stolen the baby. They ran to the trap and there he was, tearing down their valuable structure. Then the women began blame each other, "We ought not to have broken the dish. Here we are fooled. That is Fox tearing down our trap." One of the women got a salmon spear. She went after Fox and speared him right on the head. But the spear would not go though the basket. The other woman sharp stick to spear Fox from behind, but again he was protected by basket. By this time the trap was broken. The women ran to the house to get some more weapons to kill Fox, but Fox went up the bank, took off the baskets and the salmon followed him up the river.

Fox felt very big as he was going along with the salmon. At last he came to the woman and her daughter. Old Fox went to the place where they lived and made a motion for them to come down to the river. He spoke Yakima to them all the time. The women did not understand him. The old woman said to her daughter, "I wonder what this chief is saying." Fox never let on that he understood what they were saying, for he wanted to make the women believe that he was a great chief from the people of the mountains. Finally the woman guessed what he wanted to say. She went down to the river and found the salmon there. She was sure that Fox must be a great man and she thought, "How nice if he married my daughter and we should have a great chief with us. And then we should have plenty of salmon and enough to eat all the year round." The old woman said to her daughter, "You better have this chief as husband." The girl replied, "He is really too [406] old for me, but if he is so great as he seems to be, it would be a good thing to marry him. He is leading all the salmon up the river. If he is that kind of man, then it would be good to marry him, so that we may have salmon to eat all the time."

Old Fox saw that he was going to have a young wife. He married the young woman. Her mother was proud of her son-in-law, because she thought that he was a great chief and could call the salmon any time. Fox knew that the salmon would not last very much longer, probably only two or three days more. After they were married, the salmon lasted for several days and then they began to get scarce. Old Fox did not act like a big chief any more for he no longer had control over the salmon. So he got into trouble again. His wife became pregnant. Fox thought, "It is all right as long as I have this young wife for some time, then she may leave me if she wants to." This is what happened. The child was born and the girl's mother advised her to leave the old man for he was not much good after all. She left the baby with Fox and went away. And there was Fox all alone with a baby on his hands. But the baby was smart and grew up very fast, and in a few days it was a large girl. Finally chief Mountain-Sheep came down to ask Fox to let his son marry the girl. Fox was glad to see a chief come and ask for the hand of his daughter. He considered himself lucky to find someone who would take good care of his daughter. So the girl and the son of Mountain-Sheep were married. The chief asked Fox whether the girl might go over the mountains with them and Fox allowed her to go.

Fox was away from his daughter for a long time and he was all alone and not very happy, so he decided to go and see her. He went there and came to a large house made of stone where the Mountain-Sheep lived. These people were all big chiefs, so Fox thought he would have to act like a big chief too. He talked and acted like a big chief and the Mountain-Sheep people were glad to see him. They gave him to eat all he wanted and they treated him well. Fox's daughter had a baby. The child wore diapers made of *lo'paledjɛn* (a thin fat). Although Fox had plenty to eat, he wanted to eat these diapers and every time his daughter looked away he ate part of them. Finally his daughter saw him do it and she said to him, "Oh, father, don't eat that; it is dirty, your grandchild wets it." Old Fox said, "I just do this to show that I like the baby so well that I don't mind its dirt. I don't really eat the diapers. It is such a sweet baby." His daughter became very much ashamed of him.

Old Fox was beginning to get tired of the place and he wondered what he should do next." It is about time for me to go away from here, my daughter does not care for me any more. But before I go I will steal some things. "So he stole a stone mallet. He put it under his arm and went away by night so that he might be a long way off in the morning. He walked fast and he thought he was far away. Then all of a sudden he heard someone say to him, "What are you doing with that mallet? [407] How did you get it?" Old Fox said, "That is my mallet, I should not be travelling with it if it were not mine." It was still quite dark and the man followed Fox. Then Fox heard his daughter's voice and she said, "You ought to be ashamed of yourself for stealing something from people." Fox thought, "I thought I was far away and now I see that I am still in the house." He had gone right around in a circle all the time and had never left the house, while he was under the impression that he had travelled a long way. His daughter was very angry now and she drove him out; it would be a shame to have him around. When she turned him out it was light outside and he found that he had been indoors all night.

Fox then started to travel through this strange country. There was nothing but rocks everywhere and he did not know where he was going, but he walked eastward to the other side of the mountains. He walked for two or three days and he was getting very tired and hungry, still he saw nobody living anywhere.

Then he made up his mind to be happy and do something to cheer himself up. "I had better use my eyes to play with. I think it would look very nice to pull my eyes out and throw them about. They will make sparks." So he pulled out his eyes and threw them about. They made nice sparks and danced about and he enjoyed it. Although his eyes were out of his head he could see with them all the same. They came right back into his head again. But when he threw his eyes the last time, they would not come back. He said, "Go, my eyes, and come back again." But they would not come back this time. After a while he heard Raven. Raven got Fox's eyes and flew away with them to another country. Then Fox was blind and had no eyes. He would run against a bush and against stones; he bumped against sticks and rocks and all kinds of things. Magpie came along and laughed and laughed, "Oh, what are you doing there?" she laughed, "you look as if you were blind." Fox said, "Blind, nothing. I am just looking for a sharp stick for a pointer." Magpie said, "I never saw such a stick for a pointer before, you are fooling me, you are really blind." - "No," said the other, "I am not blind." Magpie said, "How can you prove it?" Fox said, "Come here, I will show you something that you can't see. Up in the sky is a little star. You cannot see it but I can. That shows that I am not blind. These little sticks I use to point at the star." He made Magpie believe that he was pointing at the star. Magpie was fooled and came right up to Fox. She thought that Fox was going to show her the star. Fox thought, "If I can get her near me, I will fix her." He kept on coaxing her to come near, "Come closer, then I will show you that little star." He took hold of her and told her to look where he was pointing. When she looked up he pulled out the poor Magpie's eyes. He put her eyes on and the then poor bird was blind. She called for help, "Fox has taken my eyes," she cried, but nobody was around to hear her. [408]

Fox travelled on, he was all right now for he had eyes again. He on and came to a very fat old woman. She was so big that she could stand up. Her name was Sickness (sko'tam'). Fox wondered why she ed herself thus. She was all alone and he went into her house. She him a good meal and treated him well, but still he wondered what he should play on her. He asked her many questions. Fox asked whether she was alone all the time. She answered, "No, I have two granddaughters." - "Where are they?" asked Fox. "They went to a big meeting over there," she said, pointing to the place. Then Fox kept on asking, "What is the gathering about?" The old woman told him that had stolen Fox's eyes and he was showing them to the meeting. asked, "What did the people do when Raven brought Fox's eyes? The woman answered that she had not been at the meeting, but that grandchildren told her about it. Each one who was invited to the meeting would have to sing some kind of song that would make the eyes sparkle more and jump about, and some songs would be better than others for making the eyes dance. The old woman told Fox that she had invited to be there the next day. Her grandchildren were going to carry her over there because she could not walk. Then Fox thought, "I can get my eyes back. This woman will tell everything about matters. Then I shall find out how I can get my eyes back." Fox asked, "How many times do you eat a day?" - "Only twice a day, "old woman replied." How do you cook your meals?" Then the woman told him how she cooked her meals. "And what do you do between meals?" And the old woman told him what she did all day and how made shredded cedar bark (*slawai*). She showed him how she made it. Then Fox asked, "Is there any other thing you do?" - "No," she said. Fox asked, "Is there any word you use when the children come back?" - "No," she said, "they just come in and sit down and tell me what they did." Old Fox made up his mind to kill the old woman. He thought, "That is the best way to get to the meeting. She has already been invited to be there and I will flay her and use the skin to put over myself. Then I shall make the people believe that I am the woman and not Fox."

He went out and found a rock to use in killing her. "I am going to kill you, I am going to smash your head with this rock." The old woman said, "Go ahead, that rock won't scare me. You will do me a favor if you would hit me with that rock. That would just suit me." Fox was surprised and scared. He thought, "Surely there must be someway of killing her." He went out and got a club. He came back and said, "I shall hit you on the head with this club of solid wood and I shall kill you." The old woman laughed and said, "That will never hurt me; you will do me a favor by hitting me with it; you can never hurt me with it." Fox was surprised again and he did not know what to use. He went out and got some water, a lot of water. He ran in and said to the woman, "I [409] shall drown you, I have lots of water here." The old woman said, "That is just what I want; water will make me strong." Then Fox wondered what he could use to kill the woman. He said, "I know what I will with you now, I will burn you, I will throw you into the fire." The woman said, "Fine, do that, that will suit me well; that will make all the stronger." Then she added, "Don't you know that I am Sickness? You will put me into the fire and I will get stronger. My name is Sickness; that will make sickness greater. Put me in the water and I will become stronger still." All the things that Fox thought of would only make her stronger because she was Sickness herself. Fox thought finally that such things would not kill her but medicine would perhaps harm her. So he went out to get some medicinal root. She said, "Go ahead, use the root, it won't hurt me." Fox went out and began to worry because he was not able to kill her. Then he asked the two little sisters inside of him. The little girls laughed at him. They said, "You always say that you know all about it when we tell you what to do. We know how you can kill her. You must take the strongest medicine." Fox said, "Well, what would that be?" The girls said, "Go and look for nettles, then give her a good whipping with that. That is the only thing that will kill her. Nothing else will kill her, but that will." Fox said, "Well, that is what I thought." He ran and got some nettles and went into the house with them. "Now," he said, "I shall whip you with these." As soon as she heard this she began crying, "Oh, I am gone, I am gone." So he gave her a good whipping with the nettles and she died. Fox said, "Everybody should know about these nettles because they will cure sickness".[112] Fox cut her open and skinned her. He did this with the greatest care, but there was a little place where he spoiled it just under one of the eyes. He tore the skin while he was taking it off the woman. After he got through he tried the skin on and he did not know whether he looked like the old woman. There was no one around to tell him; so finally he thought of the two little girls and he asked them how he looked. The girls said, "You look like the old woman, only there is one spot under the eyes that looks different. It looks as though she had been hurt. So when the granddaughters come back just tell them that you needed some wood and that you hurt yourself gathering it." Fox waited until evening when he thought that the girls would return and then he put on the old woman's skin and sat down in just the way the old woman always sat. He tried to imitate her so that every action would be just like hers. When the girls came in, they went right back into the house and the first thing they saw was her eye. "Oh, you must have hurt yourself." Fox talked just like the old woman and told them how he had gone to get firewood and how he was hurt. The girls felt very sorry about the accident. Fox replied, "I am hurt, but I want to go to [410] the meeting just the same, if you will carry me there." The girls that they would be glad to carry their mother over. So Fox waited until the next morning hoping that the girls would not discover that he was Fox and not their mother.

In the morning they started, the older one carrying him first. Fox was very heavy and it was all the girl could do to carry him. Then Fox thought how pretty the girls were and how nice it would be to have them as wives. He could not help but desire them and at the same time he tried hard not to let them know that he was Fox. Then he began to act queerly toward the girls and they did not know what to make of their grandmother's actions. The girl who was carrying him dropped him but the younger daughter felt sorry for the old woman and said, "Oh, sister, don't drop the poor old woman like that." The younger girl took her turn at carrying. Then Fox got the same feeling towards her. She was even prettier than her sister. He forgot that he was the old woman and began his strange actions again. The younger girl threw him down, she would not stand for that. Now the older girl felt sorry for the old woman and carried her again. Finally Fox became hot and began to put his penis into the girl. She felt something hard on her back and she began wondering what the old woman had back there. She thought that the old woman was getting too dirty and she threw her down again and decided not to carry her any more. The younger girl felt sorry for the old woman and began to carry

---

[112] This is the origin of the use of nettles as medicine.

her. They got nearer to the meeting and Fox thought that he had better not do this again, but he could not help himself. So he did it again and the younger girl dropped him. The elder daughter took him up and now he kept still because they were at the meeting and there were a great many people around enjoying themselves with the eyes of Fox.

They went right to the house where the gathering was. The people did not know that Fox was with them, but they thought the old woman had come. So the leader of the meeting ordered the people aside so that the old woman could have a comfortable corner. The people made room and they were all happy to see her there. They said to her, "Well, old woman, it is your turn now to give us a song which will make Fox's eyes dance well." Fox picked out a good tune which he thought would make his eyes move around in a lively fashion. Then he started singing. The words of the tune were something like this:

"Oh, my, the eyes of the great Fox,
how did the people handle the eyes of the great Fox.
Oh my the eyes of the great Fox,
how did the people handle the eyes of the great Fox."

Everybody sang with Old-Woman-Sickness who really was Fox. My, how the eyes did sparkle and dance when they sang this tune. Then the women cried, "Listen to the old woman, what a fine tune that is. I [411] thought that she would give us a fine tune." The second time sang, he thought he would call his eyes back to him. He whispered eyes, "Come, my eyes, come to me." And the eyes danced him and almost went back to their places. Then the people applauded. "Look at the way the old woman can make the eyes dance." He stopped singing, but the people asked him to keep on. Then Fox again made his eyes dance. After a while he got tired of this and was time to get away. He said to his eyes, "Now, my eyes, back to your places." Then the eyes came back to their sockets. Fox got up and started to run away. Everybody was astonished and stupified for a little while. As Fox ran he dropped the skin of the old woman. Then the people found out what had happened and they shouted, "Fox, Fox!" The two girls told how he had acted toward them. They said they thought he was the old woman and that he must have killed her. The people picked out their best runners to chase Fox. These five started out and they gained on Fox rapidly. Fox thought, "I am gone if they get me." He wondered how he could save himself. Finally he pulled out his penis. He turned around and showed it to the people who were chasing him. This caused a thick fog to envelope him. So the people lost track of him until the fog was blown away. When they saw him again they chased him anew. Again he turned around and did the same trick. This time he made more fog. The people could not see Fox at all. They lost him. Fox looked around and saw no sign of the people been chasing him. Then he thought he had better go back to the country where he had come from. He decided to be good and play no more tricks on his homeward journey.

21. THE ARROW CHAIN AND THE THEFT OF FIRE.
(*Snohomish.*)

A Snohomish man was a great canoe maker, and he would start work very early in the morning and work late into the night. The continual hammering annoyed a great chief who lived up in the sky with his people so he sent down four of his men to steal the canoe maker. Now this man was the only man who could make canoes and when the Snohomish people found out that he was gone, they looked everywhere for him. He could not be found. Nobody but an old Snohomish had seen how he had been stolen. This old man could hardly talk because his mouth was so small and he had a snout like a pig. The people made his mouth larger by cutting it open. Thereupon the old man told how he had seen four men come from the sky and steal the canoe maker.

The people wanted to go up to the sky and get the man back, so they tried to make a chain of arrows reaching to the sky so that they might climb up. But no one could shoot up to the sky. Finally a little bird [412] called *LaLeq^ucid* succeeded in shooting his arrow into the sky with help of his *skɬaletut*. He shot off all his arrows, each one adhering to end of the preceding one. After that the other people were able their arrows to the chain and they all climbed up to the sky and made hole in it to get through. When they were all in the sky they covered the hole with buckskin so that the wind of the lower world could not blow through and so that the sky people would not notice their coming. The people now began hunting for the canoe maker and two brothers, Winter-Robin and Summer-Robin, found him tied to the roof of a house. He told the Robins that he had to promise the son of the chief in the sky that in the future he would not work at the canoes at night and that he would not begin until the sun rose in the morning. He also told the Robins that he would have to suffer his punishment for one year. The little Robins got cold and went to the fire of the people of the sky. The people of the earth did not have fire then. The people got suspicious of the Robins and the latter became afraid and returned to their people. They told them all about what they had seen.

Beaver decided to try to get fire away from these people. The next morning he pretended to be dead and floated down the river to the salmon fence {weir} of the sky people. The sky people found him, took him home and began to butcher him. They cut open his belly and he was afraid of being killed. The children played around him and made Beaver smile. A little girl noticed this and told her father that Beaver must be alive, but they did not believe it. They continued to cut him up and they reached his ears. Now Beaver became very much afraid for if they cut off the point of his nose he must die. But just at the proper moment Beaver's people came and made war on the sky people. In the confusion that followed, the sky people paid no attention to Beaver and he jumped up, wrapped the fire of the sky people in his blanket and ran away with it. He did not stop until he arrived on earth. In the meantime the fight went on and the people liberated their canoe maker and took him along. They climbed down the ladder of arrows. When they were half way down, the four shamans, Grizzly Bear, Black Bear, Cougar and Wild Cat began a shamanistic performance. Their dancing caused the chain to break and all the people fell down, but they did not hurt themselves. The snake and the lizard who were behind the rest of the people did not fall down with them and could not come down until the spring.

The people on earth now had fire. The chief of the sky decided to attack the people on earth if the canoe maker did not keep his promise. All the tribes around this place were careful to adhere to these regulations and not make canoes early in the morning or late at night. The chief in the sky lived on the river which is today the milky way. [413]

22. ORIGIN OF THE PHEASANT TRAP.[113]
(*Snuqualmi : told by Little Sam.*)

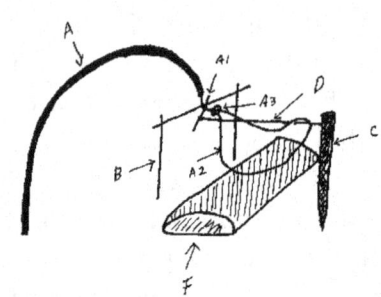

There were four brothers and one sister camping on a called *Satsqau*. The girl was a pheasant, and the men were salmon, but these were really also pheasants at that time. The woman was married to Old Log with whom she had five children, four boys and one girl. She was very fond of her husband. Old Log had two more wives These women talked so badly about Pheasant woman that the latter came to fight with them, first with one and then with the other. The brothers of the pheasant woman were married. Wildcat wanted to marry Pheasant woman, but she did not like him because he had an ugly face.

Pheasant woman also had four sisters and she asked them to get crab-apples with her. She climbed up a tree and began to sing. Wildcat saw her and shot in her anus. This did not kill her, she simply pulled out the [414] arrow and went home. Wildcat ran away because he was afraid of revenge of her brothers.

Wildcat made a trap for Pheasant woman over Old Log. Pheasant woman was caught in it. Wildcat was glad and ate her. The daughter of Pheasant woman went to the trap and saw the blood her mother. She knew that her mother had been killed and

---

[113] 1. Explanation: A is a pliable stick with a string A2 and loop A 3 of cherry bark. A was held down to the crosspiece B by means of the little stick A I attached to the string. The little stick was again held in place by means of the stick D which was set against C. F is a rotten log covered with moss. The noose was made to lie over this log and the stick D. The pheasant laid its eggs on moss like that on the log F. When the pheasant flew down upon the log the stick D would come out of place and cause A to snap up and this in turn would close the noose, catching the pheasant. This type of trap was not used by the Snohomish but was always employed by the Snuqualmi. Besides pheasants, loons and ducks were caught in it. When loons were caught salmon was put on the log. When it was set for ducks rotten salmon was the bait. When pheasants were caught two sticks wrapped in moss were stuck into the rotten log, one at each end. These were the "wives" of the log and without these it was impossible to catch pheasants. These sticks were not used for loons or ducks. This usage is explained in this story.

went home and cried. She told her uncles, Steelhead Salmon, that her mother had been killed. The youngest brother of the dead Pheasant woman went to a place where Wildcat was wont to cross a river on a log. On this log he made a trap for Wildcat. Wildcat was caught and fell into the river and was drowned.

23. ORIGIN OF THE SWEATLODGE.
(Snohomish: told by William Shelton.)

There was once a village in which many Indians lived. The chief of this village had a very beautiful daughter whom all the young men were anxious to marry. But she refused every suitor. It happened however that she became pregnant. Her father was angry and wanted to find out who her lover was. Some people were sorry for her, others however, rejoiced for they considered her too proud and haughty.

The girl gave birth to a child which cried incessantly. Her parents thought that the baby was crying for its father and that it would stop crying if he came into the house. Therefore the girl's father decided that whoever would make the child stop crying should be the husband of his daughter, because he would probably be the child's father.

Mink heard of this decision and thought that this would be a good opportunity to get a beautiful wife. He was a very cunning fellow. He dressed himself in fine clothes. His grandmother warned him not to go into the house of high class people but Mink paid no attention to her. He went in and crossed to the place where the baby was lying. Mink looked at it, but the child continued crying, so Mink had to return home without accomplishing his purpose.

All the other young men in the village went to the house, but the child kept on crying. The parents of the girl were very much surprised, for everybody they could think of had been brought before the child. Finally they remembered that there was an old man whom the child had not seen. His name was Wildcat. He was very old and his whole body was diseased and covered with sores. He could hardly walk at all and he lay by the fire all day. No one thought that he might possibly be the father of the child because nobody would have anything to do with the old man. But the child's grandparents insisted that he also be shown to the crying baby. A servant woke up the old man and bade him take hold of the baby. The old man said, "My hands are full of [415] sores and I must not touch the baby with them. Give me a blanket of feathers, and I will put it over my hands so that the baby may my sores." They gave the old man a blanket. As soon as he child it stopped crying. Everybody was very much surprised old man should be the child's father. He was asked how it came about. He answered that he had never had any relations with the girl, but possibly she may have swallowed some of his spittle. The people convinced themselves that this was is the way it happened.

The girl's father was so horrified at what had occurred that he decided to move away from the village with all his people and to leave his daughter and her baby with the diseased old man so that they might all three die of hunger. He ordered that all the houses be torn down so that no shelter should be left for them. The people prepared for the journey, putting all their possessions in canoes. Before starting they were very careful to put out all the fires so that these could be of no assistance to the girl and her child. They tried to extinguish every little spark. But there was one which escaped them. Crow had been watching in the neighborhood and he took a clamshell and quickly put it over the spark in order to save it. He stayed there and guarded it himself.

The people started out and crossed the bay. Some felt sorry for the girl but no one felt any pity for the old man. When the girl and her baby were all alone with this old man, Crow came and told them that he had saved the spark of fire. With the help of this spark they succeeded in building a fire so that the girl was able to warm the freezing baby. The old man spoke to the girl and told her how sorry he was that he had brought about such a situation. He gave the girl his only blanket and told her to wash it well and then wrap it around the child.

The next day the weather was fine. The water in the bay was quiet. Then the old man told the girl that he had decided to go away. "Don't worry about me," he said, "my life is worth nothing. Just think of yourself and the child. Perhaps I shall come back to you, but perhaps I shall never return. Above all, do not follow me." These words made the girl feel sorry for the old man. She did not know what he was about to do. The old man crawled along the sandy beach until he was out of sight. He went to a large creek which ran into the bay. At this creek he built a sweathouse. Then he started a fire and heated a large number of stones. When the stones were hot he laid them in the sweathouse and entered carrying some water. By sprinkling the stones with water he made the sweathouse full of steam. This made him perspire and gradually his dirty sores began to heal. After his sweatbath he came out and plunged into the creek. Then he rested for a few days. He repeated this sweatbath many times and after each bath more of his sores were healed.

While the old man was gone Crow came and helped the girl get some food for herself and the child. After the old man had been gone for several days she began to wonder what had become of him. She was sorry [416] for him, so one day she went out to look for him. She took the baby and went in the direction in which he had gone. She travelled along until she saw some smoke rising and she thought that that must be his camp. She wanted to go up to the place but she remembered what the old man had told her and she did not want to disobey him. After changing mind repeatedly she decided to go to the camp. She looked into the sweathouse. There she saw a fine looking young man. His body was white and clean. All the sores had disappeared, only one was still to seen on his forehead. The man scolded the girl and told her that she had disobeyed him. "Yes," she answered, "but I was so sorry for you that I wanted to find out what had become of you." The man regretted that the girl had come too soon, because he still had one sore left on his fore-head. But the girl told him not to worry about this sore and to come out of the sweathouse. The old man was young now and married the girl. She was very happy and he was full of energy and felt strong like Dō'kui- bEl, the Transformer. They went back to the old village site.

Wildcat was anxious to show the people who had left alone him and the girl what he could do. So he decided to create human beings who would live with him and his wife and would work for him. He gathered up all the rubbish that was lying about the old village site and by making a sign over it he created people. He made them of all ages. Some of these people were ordered to build houses; some went out to hunt and fish; others made canoes and split wood. Wildcat and his wife and the child now had plenty to eat and everything else they needed. The little baby had many servants to attend him. Wildcat owned the town and had people make his canoes, his blankets and baskets. All these things were originated at that time.

The people who had left Wildcat and the girl, had gone across the bay and could look back to the old village site. And they saw smoke rising there. They were very much surprised and wondered how Wildcat the girl had gotten fire. Then Crow came flying over to them and told what had happened. The parents of the girl did not know what to do. The father considered returning to the old village but he was afraid people would laugh at him. As soon as the people had heard of the success of Wildcat and his wife and their new village, their own place across the bay began to fall into decay.

Wildcat decided that the sweatbath should be of the greatest use he people. Everybody could see what it had done for him. It had cured all his sores and made him young. It should do this in the future. The sweatbath shall make people clean and shall let them regain their strength.

***

Shelton said that the following advice was given after telling this story: Do not look down upon old people just because you are young [417] and strong. You never know what may become of an old person. See how Wildcat regained his youth. If you are always kind to poor people, then you will always have good luck yourself.

24. ORIGIN OF THE EXCLAMATION "YAHŪ'!"
(Snohomish: told by Shelton.)

A long time ago, when all the animals were still human beings, the sky was very low. It was so low that the people could not stand erect. Every time they attempted to do so they would bump their heads. They called a meeting together and discussed how they could raise the sky. But they were at a loss to know how to do so. No one was strong enough to lift the sky. Finally the idea occurred to them that possibly the sky might be moved by the combined efforts of the people, if all of them pushed against it at the same time. But then the question arose of how it would be possible to make all the people exert their efforts at exactly the same moment. For the different peoples would be far away from one another, some would be in this part of the world, others in another part. What signal could be given that all people would lift at precisely the same time? Finally, the word "yahū' " {ya-haw!} was invented for this purpose. It was decided that all the people should shout "Yahū!" together, and then exert their whole strength in lifting the sky. In accordance with this the people equipped themselves with poles, braced them against the sky, and then all shouted "Yahū!" in unison. Under their combined efforts the sky rose a little. Again the people shouted "Yahū!" and lifted the heavy weight. They repeated this until the sky was sufficiently high.

This story explains the origin (dzix̱ᵘ) of the custom of shouting "Yahū!" when a number of people want to exert their combined strength in performing some strenuous work. The force is applied in unison upon uttering the last syllable, which is drawn out very long and the pitch of which is much higher than that of the first syllable. The word is used today when some heavy object like a canoe is being lifted.

25. TWO BROTHERS ARE TRANSFORMED INTO THUNDER AND LIGHTNING.[114]
(*Told by Henry Sicade*.)

A long time ago two brothers lived somewhere to the east of the present town of Enumclaw. The older brother was named Enumclaw, meaning thunder and the younger was Kapoonis. These two brothers were great hunters and travelled far and were often gone for many months. They killed game, dried the meat for future use and cached it [418] at different points to supply their wants as they travelled. They travelling in search of a spirit that would make them great medicine men.

In time Enumclaw became possessed of great strength and could throw small stones from peak to peak in the mountains. These stones in rebounding made a sharp, cracking sound. When the elder brother wanted to call the younger one, a stone thrown on the rocks served as signal.

As he grew older Kapoonis took long trips alone. At the head of the Cowlitz River he took baths every day at dawn and at dusk and in this way he finally acquired a great fire spirit.

When people crossing the mountains came near their home, Enumclaw would throw stones at the different peaks as a signal of someone's approach. The noise was terrifying and fiery flames could be seen. The people related at home that Enumclaw had caused great birds to fly at such a speed that their wings made great rumbling sounds, and that Kapoonis being possessed of the fire spirit caused lightning.

In friendly rivalry the brothers sat on the rocky ridge to the south of Tacoma facing the setting sun, and they agreed to test their powers. Enumclaw pointing to a great white rock across the ravine, offered to throw stones to the left of the rock (he was left handed) with such force that the ridge would tumble down.

Kapoonis agreed to do likewise, throwing to the right of the rock. The contest raged with such terrific force that in a short time only a sharp rock stood high in the air where the ridge had been. This rock is known now as Saw Tooth Rock and stands somewhere to the south or southwest of Longmire's Springs.

The Great Spirit saw that such dangerous playthings were not safe in the hands of human beings so he caused Enumclaw to be the thunder and Kapoonis to be lightning forever.

26. THE GIRL WHO MARRIED A DOG.
(*Skagit*.)

The daughter of the chief of the people at Niccolum Point found a little dog. She picked it up and took it home and slept with it. In reality the dog was a boy who was sent to the Skagit by his father Qē'qē (a bird) who lived in the mountains. The boy

---

[114] I. From the *Tacoma Evening News*, Nov. 1, 1916. {Sadly, this is the lone example from his 400-page collection of stories that burned up with his house.}

changed himself into a dog before he came to the Skagit. The girl became pregnant. Neither the girl nor her parents knew the cause of this. She gave birth to three dog-boys and to one girl who was a hairy dog on one side and a human girl on the other. The father, who was a high-class man was ashamed of his daughter and decided to leave her and go away with all his people. The people moved from Niccolum Point to Camano Island and took everything with them, even fire and water. The girl was left all alone with the [419] dogs and the half-dog girl. But 'a'dad, a bird and the grandmother the girl covered with a shell a little piece of burning ember, which the people had forgotten. She also saved a little bit of water in a shell. The little dogs grew very fast, but the girl was starving. The woman went out to get some clams on the beach. The second night she did this again and while she was on the beach she heard someone singing in the house. It was the old dog who had taken off his dog skin and was singing. The woman returned to the house and the dog changed himself back to a dog and when she asked who had been singing the half-dog girl replied that it was she. The third night the woman went out for clams again. This time she found a great quantity of them and again she heard the singing. Before she came home the dog-man changed himself back into a dog. This time the woman suspected that the old dog was really a man. The half-dog girl told her mother that the father was really not a dog and that he changed himself into a man during her absence by taking off his dogskin. The fourth night the woman fooled her husband. She built a fire on the beach, hung her clothes nearby, and put a digging-stick into the hands of the dummy. She herself hid in the house. When the dog-man looked out and saw the dummy, he thought that it was his wife digging clams. So he took off his dogskin and danced around fire with the other dogs. The woman now came out of her hiding place and ran after her husband with a stick and began to club him. "Why do you pretend to be a dog, while I am starving?" she cried. All now kept their dogskins off and did not put them on again. The husband was a fine looking man and he was the son of the chief Qē'qē in the mountains.

The son of Qē'qē now decided to make a new race of people. He told his children to gather up the refuse and sticks that were lying around the house and to make four piles out of this. Then he made human beings out of the refuse by singing his spirit song. He was the first man to sing this song and he had learned it from his father. He also built a house for his people. Furthermore he originated the game of shinny for his sons to play. After doing this work in the morning he went out to the woods in the afternoon. He met twenty elk, ten bucks and ten does and he killed them all by waving his stick. He told his wife that he would give her any kind of food that she desired. She said that she would like some sea food. Thereupon he took some gravel and threw it into the water and at once it became smelts. This was the origin of smelts.

The people who had left the girl with the dogs saw some smoke on the site of their old village. They wondered how it came there. They were starving and had nothing to drink. The son of Qē'qē brought this punishment upon them. Crow flew over to the people on Camano Island with two smelts. He told the people that the dog was no dog at all, but a high class man. He also told them of the great wealth that the son of Qē'qē had produced. [420]

The son of Qē'qē learned the *sL!a'lqab skłaletut* from his father and now he taught it to his wife. He told her that when she would sing this a whale would come to the beach from the ocean. He called for a high tide and then as the woman sang the *sL!alqab* a big whale came right up the beach. When the tide receded the whale lay on the beach and people butchered it.

The people returned from Camano Island. The woman pleaded with her husband not to take revenge on her people for deserting them. The man agreed not to do this, but to make them ashamed of themselves. He made his wife give them a lot of property. She also showed them the dog blanket with which the son of Qē'qē had made himself look like a dog.

27. DEER AND LOON.
(*Snohomish: told by Shelton.*)

Once Deer and Loon were together in a canoe. Deer began to sing and make a noise. "If the wolves hear you," said Loon, "they will come and kill you." Deer did not take heed. "If the wolves come," he said, "I will jump right over to that mountain." Deer continued to sing and did not listen to the repeated warnings of Loon. Soon a canoe full of wolves approached them. Deer became frightened and he was not able to jump as far he said he could. When the wolves came nearer Loon dived into the water and saved himself, but Deer was devoured by the wolves.

***

According to the informant this story ends with the teaching: Do not be boastful, otherwise you may come to grief just as Deer did.

28. FOX AND SEAL.
(*Snohomish: told by Shelton.*)

Fox was a cunning fellow. He met Seal and decided that he would like to eat him. He wondered how he could kill Seal. Finally he simulated great grief for the dead. He cried and told Seal how very sad he felt when he thought of all the people who had passed away. This made the innocent Seal cry too, but his grief was sincere. Fox suggested that they go to the top of a precipice and continue their lamentations there. They went and sat around a fire. Fox managed to make Seal sit nearest the precipice, while he seated himself on the opposite side of the fire. Now Fox moved the fire nearer and nearer to Seal with the intention of finally forcing him down the precipice. While they were wailing Fox succeeded in killing Seal in this way and then he devoured him.
[421]

***

According to the informant the moral is: Always be on your guard lest a cunning person trick you the way Fox did Seal.

29. SKUNK MARRIES FROG.
(*Skagit: told by Josephine Leclair.*)

Skunk married a girl named Frog (*wa'q!waq!*) who was very beautiful. After a year at spring time Frog started singing. Finally Skunk noticed that all the relatives of the girl were singing too. They all went to a pond and sang there. Skunk stayed at home. They did this for two days and the third Skunk wanted to go along. But his wife said, "No, you must not go, it is hard for you, you can't do it." That day they went out again. The fourth day Skunk said, "I want to go along." His wife answered, "Well, then come and try it."

So he went to the pond with his wife. She took him by the hand and went into the pond with him. He enjoyed it very much at first. His wife was singing, "I am a frog, I am a frog." Skunk sang the same song with her. At noon time he felt queer; his legs got stiff and they were cold. Towards evening his jaws were getting stiff and cold. Then he could only say, "Waiyī's, I am a frog." His wife shook him and told him to sing on. The last word he said was, "Waiyī's," and then he died.

When he was dead his body floated on the water. His brothers came out to the pond and found Skunk floating on the water. They went up to him and took him ashore. They said, "That is what he gets. We were always telling him not to marry Frog because he could not do what the frogs were doing." They took him home.

30. HOW SKUNK KILLED THE PEOPLE.
(*Skagit: told by Skookum George.*)

Skunk was wise. He knew that Dō'kᵘibɛɫ was coming. Skunk came to a river and he could see that there were people living on the other side. He wanted to kill them so he called to them to take him across. They did not hear him at first but after he had shouted repeatedly they came to get him. Then Skunk said to the people, "Patch up your house and see that all the cracks are closed up. I want to tell you about Dō'kᵘibɛɫ. He is coming to change everything." The people did as Skunk ordered. When the house was closed up tightly Skunk urinated and the stench killed all the people. [422]

31. GRIZZLY BEAR AND BLACK BEAR.
(*Snohomish: told by Shelton.*)

Black Bear and Grizzly Bear were living together at the time when all animals were human. They were both mean women, but Grizzly Bear was the worse of the two. Each had two sons and the sons of Grizzly Bear were stronger than the two little Black Bears. When they fought together the Grizzly Bears would always win. Everyday the two women would gather berries and other things. They were gone all day, and the boys stayed at home. One day Black Bear said to her sons, "Some day I shall be killed; old Grizzly Bear is getting so that she wants to kill me. So don't be surprised if I am killed some day. If I am killed, then I will give a sign by which you will know. The sky in the west will turn red. As soon as you see that sign, then you must get your bows and arrows and kill these young Grizzly Bear children. Then you must start out in this direction (pointing) up river. You have an old grandfather living there. On the road you will find some old people and they will tell you exactly where he lives. You will have with you your bows and arrows and some spears and other property. Give these things to the people, who do you a favor. I am telling you all of these things in case I do not get back, so that you may know what to do."

The next day the boys saw the sign, the red sky in the west, and they said, "Our mother must be dead, the sign is up now. We have to hurry to kill the two Grizzly Bear boys, otherwise their mother will come home and kill us. If we can get a good start then we shall be all right and we can go to our grandfather." They killed the Grizzly Bear boys with their bows and arrows. They had a great fight because these boys were strong, but finally they succeeded in killing them. The boys knew what to do because they had been instructed by their mother. After killing the boys, they started out with their few belongings. They got a good start.

Then old Grizzly Bear came home and found her two boys dead. She was very angry and wanted to eat everything. She had a fine sense of smell; she could scent much better than all the other bears. She smelt around and found the tracks of the boys. Then she followed them and as she went along she cried, "I wonder who killed my sons." She was getting closer to the boys and they knew it. They talked to each other and said, "What shall we do ? The old Bear woman is coming, surely she will eat us up." The boys thought about what their mother had told them." She told us that we should pay for favors as we went along. Whom can we pay?" The other boy said, "I tell you, we will pay the Echo to fool the old Bear woman." The first boy said, "We might give him one of our arrows so that the Bear will lose track of us and not catch us so easily." The Bear boys asked Echo to do them this service and told him that they would give him an arrow in return. Echo said [423] that it would be easy for him to fool Grizzly Bear. Echo said, "I will fool her until you get a good start, then I will let her go." The boys told him that was just what they wanted. They thanked Echo and ran away.

They travelled through the woods heading towards their grandfather about whom their mother had told them. They came to a thick crab-apple tree. One of the boys said, "This is a good place to make the Crabapple tree catch old Grizzly Bear when she comes along." Grizzly Bear had long hair. They gave the Crabapple tree their second arrow for this service. The Crabapple tree said, "I will do that well. I will hold Grizzly Bear until I know that you got a good start." The boys thanked the tree and went on.

They still had a bow and a spear to give away. Two arrows had already been given away. They said, "We have only these two things now and we want to be sure to make the best use of these two remaining things." They went on and came to an old log lying across the road. One boy said, "Don't you think it will be a good thing to pay one of our things to this log?" They discussed the matter. They decided to give the bow to the log. The log said, "I will do that. I will make Grizzly Bear fall so badly that she will lose her senses. She will stay senseless until I know that you get a good start."

Then the boys began to hear Grizzly Bear howl at her home where the young Grizzly Bears had been killed. That scared them. The one said to the other, "I don't think that Grizzly Bear will catch us now, we have so many helpers." The other said, "I am not sure, she may get us after all." They ran as fast as they could and they went through a wild wood and came to a river. The water was running fast. They wondered how they were going to get across. Nobody was living near by and no canoe could be found. Finally they came to Crane. He was living near the river. He was an old man with long grey hair; bony, tall and slim. They ran up to him and said, "Do you live here all the time? Is there any way of getting across the river?" He said, "No there is no way of getting across the river." They asked him, "What do you do here?" Crane answered, "I fish here." - "And where is your canoe, if you fish here?" The Crane replied, "I fish without a canoe, I don't need one for my legs are long and I can fish anywhere in the river without a canoe." The boys asked, "Can you get us across in any way? We want to get across." Crane told them, "Yes, I can do that very easily." The boys said, "We will give you a very valuable spear for your services. There is a Grizzly Bear after us and we want to get to our grandfather. Would you detain Grizzly Bear until you know we have safely reached our grandfather?" The Crane answered, "My dear boys, I will do all I can for you. I thank you for the spear. It is just what I need sometimes. I can use this spear to catch fish with. I don't have to reach for them." Crane proceeded to tell the boys how to cross [424] river. He said, "I will put my leg right across the river. You may use it as a bridge. You must be very careful not to step on my knee cap. If you do that you will fall at once into the water. So be very careful. When you get over on the other side then follow the river to your left and go up the mountains. There you will find your grandfather. He lives right in a mountain of stone." The boys then crossed the river on the leg of Crane and were very careful not to step on his knee cap.

When they got to the other side they turned to the left and went along the river. Far off they could hear Grizzly Bear howling and they became frightened and ran fast. They went into the mountains. At first they had some difficulty in finding the door to the house of their grandfather, but finally they saw it, a mighty rock closing the entrance. When they at last found their grandfather they told him of all their experiences. They told him how Grizzly Bear had killed their mother, how they in turn had killed the little Grizzly Bears, and how old Grizzly was pursuing them. The boys were still uneasy, for they were afraid that Grizzly Bear might get them any way, for their grandfather was old and looked very weak. They were anxious to have the door closed, but their grandfather said, "Don't be afraid, I am a great man. Nobody can enter my door without my permission. I can close it at any time and kill the person who gets between the door. The door protects me; fear nothing."

Grizzly Bear in the meantime had been following the tracks of the boys and howled and cried on her way. Every time she cried she said, "I should like to catch the boys who killed my children." The Echo heard her coming and he thought of this promise to the boys." Now Grizzly Bear is coming," he thought. Grizzly Bear was coming nearer and nearer. Echo thought, "I won't fool her right away. I'll wait a little." Grizzly Bear's hair was bushy and dishevelled and she was foaming at the mouth. She went by and Echo started to fool her. Grizzly Bear said, "I wonder who killed my children." Echo repeated these same words. Grizzly Bear heard this and thought that she heard the boys. Again she howled, "I wonder who killed my children." Echo repeated this and Grizzly Bear thought the boys were over there. Echo continued to fool her in this way and Grizzly Bear ran after Echo, thinking that she was following the boys. Echo did this for a long time until he thought that the boys had gotten a good head start. Finally Echo let Grizzly Bear go.

She took up the track of the boys. Then the Crabapple tree heard her coming and thought, "Now I will help the boys." All the limbs of the tree got ready. Grizzly Bear came along and got entangled in it. The more she tried to get loose, the more she got entangled. She lost much hair. After she finally disentangled herself she ran crying and howling after the boys. She went through wild country over a little trail. The log heard her coming and thought, "I will help the boys, and do well for what I have been paid." Grizzly Bear tried to jump over [425] the log, but Log brought her to fall and she lay there unconscious quite a while. The log did his duty very well.

When Grizzly Bear regained her senses she ran on until Crane heard her coming. Crane thought, "Now I will fix her." Grizzly Bear asked Crane, "Where can I cross this river?" Crane answered, "I don't know." Grizzly Bear ran down stream looking for a place to cross to see if she could find a canoe. She went way back and then returned to Crane and said, "I could not find a place to cross. Tell me where can get across." Crane said, "I don't know, probably it is up stream somewhere." So Grizzly Bear ran up stream. She could not find anything and she returned and said." I could not find a way to get across. I believe you know how I could get over." Crane replied, "Yes, I know how could get across. I always stretch my leg across the river every time it necessary for any one to cross the river to the other side." Grizzly Bear said, "Why didn't you tell me right away?" Crane then stretched leg over the river and said, "You must walk slowly and be sure and step on my knee cap." Grizzly Bear promised to do that and she walked it. She slipped and fell into the water. She drifted downstream until she reached the same side of the river from which she had started. She ran to Crane and he told her that she must have gone too fast." You must walk very slowly," he warned her, and with that she tried a second time. She walked very slowly and when she stepped on the knee cap she fell in again. She drifted down the river and got back to the same bank. Again she returned to Crane and now Crane told her to jump over knee cap and not step on it. She did as she was told and this time got across. She ran on, chasing the boys until she came to the door of their grand-father's house. The boys were very much alarmed and wanted to hide, but their grandfather told them not to be afraid, "Grizzly Bear won't hurt you." The boys asked their grandfather not to open the door. "No one can get through my door without my permission," said the old man. He left the door open and Grizzly Bear saw the boys inside and she could hardly restrain herself. She wanted to jump in but the old man told her, "I will let you in but you must go very slowly. If you want to get in, you must do as I tell you." Grizzly Bear wanted to jump, but she did as she was told. She walked through the door slowly. Just as she halfway through, the door crashed closed and tore Grizzly Bear to pieces.

32. THE FIVE HUNTERS.
(*Snuqualmi.*)

There were five Wolves who were all brothers. The eldest of them went hunting for deer. He travelled all day and came to an open place from which he saw smoke on the prairie." Some Indians must be camping [426] there," he thought. He went there and looked into the house. were the Stɛmta'mɫ family, the parents and two little boys and daughter. The girl was very beautiful and as Wolf looked in he thought that he would like to marry her. He went in and the girl consented marry him.

The next day the old father told the girl to go out on the prairie get food for her husband. She went out to dig roots. Then the old told Wolf to get his bow and arrows and kill a bear. Young Wolf set to hunt for bears. Meanwhile the girl had changed into a bear and Wolf not knowing that this was his wife tried to kill her, but instead she killed him.

The next morning the second Wolf went hunting and he also saw smoke and thought that probably his brother had stayed at that He went in and was killed in the same way as his brother. The happened to the third and fourth brothers. The youngest Wolf thought, "Well, my four brothers must have gotten into trouble." Before starting off to find them he dreamt. He and dressed and put good arrow points into his hair. He put red on his hands, face and trousers. He kept the four arrows in his Then he started out and when he came to the prairie he knew that was where his brothers had been killed. He looked into the house and found everything as it had been in his dream. The girl consented to marry him and she liked him very much. The old man told her to get something to eat for her husband, but she did not want to go, for she did not want to kill the young Wolf. The father urged her and finally she went. Then he sent young Wolf to hunt after changing arrows with him. "You climb up the hill," said the old man. "I'll fix you; just give me advice," thought Young Wolf. The old man noticed that this young man looked different and seemed more clever.

Wolf set out and went around the other side of the hill, and there made a fire. The old man called after him that he had gone the wrong way but Wolf paid no attention. He put the good arrow points into his shafts. The two little boys were sent to follow Wolf and they told their father where Wolf had gone. He crossed the hill and came down on the other side. There he killed the woman who had changed into a bear. He cut off the legs and paws and took them to the old man. The old man cried. The next morning the old man felt sorry for his daughter and he told his son-in-law that there was plenty of game around and that he should go to hunt. Wolf went out. Then the old man's wife and boys followed him. They came to a gulch. Wolf dressed up a stump to look like himself while he hid in the brush. The old man told his son not to be afraid of Wolf but to go right at him. Wolf killed the boy. In the same way he killed the second boy and when the old man's wife came he killed her too. The old man said, "I'll fix him, I'll eat him." Wolf shot an arrow at the old man and then another and finally he killed him. [427]

Then Young Wolf opened the body of the young woman and the hearts of his four brothers. The first one was a little bruised, others came to life again. The oldest one said, "I can hardly me die."

So the eldest brother died and Wolf buried him. His bow and arrows were then used by his younger brothers.

33. THE WOLVES AND THE FLYING SQUIRREL.
(*Snuqualmi.*)

Wolf started out to hunt. He travelled a whole day and every time he shot a bird he hung it up in a tree. When he was ready to go home he took all the birds with him. Late in the afternoon he heard girls singing on the prairie. "I'm going to wait until tomorrow before I visit the girls," he said. There really were no girls; it was Flying Squirrel who sang like a girl as he sat up in a cedar tree. Wolf camped under the cedar tree. Squirrel kept asking Wolf whether he was still awake and under the influence of this continual asking Wolf fell asleep. Then Squirrel came down from the tree, cut Wolf open and ate his heart. He threw the body into the brush.

The next day the same happened to Wolf's brother. He hung up his birds and came to the cedar tree. When he heard the girls singing he said, "That is where my brother is," and he was very glad and thought of the good time he would have with the girls. He fell asleep under the cedar tree and Squirrel cut him open and ate his heart. The third Wolf went out in the same way. When he heard the girls singing he said, "I want to go over there in the morning." Squirrel killed him in the same way. The fourth Wolf started out too and camped under the cedar tree. Squirrel tried to make him fall asleep but did not succeed until almost midnight. Squirrel thought, "He is tougher than his brothers; he stays awake so long." Then Squirrel killed the fourth brother also.

The fifth Wolf, the youngest one, dreamt that night about the death of his brothers and he said, "I will fix that bad animal." He prepared his flint arrows and travelled until he saw the dead bodies of his brothers lying in the brush where Squirrel had thrown them. But he did not let Squirrel know that he had seen them. Wolf carried big logs to make a fire and Squirrel became afraid of his great strength. Squirrel sang again in the cedar tree and it sounded like girls far out on the prairie. "Ah ha," thought Wolf, "this is how my brothers got killed. I'll fix that bad animal. "Wolf took his shirt and stuffed it with moss to fool Squirrel. Wolf hid and Squirrel asked, "Are you awake?" Wolf answered from his hiding place. At about midnight Wolf just grumbled as if he were asleep at last. Squirrel thought, "He is asleep at last." Wolf let his [428] fire die down so that it was dark. Squirrel jumped down and landed the dummy. Wolf shot two arrows at Squirrel from his hiding and killed him. Wolf knew that the world was going to be changed he said, "You are not going to kill all the Indians who are going to in this world." The next morning he cut up Squirrel and took out hearts of his brothers and cleaned them. He put the heart back into body of the fourth brother, healed the cuts by rubbing his hand over breast and stepped four times over the body. He did the same with three other brothers. The heart of the eldest brother was spoiled. became conscious but he was very weak and he said, "In the future when the world is changed, this is the way that the eldest brother always die more easily than the others." After burying the eldest brother the others I went home.[115] The youngest Wolf now cut off the nose Squirrel and threw it into the cedar and made the flying squirrel out it. For this reason the flying squirrel does not kill the Indians of today.

34. THE JEALOUS BROTHERS.
(*Skagit: told by Skookum George.*)

There were five brothers, all Wolves. They were all good hunters, but the eldest was the most successful. He always brought home mountain-goats when he hunted. His name was Q!Ebasсɛd. The younger brothers were jealous and said, "We don't want to stay with our brother; he always gets mountain-goats and we four get nothing. The best thing to do is to kill him by some trick. We can take him to a rocky place and push him over a precipice." They all went out to hunt and took him to a precipice and pushed him over. In this way the eldest brother was killed.

***

The people say that is just the way nowadays; the best hunter is always killed. All Snuqualmi families are descended from surviving Wolves.

35. THE FIVE BROTHERS.
(*Snohomish.*)

There were five brothers who were Snohomish and lived at Priest Point. The eldest one was always making canoes while the others went seal hunting. The wife of the eldest brother was very greedy and ate very much. When the hunters came home they gave her part of the supply but she always ate it all by herself and told her husband that [429] his brothers never gave her any food. This made the man angry brothers and he decided to get even with them. So he carved a seal of a cedar log and told his brothers that there was a fine seal out in water. They started out in two canoes to catch the seal. They shot harpoon points into the wooden seal which had become just like seal. The animal swam on and on and did not seem to tire. The brothers caught hold of a "duck" float but it was impossible to stop the seal, and the brothers could not let go of the float. The seal swam on and on and dragged them out through the straits. Then the seal became a log again. It was foggy and the brothers were completely lost. They drifted on and finally they came to a land where very small but very strong men lived. They landed and had nothing to eat. They saw a canoe out in the water and there was one of these pygmies in it catching halibut by diving in the water for them. The starving brothers decided to steal the fish. So just as a pygmy was diving they paddled over quickly to his canoe and took all the halibut out of it. They came back to land when the little man rose to the surface of the water. He saw that all his fish were gone and he looked around and pointed with his finger to all about him. Finally his finger stopped just where the people were. Now he knew who had stolen his fish. He paddled over to the people. They thought he was weak because he was so small, but he was really very

---

[115] I. These Wolves were the first Snuqualmi.

strong. He seized all the people, threw them into his canoe and took them home. The little man had a very small mouth and he ate only the maggots that grew in the rotting halibut.

The people were brought to the house of the little man. There were many people in the house and they all talked to one another by signs. They told the Snohomish by signs to cook the halibut for themselves. They did not let the Snohomish stay in their house but made them camp outside for four days. Then the little people told them, again by signs, that ducks, snipe, and geese came every year to make war on them. On the morning of the fifth day the Snohomish saw the enemies coming. The ducks and cranes and other birds killed many of the little people. Then the Snohomish seized some yew-wood poles and slaughtered the birds in defending the little people. Diver-duck (a woman) said to her friends, "Let's get away. These are real Indians." Then the ducks flew away. The Snohomish cured some of the little people, who had been wounded, by pulling out the feathers which the birds had shot into them. After curing the little people the Snohomish picked up the dead birds and roasted them. The little people thought the Snohomish and the birds were the same kind of people, - both human beings, - and when they saw the Indians eating the ducks they thought these human beings were eating one another. So they decided to get rid of the Snohomish. They gave them provisions and told them to stay on one side of the water, otherwise they would get lost. After they had come halfway the youngest brother said, "I am very tired. We might just [430] as well turn ourselves into blackfish (killerwhales). Then we home quickly." The others did not want to do this, but they wanted to see whether the youngest brother really could turn himself into whale. He took his spear for teeth and his paddle as a hump; then he dove into the water and came up far away as a killerwhale. The second and third brothers followed the youngest one's example and finally the other brother did the same. Then they all found plenty of food. When came back to Priest Point they took revenge on their brother who had played this trick on them. They told the salmon berries to get ripe quickly. The eldest brother followed these berries and ate and ate. He got lost and died while eating the berries. After that the other brothers went out into the sea and became killerwhales again.

36. THE SEAL HUNTERS.
(Snohomish: told by George Bob.)

Once there were three brothers who were great hunters. The was making a canoe while the other two hunted sturgeon, porpoise. Then the eldest brother went out to get some cedar from this he carved a seal. He told this wooden seal to act like a real seal and the cedar became alive and obeyed him. Then the eldest brother went home and told his brothers that there was a seal out in the water. The brothers started out in a canoe with their two sons. They speared the seal and the point stuck in the animal. The seal in this way pulled the hunters out towards the sea. The brothers did not know where they were. The seal climbed up on the beach and at once became a piece of cedar again. The brothers pulled their canoe up on the beach and suddenly they were turned into blackfish. The oldest brother who made the seal went out into the brush and died.

37. THE SUN'S DAUGHTER.
(*Skagit: told by Josephine Leclair.*)

There was a chief who had two sons. There had been a third son older than these but he had died. This man had left a widow. It was customary for a man to marry his widowed sister-in-law, so the elder of the two living sons went to bed with this woman. She became very angry at this and took the man by his long hair and dragged him to the fire. Here she burned his hair and face. His hair was all gone. The young man was very much ashamed. He wondered what he should do, for he did not want to go home in that condition. He decided to leave his native country and that same evening he started out. He walked a great distance and finally he saw smoke. He went closer and found a hut. He looked through the door and inside there was a beautiful young woman [431] but she was so bright that her sight dazzled him. She looked out door but could see no one. A second time he looked in and again brightness dazzled him. She looked out to see whether anybody the door but again she found no one. A third time he looked in and time the girl grasped the young man. She looked at him and "This must have been a very handsome boy." But now his head all burnt. She asked him what he wanted but he did not answer her. She pulled him into the house and made him sit near her. Then she asked him why all his hair was burnt off. He told her the story of how it happened. The girl said to him, "My father is the sun. Just before coming home and entering this house he throws out three flashes of light." She hid the young man among the blankets of her bed.

The girl had to make three pairs of moccasins for her father every day, for three pairs were worn out every day on his journey. She also had to mend moccasins. This kept her very busy. While the young man was hiding it was getting late in the day and soon he saw a flash of light, then a second, then a third. Finally he heard a great crash and Sun came into his house. He lit up the whole place. Sun spoke to his daughter, "Today I heard much crying while I was traveling. It must have been a chief's child that I heard crying. I looked among the graves but I could find no signs of the boy." He told his daughter that he would make a more thorough search for the boy on the following day. The next morning at daybreak Sun was off again. As soon as they were alone the young man came out of his hiding place and ate with the girl. She smeared salve on the boy's head and face to cure his burns. Then the two worked together on the moccasins for Sun. His work proved to be better than that of the girl herself. That evening Sun came in again, and the boy hid as before. Sun stayed awake that night and heard his daughter whispering with someone. He also noticed that the work on the moccasins had an unusual appearance. When Sun had arrived home that evening he had told his daughter that the family of the lost boy were crying and had cut their hair short.[116] Sun knew where the boy was, but he did not let his daughter know that he knew.

The third day Sun went out again and the boy and girl played together. Then they worked on the moccasins. The boy's burns were healing by this time and his hair

---

[116] Short hair is a sign of mourning.

was growing. In the evening Sun returned. He was weary from traveling and lay down on this bed. He said to his daughter, "Why are you hiding that boy? Do you think that I do not know he is here? Don't you know that I know everything?" At first the girl did not want to get the boy out, but after a second bidding she called him from his hiding place. Sun said that it was not right for his daughter to hide the boy in his house, then he spoke to the boy and said, "As soon as your face is better and your hair has grown long you will return to [432] your own country. I do not want to keep you here. You will take daughter with you."

The boy and Sun's daughter were married and the girl gave birth a boy. When the appointed day came they started on their journey back to earth. Before his daughter left, Sun told her that she must never near a dirty person. She must always keep away from dirty people else she would disappear. They travelled a long time and on the third day the young man saw his brother off in the distance shooting arrows. The elder brother had a bag of red paint with him. He threw the bag to the place where his younger brother was shooting. The bag became pretty bird and the younger brother shot at it, but missed it. The elder brother went to pick up the arrow. Meanwhile the younger brother followed his arrow to regain it and in this way the two young men met. The elder brother had merely used this device to meet the boy. He said, "Don't be afraid of me; I am *Sle'hem*, your elder brother." At first the boy would not believe this, but then the older boy touched his brother's hair and asked why it was short. The boy answered, "My mother did that because she thought you were dead. We have all been very unhappy since you left us." Then the elder brother said, "Go home to our parents and tell them that I am well and that I am coming home very soon. Be sure to tell them to sweep the house and make everything clean."

The boy ran to his parents and told them what had happened. parents thought that the boy was lying." No, I am telling the truth, the boy said. "I met my brother with a woman and a child. They be here very soon. He wants you to clean the house well before he comes. Then the old parents cleaned the house very carefully and asked neighbors to help them. The young couple came into the house and sat down by the parents.

The young man told his parents his experiences. While he was doing this two dirty women came into the house. They were Bluejay (*kai'kai*) and Mouse (*qᵘa'nan*). These two women were anxious to see the daughter of Sun, so they looked into the room through a small hole. This caused the brightness of Sun's daughter to diminish and finally she disappeared. This was in accordance with what her father had told her before she went away from him. Then the baby boy disappeared and finally the girl's husband also. They went back to the Sun. They came back a second time to the home of the boy's parents. Again there were dirty women about, so they disappeared again. They came a third time. Before disappeared this time the boy told his father that this time they going away for good. He said, "Sun told us that if nothing had wrong in this world, we could have stayed here. Then everything would have been better in the world than without us ; but as things are we to go back to the sky."

Sle'hem is up in the sky now and is a very pretty bird. [433]

38. THE UGLY HERO.
(*Skagit: told by Josephine Leclair.*)

There was a boy who had a skin disease. His elder brother died a widow who was a woman of high rank. She did not care to again. The younger boy was very greedy and ate so much that big, big belly. He was all covered with sores, still he was the favorite the family and they spoiled him very much. When he had grown thought one day, "I am a man now, I think I can marry my law." He went to the house where she was sleeping. It was midnight he went over and lay down on her bed. He did not sleep under the he just lay on the bed for he wanted to talk to the woman. When saw him she became angry and said, "Who could marry such you are? Nobody would want to marry a person full of sores. She pushed him away. He took hold of one end of the blanket; so the woman cut off that corner with her knife. She was afraid of the sickness the boy had and she said, "You may have that corner of the blanket which I cut off, but you may not have me. "The boy took the corner of the blanket and went home with it. He began to cry and wiped his face with the piece of blanket. At home he put it in his bed mat. He sat on his bed and thought of what the woman had said to him. He felt very badly about it. "There is no use living in this world, I will go away this very night, I don't care if I live or die."

He left that very same night and travelled toward a lake. When he came to the lake he saw that it was calm at one end, while at the other end there was a whirlpool. He made a fire and bathed in the lake. He bathed three days long. When he was through with that he went up to the whirlpool. He took three great stones and tied them to his waist. Then he dove. All at once he fell on the top of a great stone house. There was somebody in the house. When he went into the whirlpool he was looking for a spirit. The spirit inside the house said, "There must be somebody on top of my house." The people went out and saw the boy there and told the spirit that there was a boy on the roof. The spirit asked, "How is the boy? Is he clean? Has he anything in his stomach?" They answered, "No, the boy is not clean." The spirit said, "Tell the boy to go back and be really clean."

When the boy woke up[117] he found that he was not in the whirlpool. He then took another sweat bath and purged himself. After three days of bathing and sweating, he went back to the same place. He took the rocks and leaped into the whirpool. The same people came out of the house and looked at the boy. They said to the spirit inside, "It is the same boy again." The spirit said, "Is the boy well cleaned out this [434] time?" The people answered, "No, not quite, there is still a little in his stomach." The boy had a large stomach and this had to be reduced. So they turned him back again.

The boy woke up and found that he had been sleeping in the place he had slept in before. Again he bathed and sweated for days. He took the rocks and went down a third time to the stone house. The people came out as before. The spirit inside said, "How is the boy? The people said, "The boy is clean now." - "Then bring him in and him

---

[117] 1. Mrs. Leclair said: "When boys look for Skal'letut they are dreaming like."

what he can learn here." They brought the boy into the house the spirit said to them: "Turn him towards the east." When they turned him to the east the boy saw all kinds of animals. "Now turn to the west." When they had turned him to the west he saw all of berries. "Now turn him to the south," the spirit ordered. They so and the boy saw all kinds of ducks. "Now turn him to the north. There he saw all the property and goods that would come to him. The name of the spirit from the north was *he'yina*. The one from the was *ts!aiq*. This spirit made a man a great hunter.[118]

Then they let the boy go. He floated toward the calm end of the and lay there about three days, before he regained consciousness. Then he bathed himself and started home. He was altogether different now. He was no longer diseased and had long hair. It was near midnight when he reached home.

Soon after he got home his father rose and made a fire.[119] In doing so he saw somebody lying near the fireplace. The boy had not gone to bed but had fallen asleep there. The man went to his wife and said, "There is somebody lying near our fireplace." The woman went there and saw that it was their own boy whom they had thought to be dead and for whom they were mourning. They awakened the boy. He said, "I wanted to die when I went out but I have changed my mind. I thought of you old folks here. Tomorrow you will clean the house before daybreak and call in all the boys of my age and all the neighbors, as many as you can bring." Then he went to his bed.

The parents went to work and cleaned the whole house. They invited all the neighbors and towards evening the people gathered in the house. The boy did not eat all day; he had not eaten since he had obtained his spirit. Towards evening the boy rose and sang all the songs he had learned. In the morning the girl in the other house, his sister-in-law said, "Who is that boy who is singing so beautifully?" They told her, "That is your brother-in-law." She laughed and said, "Where did that ugly boy get all those beautiful songs?" They said, "He is altogether different now and you would not speak like that if you saw him now." So she went to see him. She went to that end of the house where the boy [435] was. When the boy found out that she was coming he turned around. Then she tried to approach him from the other side. She wanted to see his face. The boy knew that she was coming around, so he turned again. She tried a third time and he turned. The girl now became angry and sat down beside the boy's mother. The old woman liked the girl very much and made room for her. She sat there until the boy's song was over. Then he turned around a little towards his mother. He said, "Mother, what does that girl want? I suppose she wants that piece of blanket she cut off from her cover when she was afraid of getting my disease." The mother looked for the piece of blanket and gave it to the girl. The girl was so vexed that she went home and cried.

The boy sang for three days and nights without stopping. The people had to sing right along with him and they were getting very hungry. After the third night the boy chose several boys of his own age. He told the people that he would bring them something to eat. Then he and his comrades went hunting. They came to a lake and

---

[118] 1. The names of the spirits of the south and west are not given.

[119] 2. When parents mourn for a dead child they rise early and go some distance from the house and cry. The boy's parents were about to do this.

found a canoe. The boy said, "Now you must do everything I tell you to do." Soon some ducks came flying by. The boy simply made a sign with his paddle and all the ducks fell down. He told the boys to get the ducks. He did this twice and they had a whole canoe full of ducks. Then they went home. They fed the people on these ducks. When the ducks were all eaten the boy said to his comrades, "Let us go out again." They went toward the mountains. There he just made a sign and said a word and elk, deer and goats fell down dead. They brought home the game and fed the people with it. The next day he said, "The people are tired of meat, let us go and get berries." It was not the season for berries, but nevertheless the boy took his companions to a place where there were plenty of berries. They picked them, took them home and fed the guests. The boy had done all this because he wanted to show the people what he could do.

The girl had gone home with the piece of her blanket and cried. She wiped her face with the piece of cloth and from it contracted the same disease the boy had had. Her body was all covered with sores and her hair began to fall out. The beautiful girl now became homely.

***

It does not matter what kind of person you are, whether you are beautiful or of high rank, you should never despise the lowly.

39. LOON AND THE CANNIBAL WOMAN.
(*Snohomish*.)

Loon was a young Snohomish man. The *Sxwayok!ᵘ* woman who was a cannibal wanted to capture him. She had a powerful love-magic and [436] went down to where the young man lived and by means of this magic made him come out of the house. Her magic made Loon fall passionately in love with her. "There never was such a beautiful woman before," he thought. He went up and tried to embrace her. As he did this, she seized him and put him into her basket, and ran off with him. She ran up the river and he saw that he had been deceived and began to cry. The woman took him home. She lived with her grandfather, Black Bear. She roasted some camas and fed them to the stolen man.

In the morning *Sxwayok!ᵘ* went out to bathe. She told her grandfather to look after the man. But when she had gone, Black Bear told Loon to beware of *Sxwayok!ᵘ*, who was a bad woman. He pulled out the man's finger nails and gave him his bear claws instead. He also gave him his strong teeth and his tough hide to wear under his buckskin. When *Sxwayok!ᵘ* came home, she was anxious to sleep with her husband. When she embraced him she found that he was very strong and she became alarmed. As she embraced him they bit one another. In the morning she roasted some more camas. Loon pretended to eat very much in order to make *Sxwayok!ᵘ* think he was a very strong man. In reality he stuffed the camas into a concealed bag which Black Bear had given him to tie around his waist. *Sxwayok!ᵘ* said, "You are the first whom I have seen eat so much." Loon however replied, "I am still hungry." Then he went out of the house and dumped the food out of the bag and buried it.

Sxwayok![u] again went away and Black Bear told Loon to be careful, because *Sxwayok!*[u] was going to roast him and eat him. He told Loon to run off towards the west." There you will come to Thunder and Flint; they are cousins of your father. Give them my finger nails and they will return your own to you." Loon did as he was told. He ran towards the west and came to a prairie where he met Mole and her daughter digging camas. The girl noticed Loon first and told her mother. Mole bade her daughter take the man to Thunder and Flint. The girl packed Loon on her back and ran to Thunder and Flint.

While *Sxwayok!*[u] was digging for roots her digging stick broke. This told her that there was something wrong at her house. She ran home. Black Bear had twelve hollow cedar trees for his houses. He hid himself in the last one. When *Sxwayok!*[u] came home she looked for her grandfather. She went to the first tree and asked, "Grandfather, are you at home?" - "Yes," answered the tree, for Bear had told the trees to answer that way so that *Sxwayok!*[u] would be delayed in chasing Loon. *Sxwayok!*[u] broke open the tree and did not find her grandfather in it. She then went to the second tree and there got the same answer. She tore the tree open but again found it empty. In this way she tore open four trees. Then she ran back to the house. There she saw the tracks of Loon. She followed his trail until she reached the prairie where Mole lived." Have you seen my husband, Loon?" she inquired. "Yes," said Mole and sent her to Thunder. *Sxwayok!*[u] ran on and came to Thunder [437] and asked him, "Have you seen my husband?" - "No," said Thunder, "probably he is at Flint's house." Thunder himself was not powerful, he could only make a noise, so he sent *Sxwayok!*[u] to his more powerful brother Flint. "Is my husband here?" she asked again." Yes, here," answered Flint, "come right in." But the door of Flint opened and closed and *Sxwayok!*[u] was afraid to go in. Flint told her not afraid if she wanted to see her husband. Finally *Sxwayok!*[u] became raged and rushed into the house, but just as she was halfway through door, it closed and cut her to pieces. They buried her in the ground. Thunder was delighted and produced thunder and lightning. Flint gave Loon his own finger nails back and took the bear claws from him.

The father of Loon went out to find his son. Finally he came house of Thunder. He was told that his son was there and had married the daughter of Mole. Loon and the Mole girl returned to his home and they had a little boy.

40. THE STOLEN CHILDREN.
(*Told by Snuqualmi Jim.*)

A great many people were camping near a river and there were many children with them. The children went out to play together. There was a little humpbacked boy among them whose name was *Askek*[u]*itc*. This boy would sing, "You watch out, you girls, the big animal will carry you away in his basket." The oldest girl said to him, "Don't say that, the wild animal will get you too." The name of this animal was *Sxwayōk!*[u] and it was a woman with a large basket on her back. This woman came down and got the little humpbacked boy first of all. Then she got the other children too. The basket was full of children and the boy climbed up and held onto the rim of the basket. *Sxwayōk!*[u] took the children to her house in the woods. On the way she brushed against a branch. The boy held on to it but the woman shook her basket and he fell back. This happened five times. Finally the boy clung to the limb of a tree and the woman did not notice it. Then when the woman was out of sight he let himself down and ran home to tell his people. He told them that *Sxwayōk!ᵘ* had stolen all the children, "I saved myself by getting hold of the branch of a tree while the woman carried us in her basket." The people chased after the woman with spears to kill her.

The woman carried the children into her house and made a fire. She made stones hot to cook them. She began to dance around the hot stones and sang, "The stones are hot; I shall eat the children." *Sxwayōk!ᵘ* closed her eyes as she sang and danced. The oldest girl said, "How would it be if we pushed her on the hot stones?" As soon as the woman came dancing around to the place where the oldest girls were, they pushed her over on the hot stones. She cried, "My children, help me [438] get me off the stones, I will send you back to your people." But the did not believe her and they took a forked stick and held the down on the stones until she was cooked. Then the oldest girl took children back home. Just as they were halfway home they met people coming after them with the little humpbacked boy leading way. The people were glad to see their children again and they asked they had escaped. The girls told how they had killed the woman, but old people would not believe it, so the children took them to the woman's house and they saw it for themselves. Then they all went home together.

41. THE WOLF SKLALETUT.
(*Skagit: told by Josephine Leclair.*)

One fall my grandparents and my uncle travelled up a river in a canoe. They came to a portage. One day my grandmother came to a place where she heard a wolf howling. My grandmother went up to the wolf and found that he was in agony. He had a big bone in his mouth and could not close his jaws. My grandmother shoved her digging stick between the wolf's teeth and pulled out the bone. Then she patted the wolf and said, "You need not pay me now, but remember me and give me something later."

When they got back to this place the following year they found a fine buck lying there dead. Five years in succession they always found a buck at this spot. After that the wolf must have died.

The guardian spirit of my grandmother was a wolf. She got this while she was out fasting and bathing when she was a young girl. For this reason she was not afraid of the wolf.

***

Mrs. Leclair told this as a "true story" saying that her grandmother had told it to her. Evidently Mrs. Leclair herself believed it.

PROTAT BROTHERS, PRINTERS, MACON (FRANCE). – MCMXX

Mythology of Puget Sound. Journal of American Folk-Lore
Jul. - Dec., 1924, Vol. 37, No. 145/146 (Jul. - Dec., 1924), pp. 371-438.

Index

#f = scattered entries before and after this page number
#0 = scattered entries for ten pages after this page number: 10f, 20f, ... 70f, 120f

Index

Help Zap Away Typo Gnomes

Sold @ Amazon.com

ACCULTURATING AMELIA ~ Round Valley 1937 California
ALASKA EDGE ISLAND ~ Siberian Yupiks of St Lawrence Island
ALLIED MOUNDS ~ Touching the Earth, Modeling the World, Reaching the Sky
ANIMAL PEOPLE ADVENTURES ~ Native North American Tribal Stories
AT BAY ~ Cultures Converging through Southwest Washington   > 5
CHACO ECHOES ~ Pervasive Keresan Priesthoods
CHACOKIA ~ Chaco, Cahokia, Cities & Ceremonies ~ Bundles & Blood Lines Centuries Ago
CHINOOK CONCERNS ~ Emma Millett Luscier, Isabella Bertrand, Verne Ray
CIRCLING FOUR CORNERS ~ Re-Viewing Native American Indiens   > 10
CROSSING ~ LINES: An Educational Memoir of Native North America
DEL-AWARE ~ Lenape Legacies
DELAWARE INTEGRITY ~ Rituals, Removals, Reforms by Lenape Indiens
DISCLAIMING TREATIES I ~ Puget Tribes 1927 Testimonies
DISCLAIMING TREATIES II ~ Puget Tribes 1927 Testimonies   > 15
ELDERS' DIALOG ~ Ed Davis & Vi Hilbert Discuss Native Puget Sound Language, Culture, & Heritage
EVERGREEN ETHNOGRAPHIES ~ Hoh, Chehalis, Suquamish, and Snoqualmi of Western Washington
FEDERAL FISH FILES ~ Swindell 1942 Treaty Rights Report
GEORGE GIBBS NORTHWEST ARRAY ~ Full Reports, Place Names, Word List, Artifact Names, and Guide
GRASSROOTS JANET ~ Advancing Salish and Traditional Cultures   > 20
HERMAN HAEBERLIN REGAINED ~ Anthropology and Artifacts of Puget Sound 1916-17
HERSTORY NW ~ Women Upholding Native Traditions
INDIEN ~ ETHNOGRAPHY: Cultural Traditions of Native North America
INDIEN ~ ETHNOLOGY: Grounded, Gendered, Meaningful Cultural Traditions
LESCHI IN LOVE ~ A Novel of Native Puget Sound > x2   > 25
MARCO MUCK MASKS ~ Frank Cushing on Marshes and Mounds
MINTER BAY ~ Land, Lore, Loss, and Lucre in the South Salish Sea
NATIVE MET HOW ~ Improving Posterity
OLD LUKH ~ A Novel of Native Puget Sound Daily Life, Places, and Stories
OVER THE FALLS ~ Sdoqwalbixw Survivance Surrounding Seattle   > 30
PACIFIC PLATEAU PORTRAYALS ~ People Places Ponderings
RAY'S ARRAY ~ Raymond D Fogelson's Works
RIGHTING NATIVE PLACES ~ Adventures in Northwest Geography
SAHAPTINS STUDIES ~ Columbia River Plateau, Cora Du Bois, Homer Garner Barnett, Gerald Raymond Desmond
SDOQWALBIXW   > 35
SOUND SALISH STRAITS ~ Central Salish Sea Cultures
UNSETTLING SEATTLE ~ Arresting Local Talent and Academic Illiteracy
WRITING WORDS IN WARY WORLDS ~ World Wide Improved Spellings of Native America Languages

JONA Memoirs

RESCUES, RANTS, & RESEARCHES ~ A Re-View of Jay Miller's Writings on Northwest Indien Cultures ~ #9
TRIBAL TRIO of the Northwest Coast by Kenneth D Tollefson ~ #10   > 40
INTERWEAVING COAST SALISH CULTURAL SYSTEMS ~ Collected Works of Pamela Thorsen Amoss ~ #14

University of Nebraska Press

ANCESTRAL MOUNDS ~ Vitality and Volatility Crossing Native North America 2015
HONNE ~ The Spirit of the Chehalis 2015

From: Ira Jacknis
Subject: Re: HKH himself
Date: Sat, 23 Jan 2021 09:07:41 0800

Dear Jay

Well, there is a back story there about that picture. This was the only photo of Haeberlin that I could find. I'm sure that I had checked at Columbia, AMNH, and the National Anthropological Archives. Of course, that was back in the early 90s, when we still used letters sent through the mail.

The only picture that I could find was this one, which Freddy used in her AAA anthology, published by the AAA.[120] So I wrote to the AAA, and they sent me the original print that they had used for the 1960 publication. I'm not sure where they got their copy. I sent my print to the University of Washington Press through my editor, Janet Berlo. Then after the book was published, I wrote to her asking for the print to be returned to me, so that I could send it back to the AAA. She told me that UW had destroyed it or thrown it out, and that nothing could be done. As you can imagine, I was crushed, and Iâ€™ve never forgotten this lapse.

So, as far as I know, my reproduction in this book is the only image that we will ever have of HH (although I assume that there is an original somewhere). At least it came out at a fairly good resolution, so could be repurposed, I suppose.

And I commend you for your research and publication on Haeberlin. In doing my research on him, decades ago, I came to have a tremendous admiration for him. While admittedly his early death prevented him for leaving a large reputation in American anthropology, I've always thought that he was quite important and deserved more attention, as you are now doing.

Regards, Ira

---

[120] Frederica de Laguna, *Selected Papers from the American Anthropologist 1888-1920*, American Anthropological Association 1960 reprinting his SBETETDA'Q 1918.

Herman Karl Haeberlin
1890-1918

www.ingramcontent.com/pod-product-compliance
Lightning Source LLC
Chambersburg PA
CBHW081100290526
45795CB00006B/1934